Content

Key Questions
in Education

ALSO AVAILABLE FROM BLOOMSBURY

Multiculturalism and Education, Richard Race
Education and Constructions of Childhood, David Blundell
An Introduction to Education Studies, edited by Sue Warren
Challenging Perceptions in Primary Education, edited by Margaret Sangster

Key Questions in Education

Historical and Contemporary Perspectives

JOHN T. SMITH

Bloomsbury Academic
An imprint of Bloomsbury Publishing Plc

B L O O M S B U R Y
LONDON · OXFORD · NEW YORK · NEW DELHI · SYDNEY

Bloomsbury Academic

An imprint of Bloomsbury Publishing Plc

50 Bedford Square	1385 Broadway
London	New York
WC1B 3DP	NY 10018
UK	USA

www.bloomsbury.com

BLOOMSBURY and the Diana logo are trademarks of Bloomsbury Publishing Plc

First published 2016

British Library Cataloguing-in-Publication Data

A catalogue record for this book is available from the British Library.

ISBN: HB: 978-1-4742-6874-5
PB: 978-1-4742-6873-8
ePDF: 978-1-4742-6875-2
ePub: 978-1-4742-6876-9

Library of Congress Cataloging-in-Publication Data

A catalog record for this book is available from the Library of Congress.

Typeset by Fakenham Prepress Solutions, Fakenham, Norfolk NR21 8NN

For Spike and Alan, two inspiring teachers who believed in me so much at very different stages of my life, who both showed a path and gave me the courage and confidence to follow that path. My eternal gratitude.

List of Illustrations

Preface

Above all things we must take care that the child, who is not yet old enough to love his studies, does not come to hate them and dread the bitterness which he had once tasted, even when the years of infancy are left behind. His studies must be made an amusement.

(QUINTILIAN, 29)

This book centres on the nature of childhood and on the comparative responsibilities and rights of parents, politicians and teachers to nurture young people. The chapters are framed in the form of twelve key questions and they trace past echoes and present discussions on how these might be answered. All the questions are still receiving current and often impassioned debate, in Parliament, staffrooms and the blogosphere, and their longevity shows something of their intractability. They include age-old debates on the conception of childhood, adult expectations of schooling, the extent of state involvement, the exasperations at underperformance and misbehaviour, and even the appropriateness of religion, citizenship lessons, sex education and free dinners in schools. The questions posed within the chapters constituted the subject area for an undergraduate module which I taught at the University of Hull for many years and which stimulated heated discussions among students from a variety of disciplines – politics, social science, music and drama, as well as education. The questions also appeared in professional studies modules on my PGCE courses (both primary and secondary), in compliance with the specifications of a variety of QTS manifestations, and indeed proving somewhat more resilient than the 'standards' themselves which regenerated five times between 1997 and 2011. As a history teacher and a parent, I had encountered such issues in school staffrooms and in playgrounds, as colleagues or parents expressed exasperation at why boys were so poor, why certain children misbehaved, why a secretary of state had assumed such power and why teachers had to cover subjects about which they knew little. Overall was the suspicion that neither teachers nor parents were still trusted by politicians.

The book itself is not intended solely for trainee teachers. Its origins were from undergraduate as well as PGCE modules. The current Teachers' Standards for England and Wales (2011) apply to all teachers regardless of their career stage: trainees working towards QTS or completing their statutory induction period and also those covered by performance appraisal arrangements. All teachers are rightly expected to practise appropriate self-evaluation, reflection and professional development. The content of the book does map many of the current standards. **Standard 1** expects teachers, among other targets, to inspire pupils and set goals that challenge regardless of 'backgrounds, abilities and dispositions'. Chapter 7 discusses one of the most significant variations in achievement, that signified by gender, and shows the arguments in particular about underachieving boys. **Standard 2** demands that teachers promote good progress, and there are discussions in Chapter 1 of the nature of childhood and in Chapter 6 of how pupils learn which address some of the issues prescribed. **Standard 3** calls for good curriculum knowledge, and there are reflections of the specified teaching of literacy and the use of phonics in Chapters 2 and 6. **Standard 4** expects a reflection on the effectiveness of approaches to teaching, and these are also mentioned in Chapter 6, which shows the variety of ways in which children have been taught in classrooms. **Standard 5** also expects teachers to respond to the needs of all pupils, with a 'secure understanding' of how a range of factors can inhibit their ability to learn. A number of these factors are dealt with in Chapter 1 and in Chapter 7 on gender; the discussion of the issue of food in Chapter 10 again has a similar echo of what can inhibit learning and will assist teachers to be aware of the wide variety of factors affecting children's progress. **Standard 7** requires teachers to manage behaviour effectively, and Chapter 5, addressing the history of misbehaviour, can be mapped directly onto this, with its stress on rules and routines for behaviour, frameworks for discipline and ways to motivate children. **Standard 8** and **Part 2** of the *Teachers' Standards* deal with wider professional responsibilities, with the latter covering 'personal and professional conduct'; they also specify that a teacher must show an understanding of statutory frameworks. These map directly onto Chapter 11, which discusses the professionalism of teachers; Chapters 3 and 4 analyse frameworks and faith education, while Chapter 9 explains the development of sex and relationships education – all stressing the need outlined in the *Standards* to communicate effectively with parents and to make a positive contribution to the ethos of the school; Chapter 8 deals with citizenship, covering the Part 2 specification that teachers must not undermine 'fundamental British values, including democracy, the rule of law, individual liberty and mutual respect and tolerance of those with different faiths and beliefs'. Throughout the book there is an encouragement for teachers to reflect on the questions posed, and the final chapter is anticipated to stimulate debate on the very future of schooling.

The book is intended as much for the general reader, the parent and indeed anyone who might wish to hold schools and politicians to account.

The historical context is often ignored in modern scholarship and yet it throws light onto often murky arguments and onto presumptions that present practices have no alternatives. The quotation cited at the beginning of this section sounds remarkably modern. It is a reflection of the unchanging nature of many aspects of education. The Roman teacher of rhetoric Quintilian (35–88 AD) found two millennia ago that teachers could encourage a joy in learning, or alternatively could destroy a child's interest for the rest of its life. Socrates, 500 years before him, claimed: 'I shall only ask him, and not teach him, and he shall share the enquiry with me ... see if you find me telling or explaining anything to him, instead of eliciting his opinion' (Plato, 1892: 45). In China Confucius was advising that the wise teacher guides his students but does not 'pull them along'; he urges them 'to go forward' and 'opens the way but does not take them to the place ... if his students are encouraged to think for themselves we may call the man a good teacher' (c. 510 BC). These commentators pre-empted the modern idea that pupils should work out their own solutions, own their own learning. Their sentiments would not be out of place in a modern book of 'method'. John Tosh, when looking at the value of historical studies per se, suggests that the past can 'illuminate the contours of the present' and that this knowledge can make us 'better equipped to make intelligent decisions about difficult public issues' (Tosh, 2008: viii). The issues discussed here are undoubtedly difficult to resolve and at the very least a look back to the past might stimulate future debate.

Acknowledgements

My thanks go to many librarians and archivists over the years who have beavered away to field my sometimes strange enquiries and to help wherever they can. Their work in preserving at times one of the only copies of a volume still extant, and thus the last remaining memories of the ideas within its covers, cannot be underestimated. In the present case, I would also particularly acknowledge those who have tried to help with illustrations. Stuart Brenner was most encouraging at the Southlands Archive, as was Alison Cullingford at Bradford University, Julie Woodward at the Shipley College Saltaire Archive and Neil Maw at Shrivenham Heritage Centre. Thanks also go to Gordon Clitheroe of the Beck Isle Museum and to David Harrison at St Joseph's School in Pickering. I was touched by Grizelda's offer to redraw her cartoon for me, should I be unable to locate the original. My sincere gratitude goes to Rachel Shillington and Maria Giovanna Brauzzi at Bloomsbury for their guidance, patience, encouragement and expertise. As mentioned in the dedication, my heartfelt thanks go to two of my most inspiring guides: Spike Johnson, the first teacher I ever met at my grammar school as I arrived late on my first day as a pupil over fifty years ago, whose love of history was to light my path for those fifty years and whose kindness and dedication to his pupils was always an example to follow in my own teaching; and Alan McClelland, who similarly loves history and whose guidance over a quarter of a century led me to a Masters degree, a Doctorate and a second career. And most of all my family, Susan, Matthew and Ruth, for allowing me some access to my computer to finish this work.

Abbreviations

ABCS	Associated Body of Church Schoolmasters
ACT	Association for Citizenship Teaching
ATL	Association of Teachers and Lecturers
BFSS	British and Foreign School Society
BHA	British Humanist Association
CCT	Commercial Competitive Tendering
CLEX	Committee of Inquiry into the Changing Learner Experience
DCSF	Department for Children, Schools and Families
DES	Department of Education and Science
DFE	Department for Education
DFEE	Department for Employment and Education
DFES	Department for Education and Skills
ETHOS	Electronic Theses Online Service
GTC	General Teaching Council
NASUWT	National Association of Schoolmasters and Union of Women Teachers
NUET	National Union of Elementary Teachers
NUT	National Union of Teachers
POST	Parliamentary Office of Science and Technology
PSHE	Personal, Social and Health Education
QCA	Qualifications and Curriculum Authority
QTS	Qualified Teacher Status
SACRE	Standing Advisory Council on Religious Education

SAT   Standard Assessment Tests

SIC   Social Integration Commission

SPCK   Society for Promoting Christian Knowledge

SRE   Sex and Relationships Education

STOPP   Society of Teachers Opposed to Physical Punishment

TDA   The Training and Development Agency for Schools

TTA   Teacher Training Agency

1

Does childhood have a future – or a past?

Childhood is under threat in modern society, challenged by fears of 'stranger danger', consumerism, peer pressure, internet hegemony, and school pressures from an increasingly early age. This chapter analyses how childhood is perceived in an age of such toxicity, and compares these concepts with those of the past. In doing so, it discusses the constructions of children as inherently innocent or wicked and also shows the continuing importance and resilience of play in their lives.

How does current society see children?

Neil Postman began the debate on the well-being of contemporary children with his book *The Disappearance of Childhood* (Postman, 1982). He blamed the visual culture, then largely television, for fostering a declining respect for adults, a lack of a sense of shame in sex and the increasing prominence of children in crime statistics. His thesis reflects a long history of fears that children could be corrupted by accessible and cheap means of communication, with Victorians 150 years before fearing the corrupting influence of reading 'penny dreadfuls'. Sue Palmer renewed the debate twenty-five years later (when Postman's children were themselves parents) with her book *Toxic Childhood* (Palmer, 2007), which, alongside the newer phenomenon of computer games, listed many new potential causes for the disintegration of childhood. Educational competition, modelled on the competitive ethos of big business, had expanded to include a burgeoning focus on the child's earliest years, both in the UK and in America. Literacy initiatives were targeted at younger and younger children, leading to over-pressure, and, for Palmer, 'blinding adults to children's biological needs'. The worries of 'stranger danger' led to a 'retreat inside', with unremitting adult surveillance and outdoor play disappearing. She felt that this left children poorly socialized with little social responsibility, and that 'self-realisation' had become 'the only guiding star in a darkling sky'. The older child was threatened with obesity through the cheap availability of junk food. Constant noise and ever-present television were seen to interfere with children's ability to hear their parents and consequently to develop speech. As extended families and the propensity for multiple siblings had died away, parents no longer had practice at raising children before their own were born and had become novices at child-rearing. Palmer even pointed to baby slings and outward-facing pushchairs which diminished eye contact with the parent and broke the 'triangle of relatedness'.

The concerns for the death of childhood gathered momentum and in a letter to the *Daily Telegraph* in September 2006, one hundred professionals added their voices. They were from many different fields, with children's authors Philip Pullman, Jacqueline Wilson and Michael Morpurgo, environmental campaigner Sir Jonathan Porritt and the commissioner for London schools, Professor Tim Brighouse, as well as many child psychologists. Their concerns reflected many of the above issues.

> Our society rightly takes great pains to protect children from physical harm, but seems to have lost sight of their emotional and social needs ... They still need what developing human beings have always needed, including real food (as opposed to processed 'junk'), real play (as opposed to sedentary, screen-based entertainment), first-hand experience of the world they live in and regular interaction with the real-life significant adults in their lives. They also need time. In a fast-moving hyper-competitive culture, today's children are expected to cope with an ever-earlier start to formal schoolwork and an overly academic test-driven primary curriculum. They are pushed by market forces to act and dress like mini-adults and exposed via the electronic media to material which would have been considered unsuitable for children even in the very recent past. (*Daily Telegraph*, 13 September 2006)

The signatories expressed their deep concern at the escalating incidence of childhood depression and behavioural and developmental problems, claiming that, as children's brains were still developing, they could not adjust to 'ever more rapid technological and cultural change'. In the same month as the *Telegraph* letter, the Children's Society (2006) expressed its increasing concern about the way in which childhood was both experienced and understood, and launched *The Good Childhood Inquiry*, questioning 8,000 children about their views. Introducing the primary phase of the enquiry, the Archbishop of Canterbury, Rowan Williams, claimed that young children seemed assured of their parents' care (though not in their understanding), but expressed growing anxieties and fear of failure, with one in ten suffering from mental health problems. The inquiry itself called for a freeing of children from school pressures: bullying, overloaded curriculum, and the annual testing of teenagers. Their major criticisms were surprisingly not on the easy target of the video game culture, but on the more insidious commercial pressures that aimed to make them consumers at an increasingly early age. The archbishop reiterated their constricting freedom and their growing suspicion of all adults. He concluded that the root of the problem was a shared unwillingness to let children be children long enough.

The concerns have continued to the present day. A report commissioned by the National Union of Teachers (NUT) in June 2015 claimed that children were suffering from 'increasingly high levels of school-related anxiety and stress, disaffection and mental health problems' caused by pressure from testing and greater awareness at younger ages of their own 'failure'. The increase in diagnoses of ADHD was even seen to stem from the school environment, which now allowed less movement and practical work and required children to sit still for long periods (Hutchings, 2015: 5).

Alongside this fear of the death of childhood, there is however a contradictory conception that adolescents are becoming dangerous and unmanageable, with the creation of new phenomena, such as hoodies and ladettes. In October 2008, the UN Committee on the Rights of the Child reported that British children were at risk of being treated unfairly because of a 'general climate of intolerance' towards them and that there needed to be urgent measures to address the demonization of children, especially adolescents, within society and the media. In November 2008 a YouGov poll of 2,000 adults, commissioned by the charity Barnardos, found that 49 per cent believed children posed an increasing danger to society, 54 per cent said young people were 'beginning to behave like animals', and more than a third felt the streets were 'infested' with them. Martin Narey, the charity's chief executive, condemned the daily use of such words as 'animal', 'feral' and 'vermin' in reference to children, and claimed that these appeared to be a condemnation not of a small minority of children, but 'the public view of all children'. He claimed in exasperation: 'Despite the fact that most children are not troublesome, there is still a perception that today's young people are a more unruly, criminal lot than ever before.' Adolescents, for example, were thought to commit half of all crimes, although in reality they were responsible for only 12 per cent (Barnardos, 2008). This perception of a feral youth was intensified in the aftermath of the August 2011 riots which enveloped English cities. Many of the rioters were again seen to be out-of-control children, some as young as nine, who looted shops for the consumer goods that were held in such high regard: electrical goods, branded trainers and designer clothes. At a time of economic recession, the prevalent and continuing commercialism in society, with its persuasive advertising images, was again blamed for turning children into self-absorbed materialists without social conscience. Looking at the context of the UK, Sweden and Spain, UNICEF concluded that:

> Materialism is thought to be a cause, as well as an effect of negative well-being… children are more likely to thrive where the social context makes it possible for them to have time with family and friends, to get out and about without having to spend money, to feel secure about who they are rather than what they own, and to be empowered to develop resilience to pressures to consume. (Ipsos MORI, 2011: 71)

Young people were, however, perceived as no longer able to wait to obtain desired objects and the prevalence and immediacy of advertising images was seen to be damaging the very concept of delayed gratification in children.

Was there a 'good childhood' in the past?

The words 'good childhood' could hardly be used to describe the experience of children in much of history. There have been fundamental disagreements among historians as to the development of relationships between adults and children throughout the past. Philippe Aries began the debate in 1962 in *Centuries of Childhood*, suggesting that the very concept did not exist in medieval times (Aries, 1962). He studied artistic representations to show how images of children always showed them as shrunken adults and argued that the concept appeared slowly in the upper classes only in the sixteenth and seventeenth centuries. After the age of infancy, he argued, every able person was expected to contribute to the economic well-being of the household. Childhood scarcely began for a child of a landless labourer before it was curtailed by the need to work, with even the youngest children employed in the fields to scare birds. Even clothes, he argued, were those of mini-adults, with special dress for children only appearing at the end of the eighteenth century.

> In medieval society the idea of childhood did not exist; this is not to suggest that children were neglected, forsaken or despised. The idea of childhood is not to be confused with affection for children; it corresponds to an awareness of the particular nature of childhood, that particular nature which distinguishes the child from the adult, even the young adult. In medieval society, this awareness was lacking. (Aries, 1962: 125)

Aries' work was important in postulating that childhood was not a natural phenomenon, but a socially constructed one. Other historians have supported some of his views. Lawrence Stone in *The Family, Sex and Marriage in England, 1500–1800* argued that the short life expectancy of young children led to a detachment from parents, at least in the precarious first two years of life. Edward Shorter went further in 1976 in *The Making of the Modern Family*, seeing the rapid improvement in adult–child relations only developing in the modern era, and claiming that 'good mothering is an invention of modernisation' (Shorter, 1976: 33). He described what he discerned as a surge of sentiment in middle-class French families in the mid-eighteenth century and freer interaction between mothers and babies shown by maternal breast-feeding, an end to the use of wet-nurses and the abandonment of swaddling (the binding of the baby in cloth strips). The latter has been condemned as cruel and restricting for children, although to contemporaries it may have appeared to offer a baby security and warmth and to keep it from harm. From the seventeenth century babies were rarely swaddled beyond three months. The giving of the Christian name of deceased brothers or sisters to a new baby has been seen as evidence of a distance between parents and children, although before 1600 the Christian name was commonly given by godparents.

Aries has been challenged by many historians, including Shulamith Shahar, who in *Childhood in the Middle Ages* (1990) criticized his use of very limited sources (the diaries, letters and pictures of French aristocratic homes) to draw universal conclusions on childhood. Shahar insisted that medieval thinkers saw childhood as composed of several stages, and shows the enduring care for children in the period, with even a body of theory existing in relation to pregnancy, childbirth, infant feeding, weaning and rearing. (The medieval view was that birth should take place in a darkened room to ease the transition to the world outside the womb.) She quotes the fourteenth-century St Ida of Louvain, who describes the vision of bathing the infant Jesus, reflecting what must have been common practice in fourteenth-century child-rearing:

> When the Holy Infant was seated in the bath, he began to play as is the way of infants. He made noise in the water by clapping hands, and as children do, splashed in the water until it spilled out and wet all those around … On seeing the water splashing all around, he began to shout with joy in a loud voice … and when the bathing was complete, she lifted the child from the bath, dried him, and wrapped him in his swaddling bands. She seated him on her lap and as mothers do, began to play with him. (Cunningham, 2005: 30)

The concept of the seven ages of life appears frequently in the works of the Middle Ages, which gives some indication that people recognized a difference in attitude toward the young. A separate stage of childhood, *infantia*, was seen to last up to seven years old. Linda Pollock in *Forgotten Children* (Pollock, 1983) argues, from the discipline of anthropology and using studies of primates, that 'children require a certain amount of protection, affection and training for normal development' and that parents everywhere try to supply this. She identifies the period from seven to twelve years for girls and to fourteen for boys as a time for education, not necessarily in schools but through apprenticeship on the land or, for girls, in the home with their mothers. Children were not at this stage held to be fully criminally responsible and if they did commit crimes they were given more lenient penalties. From the thirteenth century, preaching manuals contained model sermons specifically addressed to issues of childhood, and these too recognized the concept, urging education and stressing the desirability for moderation in punishment. Anselm, for example, in the eleventh century had emphasized the child's need for 'loving kindness from others, of gentleness, mercy, cheerful address, charitable patience and many such-like comforts'. However, the constant repetition in such treatises suggests that parents did not always act with affection, much as today.

A study of Montaillou in France in the thirteenth and fourteenth centuries shows how parents cared for infants, even enjoying their company and expressing grief at their loss. One woman described how her brother's baby was dying and 'he sent for me when I was going to the woods to gather firewood, so that I could hold the dying child in my arms. So I did hold it from morning until evening when it died' (Ladurie, 2002: 212). There is little discrepancy between these reactions, 700 years ago, and those of today. Recent writers have even questioned the view that parents withdrew emotionally from young babies because of the threat of high infant mortality. Parents did grieve and many wrote of their grief. Ralph Josselin wrote of the death of his eight-year-old daughter in the 1640s:

My little Mary, very weake, wee feared shee was drawing on, feare came on my heart very much, but shee is not mine, but the Lord's, and shee is not too good for her father, shee was tender of her mother, thankefull, mindefull of god, in her extremity, shee would cry out, porre I, poore I … it was a pretious child, a bundle of myrrhe, a bundle of sweetnes, she was a child of ten thousand, full of wisedome, womanlike gravity, knowledge, sweet expressions of god, apt in her learning, tender-hearted and loving, an obedient child to us … free from the rudenesse of little children, it was to us as a boxe of sweet ointment, which now its broken smells more deliciously then it did before. Lord I rejoice I had such a present for thee. (Cunningham, 2005: 51)

Adam Martindale recorded of his son John, who died in 1663, that he was 'a beautiful child and very manly and courageous, for his age', who at only two years old would challenge 'a wanton tearing calfe' that chased other children and knocked them over. He took pride that his boy would 'stand his ground stoutly, beat it backe, and triumph over it, crying caw, caw, meaning he had beaten the calfe. I doe not think one child of 100 of his age durst doe so much' (Cunningham, 2006: 74). Linda Pollock found in diaries and autobiographies no evidence that parents before the eighteenth century were indifferent to the death of the young. She felt that brutality to children appeared an exception rather than the rule and that advice books recommending severe beatings did not always reflect actual practice (Pollock, 1987).

The experiences of many children in the nineteenth century were, however, horrendous. The evidence gathered by Evangelical reformers about child labour in factories and mines, on farms and as chimney sweeps, makes painful reading for modern eyes. Children were forced to work hard on farms, often because the family needed their wages. One father described the effect of farmwork undertaken by his daughter from the age of nine in the 1840s:

> She has complained of pain in her side very often … they force them along, they make them work hard. Gathering stones has hurt my girl's back at times. Pulling turnips is the hardest work; they get such a hold of the ground with their roots; when the land's strong it's as much as we can do to get 'em out, pull as hard as we can pull. It blisters their hands so that they can hardly touch anything … My girl went 5 miles yesterday to her work, turniping; she set off between seven and eight; she walked; had a piece of bread before she went; she did not stop work in the middle of the day; ate nothing till she left off; she came home between 3 and 4 o'clock … she is sometimes so tired, she can't eat no victuals when she comes home. (Pinchbeck, 1973: 393)

Another observer described a visit to Whitehaven coal mines in 1813, where he saw horses always driven by young girls who were 'ragged and beastly in their appearance'. At the age of five or six, many girls and boys spent the entire day in darkness as 'trappers' looking after the ventilation doors. Slightly older children dragged heavy loads of coal along passages, 'chained, belted and harnessed like dogs in a go cart, black, saturated with wet, and more than half naked, crawling on their hands and feet and dragging their loads behind them, they present an appearance indescribably disgusting and unnatural' (Pinchbeck, 1973: 401). In the factories, child workers suffered a similar plight, as one contemporary described: 'in stench, in heated rooms, amid the constant whirling of a thousand wheels, little fingers and little feet were kept in ceaseless action, forced into unnatural activity by blows from heavy hands and feet of the merciless over-looker.' Lord Shaftesbury, who championed the cause of child workers, described seeing children in the 1840s coming out of the factory gates 'a set of sad, dejected, cadaverous creatures ... the sight was most piteous, the deformities incredible ... such were their crooked shapes, like a mass of crooked alphabets' (ibid.: 403).

As early as the seventeenth century young boys were employed by chimney sweeps to clean inside flues with hand brushes. After the Great Fire of London and with the increasing use of coal as a fuel, the design of chimneys was altered, making them often angular and narrow, the usual dimension of a domestic flue being nine inches by fourteen inches. As the master sweep was unable to climb into such spaces himself, he employed small climbing boys, as young as seven years old, to go up the chimneys to dislodge the soot. The boys often 'buffed it', climbed naked, propelling themselves by their knees and elbows which were scraped raw. Sweeps' boys were usually parish children or orphans, though others were sold into the trade by their families. There were numerous reports of casualties, with boys becoming stuck in flues or choked by soot inhalation, and there were long-term effects such as cancer of the testicles. The boys were seldom washed, sleeping in cellars on bags of soot. Lord Shaftesbury devoted many years to campaigning for the end of the employment of children, introducing a number of Factory Acts, but it was not until 1864 that he secured the Act for the Regulation of Chimney Sweepers which established a penalty of ten pounds for offending sweeps.

Angels or monsters?

James, Jenks and Prout (1998) have argued that there were various construc-tions of children in the past, which understood them to be either inherently wicked or inherently innocent – the Dionysian child and the Apollonian child. The first conception describes children entering the world with 'a wilful material energy', which could become anarchistic and threaten social order. The second sees the child as pure and naturally good, but liable to be corrupted by the world. The modern dichotomy of view about the nature of infants and adolescents is reflected in these two diverse views of childhood which appear to be mutually contradictory. There appears to be an oscillating emphasis on these ideas throughout history, with the former bringing with it the frequent use of corporal punishment. The doctrine of original sin did not emerge until St Augustine in the fourth century, but the conception that babies were born in sin remained until the twelfth century and reappeared with Luther in the Reformation. The belief in children's innocence was however also rooted in Christian tradition, with Jesus asserting: 'unless you become as little children, you shall not enter the Kingdom of Heaven.'

Renaissance thinkers wrote extensively about children. Erasmus emphasized the need to teach good behaviour and gave advice on sneezing, spitting, urinating and table manners from the earliest years. He did not accept original sin, although he acknowledged their 'disposition to evil' and blamed adults for corrupting young minds, He compared a child to wax which might be moulded by early education. Nature had implanted a desire for knowledge in children, but 'the child ... is nothing but a shapeless lump, the material is still pliable, capable of assuming any form, and you must so mould it that it takes on the best possible character. If you are negligent, you will rear an animal, but if you apply yourself, you will fashion ... a godlike creature' (Cunningham, 2006: 111). The child would turn out to be 'an unproductive brute unless and at once and without delay he is subjected to a process of intensive instruction'. He even claimed in 1497 that enjoyment had to be intermingled with studies 'so that we think of learning as a game rather than a form of drudgery'. One example given is of a father who noticed his son's interest in archery and so had a set of bows and arrows decorated all over with the letters of the alphabet; if the boy hit the target and pronounced the letter, he was rewarded with a cherry, and within a few weeks he had learnt them all.

There were many advice books in the Reformation which took the alternative view of the child, complaining of over indulgence. Conrad Sam wrote of Ulm that as soon as a child could move about, 'one throws a ragged frock on him and treats everything he does in the same unjudgemental way ... Soon there are outbursts and tantrums, but these only delight the old, since they come from a dear little son, who can do no wrong. Where one sows thorns and thistles in this way, how can anything other than weeds be expected to grow?' Thomas Becon in 1563 criticized parents who regarded childhood as 'a time for fun, joy and amusement' and reminded them that 'a child in Scripture is a wicked man, as he is ignorant and not exercised in godliness' (Becon, 1823: 414). A Nuremberg catechism in use in England asserted that even unborn babies in the womb had 'evil lusts and appetites', while a German sermon of 1520 claimed: 'just as a cat craves mice, a fox chickens, and a wolf cub sheep, so infant humans are inclined in their hearts to adultery, fornication, impure desires, lewdness, idol worship, belief in magic, hostility, quarrelling, passion, anger, strife, dissension, factiousness, hatred, murder, drunkenness and gluttony' (Heywood, 2001: 33). Catholicism saw this nature being purified by infant baptism, although this was rejected by Protestants, who saw only the salvation by faith, and hence the necessity for disciplining. John Robinson, a pastor of the Pilgrim Fathers wrote:

Surely there is in all children ... a stubbornness, and stoutness of mind arising from natural pride, which must, in the first place be broken and beaten down: that so the foundation of their education being laid in humility and tractableness, other virtues may, in their time, be built thereon. For the beating and keeping down of this stubbornness parents must provide carefully ... that the children's wills and wilfulness be restrained and repressed. (Robinson, 1851: 246)

Because of this perceived inherent wickedness, the regular use of the rod was approved as a biblical punishment. Hugh Latimer in 1552 typically preached: 'suffer not your children to lie, take him up, and give him three or four good stripes and tell him that it is naught; and when he maketh another lie, give him six or eight stripes and I am sure when you serve him so, he will leave it.' Thomas Becon, in his *Catechism* written for his five-year-old son in 1550, saw corporal punishment as 'necessary as meat and drink' (Becon, 1844: 353), although he was more temperate than his contemporaries in claiming that correction ought to be 'gentle and favourable ... according to the fault and also according to the nature of the child that offendeth'. Before punishing the child, he urged parents to explain the nature of the fault and the reason for the punishment and that there should be moderation 'both in words and stripes; that the wits of the children be not dulled, nor they driven to such an hatred of their parents that they begin no more to love as parents, but to hate them as tyrants and hereof take an occasion to run away from them' (ibid.: 354). He criticized the over-indulgent father, but, reflecting on the experiences of many a sixteenth-century child, he condemned those many parents who 'furiously rage against their children, and without consideration beat them as stock fish'. Such parents were 'rather butchers than fathers'.

In the seventeenth and eighteenth centuries there was a decline in the acceptance of original sin and, instead of being seen as innately evil, young children began to be regarded as angelic in their innocence. John Locke, when advising on the education of upper-class boys, questioned the use of corporal punishment, but accepted it as necessary for those who showed 'obstinacy' and 'rebellion', as the aim was for them to 'submit their will to the *reason* of others', to produce adults who would know how to submit their passion to their own reason. In *Some Thoughts Concerning Education*, Locke sees the child as a blank slate only in respect to knowledge and not in respect of abilities and temperament. For him, no two children were alike, having 'various tempers, different inclinations and particular defaults' which must be discovered in watching them play. Their curiosity should be encouraged and their questions carefully answered. Learning should be made 'a play and recreation' (Locke, 1693: 261, 174) and 'all their innocent folly, playing, and *childish actions*' were to be left 'perfectly free and unrestrained, as far as they can consist with respect due to those that are present' (ibid.: 62). This recognition of children's individuality, partly fostered by the increased privacy of family life, was a step towards a more child-centred society. During the eighteenth and nineteenth centuries, literature appeared to stress the concept of original innocence. Jean-Jacques Rousseau's novel *Emile* of 1762 attacked the dominance of the fathers in child-rearing:

> You say mothers spoil their children and no doubt that is wrong, but it is worse to deprave them as you do. The mother wants her child to be happy now. She is right, and if her method is wrong, she must be taught a better. Ambition, avarice, tyranny, the mistaken foresight of fathers, their neglect, their harshness, are a hundredfold more harmful to the child than the blind affection of the mother. (Rousseau, 1918: 2)

Rousseau felt that, until the age of twelve, education should be merely negative: 'Leave childhood to ripen in your children … beware of giving anything they need today if it can be deferred without danger to tomorrow … childhood has its own ways of seeing, thinking, and feeling'; it was 'the sleep of reason'. He also questioned the point of so forcefully preparing children for adulthood when many would die young, and he therefore championed the right for a child to be a child:

> Love childhood, indulge its sports, its pleasures, its delightful instincts. Who has not sometimes regretted (missed) that age when laughter was ever on the lips, and when the heart was ever at peace? Why rob these innocents of the joys which pass so quickly, of that precious gift which they cannot abuse? Why fill with bitterness the fleeting days of early childhood, days which will no more return for them than for you? (Rousseau, 1918: 44)

William Wordsworth's 'Ode on intimations of immortality' similarly stressed the loss of childhood innocence and the loss of insight that went with it.

By the early nineteenth century the Evangelical Revival saw the reassertion that the child was naturally sinful and needed to have its will broken by stern discipline. The *Evangelical Magazine* of 1799, for example, stressed that children were 'sinful, polluted creatures', and Hannah Moore warned about treating children as if they were innocent. John Wesley revived the belief of early Calvinists that all children were by nature evil and that parents had to check their passions. His ideas of child-rearing came from his mother, Susannah, who described her practices to him in a letter of 1732. Her children were kept on 'spoon meat' until the age of six, to allay 'the angry passions', and when they were a year old they were taught to fear the rod, and to cry softly. Susannah wrote that the 'most odious noise' of the crying of children was rarely heard in her house. Her discipline was stern, but 'leavened with kindness', with a combination of rewards and punishments. Every act of obedience, 'especially when it crossed upon their own inclinations', would be commended and frequently rewarded. There was to be no room for self-expression:

> In order to form the minds of children, the first thing to be done is to conquer their will, and to bring them to obedient temper ... As self-will is the root of all sin and misery, so whatever cherishes this in children insures their after-wretchedness and irreligion; whatever checks and mortifies it promotes their future happiness and piety. (Wesley, 1732)

In middle-class Victorian households in particular there was often a reversion to this more authoritarian family type, although fused with an intense religious concern for the children's welfare. Only in the closing decades of the Victorian period was there a gradual move to greater child-centredness and permissiveness, arguably caused by the decline in religiosity and new psychological theories of child development. The influence of Freud and other scientific studies fostered the belief that psychological origins were the triggers for delinquency in childhood.

The resilience of play

Play has been seen as almost synonymous with childhood. Vygotsky wrote of unstructured play being a powerful learning tool and Bruner in 1983 described it as 'a test frame, a hot house for trying out ways of combining thought and language and fantasy – play under the control of the player gives to the child his [sic] first and most crucial opportunity to have the courage to think, to talk, and perhaps even to be him' (Bruner, 1983: 69). It is without frustrating consequences and gives the child freedom to experiment, freedom to explore and the freedom to fail. One of the major current concerns is the disappearance of outside play.

Throughout history, and regardless of how adults saw them, children seem to have created opportunities for play. During the medieval period, they created toys such as marbles, balls and dice, balancing devices, swings, see-saws and spring-boards, known as 'totters' and 'merry totters' (Orme, 2003: 179). Martin Luther's letter to the *Mayor and Aldermen* mentioned children's natural desire to be active, running and jumping and using other games, which, he advised, should not be restrained: 'let no-one think himself too wise, and disdain such child's play' (Painter, 1889: 154–5). Medieval

Fig. 1: Fifteenth-century children snowballing, from A Book of Hours. *Courtesy of Walters Art Museum, Baltimore*

artists depicted little children at play outside with hobby-horses, windmills, birds on a leash and dolls. Manuscripts show them snowballing and playing a variety of games. Pieter Bruegel's painting *Children's Games* of 1560 is clear evidence of a remarkable resilience of similar kinds of play as today. In 1665, the *Maison des Jeux* by Sorel lists hockey, spinning tops, ladders, shuttlecock and blind-man's buff and there were also 'rhymed dialogues', similar to the rhyming games in modern playgrounds. Toys might be made by parents or crafted by the children themselves. While there were no toy shops in England in 1730, they were widespread by 1780, with toys made specifically for richer children. Books dedicated to children were rare until the eighteenth century, as they were expected to read the Bible and religious treatises, although one London publisher, John Newbery, began to produce 'little pocket books' with the story of Jack the Giant Killer from 1744. From 1780 authors began to write specific children's literature and chapbooks were common in the nineteenth century.

Children themselves had very little voice to give their evidence from the past. However, one cannot read Jean Froissart's recollections of his boyhood in 1363 without feeling that there is something never-changing about this period of life. He remembered with affection the fun, games, dances and carolling:

> I was never tired of playing games ... In a brook I would make a little dam with a tile and I took a small saucer and made it float down. And in the hollow by the brook I often built a mill out of two tiles. Then we ... got our coats and hats and shirts wet in the brook. Sometimes we made a feather fly down the wind, and I have often sifted earth with a shell onto my coat, and I was skilled at making mud balls. I often amused myself by making a straw pipe and I was very good at chasing butterflies. When I caught them, I tied threads to them, and when I let them go, I could make them fly as I pleased. I did not care for chess, dice, tables and other grown-up games, but I did like to make mud pies, round loaves, cakes and tartlets ... And when Lent came I kept under my stool a great storehouse of shells for which I would not have exchanged for any amount of money ... And when the moon was bright, we played at 'Pinch Me' ... we played games called 'Follow the Leader' and 'Trot-trot Merlot', and pebbles, and Hockley, and 'Heads or Tails' ... and when we were together, we all ran and played 'Robber Enguerrand', and 'Brinmbetelle' and 'Deux Bastons qu'on Restelle'. And I often made a horse called Grisel out of a stick. (Froissart, 1870: 87–9)

Even in the nineteenth century, and in spite of the prevalence of child labour, there was still much evidence for childhood pursuits, even for the poor. In the countryside, children would roam the fields searching for flowers and birds' nests and go fishing with improvised lines. Flora Thompson remembered the girls meeting regularly on summer evenings to participate in dancing and chanting games. School log books show how often Victorian children played truant to see a one-man band, a fair, a local meet of hounds or even a band of soldiers marching. Robert Roberts recalled how he and his friends used their imaginations to make everyday objects into playthings, constructing 'hamlets of thatched cottages' by covering gas mantle boxes with straw, using lumps of washing soda to make cliffs and flour and salt sweepings from the shop floor to create snow in their village. This was peopled with figures carved out of pop bottle corks (Roberts, 1997: 26–7).

By the twentieth century, Froebel placed a new emphasis on growth through play, devising a series of toys or 'gifts' and 'occupations' intended

Fig. 2: Southlands schoolroom in c. 1890 with pupils' chalked drawings on the wall and a rocking horse in the class. Courtesy of Southlands College Archive

to promote 'the harmonious growth of the intellectual, moral and physical powers of the child'. Play was not seen as a waste of time, but a way of development. Froebel favoured allowing the child to work out its own development. John Dewey recognized the importance of Froebel's ideas of growth, and placed great emphasis on activity, including play, for its own sake, challenging the idea of forcing the child to develop in a specific way by mechanical applications. The child should determine its own growth rather than being guided towards a completed product.

The 1950s are often idealized as a golden era for children and their play. Paul Feeney recalls that, even a decade after the Second World War, there were dilapidated houses and bomb ruins everywhere in many towns and cities and that these became the forbidden playgrounds of youngsters (Feeney, 2009). Nothing was planned and if someone had a ball, games of football would be started in the middle of a road, with jumpers for goalposts. There would be no rules and boys would join in as they arrived in the street. Children spent most of their summers outdoors, in all weathers. Feeney notes that the camaraderie of wartime was still evident, creating this sense of belonging. But he also recalls the ever-present prospect of a 'wallop' from a policeman or a parent, and the cold, draughty houses, tin baths, outside toilets and being trapped inside in dark winters, having to rely on the fledgling radio programmes or, in the early 1960s, the television for entertainment. There was, though, still pressure to compete in primary school for the coveted grammar school places and children still suffered from poverty, dirt and disease. Iona and Peter Opie recorded the games they saw in the playground in *The Lore and Language of Schoolchildren* (1959) and in *Children's Games in Street and Playground* (1969). When the issue was revisited in 2010, Stephen Roud discovered, after interviewing several hundred children, that they were still playing and creating their own traditions, with fifteen versions of 'tig' in one playground alone and the persistence of elaborate, skilful clapping chants and skipping sequences (Roud, 2010).

One cannot ignore the hardness of childhood in previous generations. Children were often seen as subject to original wickedness which had to be beaten out of them and they consequently suffered harsh and, at times, barbaric punishments for misdemeanours. For many children before the twentieth century, childhood *per se* ended with early working life in poor conditions in mines and factories or up chimneys. One is left to ponder if there ever was such a thing as a good childhood in the past for the majority of children. There were, though, certainly different childhoods. There has been a presumption in current thinking that childhood is socially constructed, a period of special treatment that adults allow to children, but there is an alternative view that childhood is a developmental imperative in a human child, and that, regardless of their social conditions, children – like Jean Froissart – will create this for themselves, by playing, investigating, questioning, learning about the world and learning to socialize, from which they find their roles in adult society. After his very detailed study of medieval play, Nicholas Orme concluded tellingly: 'Most of all, children went on playing, despite all their elders' attempts to control what they did. Boys after all will be boys, and girls will be girls' (Orme, 2003: 197). In that there may still be hope for a new generation of children.

Chapter 1

How far do children make their own chidhood and how far is it foist upon them?

Why has there been such an outcry at the supposed death of childhood and simultaneously an intolerance of a burgeoning feral youth?

How important is play for the young in contemporary life?

2

What does society expect from schooling?

Mother: 'Head Master, what do you prepare your boys for?'
Headmaster: 'Death, Madam, death.'

(DR ALINGTON, HEADMASTER OF ETON COLLEGE)

The expectations of schooling are not always clearly articulated by politicians, parents or even schools themselves. However, such aims are important in consciously or unconsciously determining many aspects of school life. This chapter analyses the potential purposes of schooling *per se*, investigating the concepts of instrumentalism and non-instrumental or liberal education, looking at the development of these two strands over time and the influence of social class on determining them, and finally, investigating recent trends in government thinking on the issue.

The above quote was made to a parent almost a century ago and shows a view that is at variance with any modern conception of the aims of schooling. It is not easy to discern the aims of a particular school, let alone of a nation's schooling. They are not always clearly articulated, they can be implicit as well as explicit, and they can be subject to heated disputes between the various interest groups such as government, business leaders, parents and the teachers themselves. Like Russian dolls, a stated objective can frequently mask a deeper, sometimes more prosaic, one. The foreword to the 2003 DfES strategy for primary schools, *Excellence and Enjoyment*, for example, stated that enjoyment was 'the birthright of every child', although this laudable sentiment was immediately linked in the text with its effect on outcomes, that 'children learn better when they are excited and engaged' (DfES, 2003: 3). The enjoyment is a vehicle, not a destination. However, defining these objectives is important. The Office for Standards in Education (Ofsted) inspects schools to discover if they are achieving the many state-imposed objectives, which have in recent years been clearly target-driven. Chris Winch goes so far as to claim in *Key Concepts in the Philosophy of Education* that the aims of schooling determine the character of everything else: curriculum, pedagogy, assessment and resourcing, especially the precious resource of time (Gingell, 1999: 10–11).

There are various ways of categorizing aims, with the tradition used in the present chapter being that which acknowledges a division between instrumental and non-instrumental objectives. These are not mutually exclusive, but provide a useful tool to analyse what society expects from schooling. The instrumental sees schooling as vital for utilitarian aims, with vocational and personal skill acquisition intended primarily to benefit society. In the instrumentalist view, schools as institutions supported by the taxpayer are a means to promote socioeconomic growth. Such utilitarians argue that there is little value in knowledge and understanding for its own sake and that the acid test of fitness for any inclusion in the school curriculum needs to be social or economic advantage. Education is therefore seen as a means to an end, not as an end in itself (Carr, 2003: 15). It follows from this viewpoint that schools should train children primarily to acquire skills needed for successful employment, with language, numeracy and ICT skills given priority in the modern world. In the sense of social utility, schools also train children to become integrated into a society, with the need to be inculcated with those values treasured by the society itself, yet which might not be acquired in the home or local community. In Durkheim's phrase of 1922, education 'far from having as its unique or principal object the individual and his interests, is above all the means by which society perpetually recreates the conditions of its existence' (Durkheim, 1956: 123). Even in a contemporary, diverse and pluralist society, schools attempt to fulfil this need with a cross-cultural consensus on 'core' values. As David Carr writes, 'a time-honoured way of thinking about education would regard schools and teachers as perhaps the principal agencies of moral formation in society – in a way that goes beyond mere accountability to current social trends or parental predilections' (Carr, 2003: 73).

The alternative, non-instrumentalist (often termed *liberal*) view focuses on the intrinsic value of education for the individual child, with schooling seen as good for its own sake. Socioeconomic concerns are therefore regarded as secondary in importance to an entitlement for all children to their cultural inheritance. It is seen as a duty of schools to acquaint every child, irrespective of differences of ability and social background, with the best that has been thought and said. This presumes that there is a literature and a history, as well as scientific ideas, that are universal educational requirements. Carr, for example, sees schooling as enabling pupils to acquire some grasp of 'how the world actually is, as well as of who they themselves are by virtue of some appreciation of the cultural traditions and events that have made them who they are' (Carr, 2003: 127). The beneficiary of this education is the individual child, and only in a subsidiary sense the society itself.

The conception of a 'liberal' education was in the past limited to a social elite, rather than an accepted goal for all learners. This division of aim was reflected in the twentieth century by the Norwood Committee, the precursor of the stratification of secondary schools in the 1944 Education Act, which recommended different kinds of curriculum in different schools for different classes of children. Its report claimed that certain types of pupils needed to receive the training best suited for them and 'that training would lead them to an occupation where their capacities would be suitably used'. The curriculum here would concentrate on the skills associated with a particular kind of occupation, 'its outlook and its methods would always be bounded by a near horizon clearly envisaged ... closely related to industry, trades and commerce in their diversity'. The majority of children would have such a curriculum, while a much smaller number, in grammar schools, would have a curriculum 'of which the most characteristic feature is that it treats the various fields of knowledge as suitable for coherent and systematic study for their own sake apart from immediate considerations of occupation' (Board of Education, 1943: 4).

Both strands can be seen in varying degrees in most schooling, although state educational policy has been dominated by this instrumentalist mindset. In the 1970s, the Great Debate on education fostered by Prime Minister James Callaghan's Ruskin College speech stressed the need for a more technological bias in science teaching 'that will lead towards practical applications in industry rather than towards academic studies'. The prime minister reiterated the concern of industrialists about the poor numeracy of school leavers and asked: 'is there not a case for a professional review of the mathematics needed by industry at different levels?' He expressed exasperation that there were 30,000 untaken places for science and engineering in universities and polytechnics, while humanities courses were full (Callaghan, 1976). The Department of Education reflected the sentiments in the following year:

It is vital to Britain's economic recovery and standard of living that the performance of manufacturing industry is improved and that the whole range of government policies, including education, contribute as much as possible to improving industrial performance and thereby increasing the national wealth. (DES, 1977: 6)

The election of Margaret Thatcher as prime minister in 1979 brought a hard-headed reassertion of the connection of schooling to socioeconomic goals. If any economy was to operate effectively in an increasingly competitive global market, it was posited that a skilled workforce had to be supplied by schools. The 1985 DES White Paper *Better Schools* emphasized that schools must always remember that preparation for working life was 'one of their principal functions', and two years later Thatcher herself iterated instrumentalist educational aims in a speech to the Institute of Directors, which stressed the 'habit of enterprise':

> Part of our response today must be to enhance the skills and abilities of our people. For even at a time of high unemployment, employers tell us they are unable to find people to fill some vacancies because so many of those seeking work do not have the skills or qualifications needed in today's world ... it all begins at school. So we are working to strengthen standards of numeracy and literacy, and a programme to encourage technical and vocational education is now being introduced into our secondary schools right across the country ... I know you will feel frustrated, as I do, that with such massive amounts of expenditure of both private and public money the process of matching jobs to skills is so painfully slow ... we must in fact take the steps which I have enumerated to see that children, after eleven years of compulsory education, come out properly equipped ... for the world of work which they will face. (Thatcher, 1987)

Under Thatcher's successor John Major, the 1996 DfEE consultative document *Equipping Young People for Working Life* claimed again that the reforms of the previous years had been 'in line with the needs of a modern competitive economy' and that the prosperity of the country depended on the skills of each individual being developed through education. It concluded: 'We must do all we can to help ... young people to acquire the skills, knowledge and understanding they will need to be part of a highly adaptive workforce' (DfEE, 1996: 1). Tony Blair, as Labour prime minister from 1997, emphasized literacy and numeracy initiatives and in the 2001 election campaign outlined his priorities, purporting to be an amalgam of objectives:

> Our top priority was, is and always will be education, education, education. To overcome decades of neglect and make Britain a learning society, developing the talents and raising the ambitions of all our young people. At a good school, children gain the basic tools for life and work. But they ought also to learn the joy of life: the exhilaration of music, the excitement of sport, the beauty of art, the magic of science. And they learn the value of life: what it is to be responsible citizens who give something back to their community. (Blair, 2001)

One contemporary analyst was led to remark at the time that, in spite of those who wanted to reclaim education as a 'humanizing, liberalizing, democratizing force' directed to the full development of the human personality, schooling had become subject to a 'tawdry subservience to market forces' and that 'the notion that educational institutions had any purpose other than an economic function had almost completely disappeared from policy making discourse' (Tomlinson, 2001: 170–1). Blair's education secretary, Charles Clarke, himself in January 2003 pronounced that education for its own sake was 'a bit dodgy' and his priorities were clear in his condemnation of the idea that students could learn about the world sitting in a study 'just reading books', without a 'relationship with the workplace'. The economic collapse of 2008 and the consequent economic recessions have made it even more difficult for educationalists to secure a less instrumentalist approach to the teaching of children.

The aims of past schooling

Utilitarianism permeated the early history of education in England. In medieval society education took place predominantly within the family, with a father's duty to instruct his sons in their trade, and a mother's to prepare daughters for their domestic duties. Basic religious education came through the church, although most of the ordinary clergy themselves had little schooling and probably shared the illiteracy of the population at large. Among laymen, literacy was confined to a few noblemen brought up in the bishops' households or in monasteries. Book knowledge and writing were irrelevant in a poor and primitive society, in which the vast majority had to struggle on the land for their families to survive. Story-telling and poetry was transmitted orally and there was no need for reading for peasants, whose own language was in any case local dialect. Books were rare, having to be copied by hand in the monastic scriptoriums and were generally in Latin rather than English until the 1250s. Writing was an even more sophisticated skill and was not seen as of use to society. Apart from a small body of clerks needed in the king's service, it was the monopoly of monks. Most of the Anglo-Norman barons were hardly more literate than the peasantry and French, not English was the language of the court. Religion though was always seen to be of value in this society. In the year 960 King Edgar required that teaching religion was one of the pastoral duties of priests, and other laws at the end of the millennium enjoined priests to keep free schools so that 'every Christian man zealously accustom his children to Christianity and teach them the Pater Noster and Creed' (Leach, 1971: 35). This teaching was given orally from the pulpit on Sundays, with priests using the ubiquitous wall paintings, statues and religious dramas. It was still the duty of the parish priest in the eleventh and twelfth centuries to 'keep schools in the villages and teach little boys *gratis*' (ibid.: 34). In 1281 Archbishop Pecham's *Ignorantia sacerdotum* (reissued until the sixteenth century) prescribed that the ten commandments and the seven sacraments should be taught in English four times a year. From about 1300, monasteries provided a form of lay education at song schools and grammar schools. From the late fourteenth century, chantry schools gave the rudiments of English reading, although they were small, with fewer than twenty boys who were usually the sons of affluent tradesmen or yeomen. Until 1406 a bondsman could only send his son to school if he was intended to become a priest, reflecting the utilitarian expectations of society. Poverty denied schooling to the great mass of the rural population living at subsistence level, with parents unable either to afford school fees or to forego their children's earnings or labour.

The sixteenth-century religious revolution of Henry VIII brought significant changes in the 'instrumental' demands of education. The Reformation saw the attempt to create a religion based on the reading of the Bible, at variance with Roman Catholicism which emphasized the interpretation of the Bible given by the Church. There was therefore more pressure to create a society based on a literate population. The convocation of Canterbury in 1529 ordered that all priests should teach boys the alphabet, reading, singing or grammar. The invention of printing in the sixteenth century brought the widespread use of the printed Bible and prayer books. During Queen Elizabeth I's reign, Justices of the Peace and town officers were empowered to establish workhouse schools and to take in the children of paupers who might become a charge upon the parish. An interesting example came from Norwich after 1570, where some 900 children of the poor were organized in an employment training scheme for which they received six pence a week, with women appointed in each ward of the city to instruct the children in spinning and other skills.

For those children who were fortunate enough to have any schooling, the alphabet and the fundamentals of the Christian faith from the Bible and prayer book were the subjects of study. The value of education was not always clear to parents themselves however and they often took their children away from school. Charles Hoole in 1659 claimed that children of 'the poorer sort' were taken away from the petty school as soon as they could read 'any whit well' and permitted to run wilding up and down without any control' (Hoole, 1913: 25). The majority of the population continued to be unable to read and write. In rural areas with no petty school, the richer boys might go straight to a grammar school, to be taught the basics by the usher within the grammar school itself. The result was that by 1640 the gentry and merchant class were generally literate, and in the New Model Army of 1645 the majority of the cavalry could write, while the most of the poorer infantry privates were unable to sign their names.

By the eighteenth century, there was a variety of schooling in England with private, petty and parish schools all giving elementary education in religious matters, reading and writing. Dame schools, run by widows or spinsters, gave some form of schooling, with the 'dames' undertaking this work to avoid beggary. They looked after the village children at home and taught them to read, knit and sew for whatever their parents could afford to pay each week. The century also saw the start of charity schools, with the Society for Promoting Christian Knowledge starting its first schools in 1699 to spread practical Christianity and Anglicanism among the very poorest children. They were supported by subscriptions, appeals and collections. The exact role of the SPCK in the provision of charity schooling has been a matter of some dispute, although the instrumental benefits of this schooling were expressed by its supporters, who argued that they acted as a protection of property by keeping poor children off the streets and farms. Pupils were trained to be good Christians, loyal citizens, and industrious workpeople, with particular emphasis placed on the learning of the catechism as a bulwark against Roman Catholic doctrines. Deference and piety were expected. Writing and arithmetic were sometimes taught to boys to prepare them for apprenticeship or other employment, whilst girls received instruction in household matters. In some there was sufficient money to pay the teacher and to provide the children with uniforms, boarding and entry into apprenticeship. There were many critics of the charity schools, however, including Bernard Mandeville, who questioned the value of teaching reading, writing and arithmetic *per se* to the children of the labouring poor. In an essay of 1724, he argued that the charity schools were simply repeating the errors of excessive school provision of the previous centuries, though at a lower social level:

> Going to school in comparison to working, is idleness, and the longer boys continue in this easy sort of life, the more unfit they will be when grown up for downright labour, both as to strength and inclination. Men, who are to remain and end their days in a laborious, tiresome and painful station of life, the sooner they are put upon it at first, the more patiently they'll submit to it for ever after. (Mandeville, 1724: 258)

Mandeville felt that these children would never make a 'good hireling, and serve a farmer for a pitiful reward' following 'the plough and dung-cart', as they would if they had never been educated. The instrumentalist mindset is clear in both views.

As an alternative to the charity school, John Locke, in a report of 1697 to the Board of Trade, suggested the establishment of working schools in every parish. These would be attached to workhouses and cater for all unemployed children between the ages of three and fourteen. Training and work would be provided on weekdays with compulsory attendance at church on Sundays for religious and moral instruction. He did not recommend over-education for the poor, commenting that 'mental culture' was not for men of low condition, but only for those with means and leisure, 'who by the industry and parts of their ancestors have been set free from a constant drudgery to their backs and their bellies' (Lawson, 1973: 175).

There was a new direction in schooling with the creation of the Sunday school movement which grew rapidly from the 1780s. The founder, Robert Raikes saw the instrumental need to reform society, through the Sunday school, 'by establishing notions of duty and discipline at an early stage.' He found the streets full on Sundays of 'multitudes of these wretches who ... spend their time in noise and riot, playing at chuck, and cursing and swearing in a manner so horrid' (Goldstrom, 1972: 16). He intended that his schools should undertake 'botanising human nature' (ibid.: 18). Raikes and his contemporaries promoted salvation, preservation of property and the peace of the sabbath, and some historians stress their concern to produce an amenable workforce. Sunday schools were again an important means to create habits of punctuality, regular attendance, honesty, deference and sobriety, which were essential to factory employment. They were also pervasive, with over a million children enrolled in them by 1831. In 1839 a general survey of handloom weavers showed that five times as many of their children attended Sunday school as weekday school. The widespread evangelical movement encouraged inter-denominational schools based at church or chapel, organized by clergy, their wives and daughters and continued to impart religious and moral instruction.

Among the ruling elite there remained a strong view throughout the eighteenth and early nineteenth centuries that too much literacy among the population at large was a danger to the established order, which had been 'divinely ordained' and depended on a plentiful supply of labourers and servants. If children were educated above their station, they might become dissatisfied with their lot and cause social disruption. Farmers in particular opposed the development of schools in rural areas and Sunday schools were described in Hull in 1788 as 'a preposterous institution, replete with folly, indolence, fanaticism and mischief' (Hadley, 1788: 378). As one contemporary exclaimed at the time:

> There is a degree of ignorance necessary ... to make them useful to others or happy in themselves. What ploughman who could read the renowned

history of *Tom Hickathrift, Jack the Giant-Killer, or the Seven Wise Men*, would be content to whistle up one furrow and down another, from dawn in the morning, to the setting of the sun? (Hadley, 1788: 381)

Even Henry Brougham, the Lord Chancellor, who saw the value of education for its own sake, still recognized the instrumental advantages, chiefly as an insurance *against* social convulsion. He believed that the acquisition of knowledge would do more than anything else to secure peace and order and to maintain the stability of the government, by instilling a respect for property into the minds of the poor. In 1833 he told the Lords that there was a clear diminution of violent crime in areas of good schooling, and two years later argued that crime itself originated from a lack of reasoning and the failure to control the passions which could be overcome if children under the age of seven were brought under the influence of the schoolteacher:

> where the acquisition of vicious habits may be effectually prevented and the principle of virtue may thus early be instilled into the mind ... where, above all, the habits of prudence, industry and self control may be taught at a season when lasting habits are acquired ... It is not merely the teaching of reading, writing and cyphering that profits the child: the regular school attendance is far more material for its improvement. Six days in the week, at six hours in the day, is a vast advantage in this training. (Hansard, 1835: 1314, 1296)

Brougham believed that it would do more to eradicate crime than either the gallows, the convict ship or the treadmill. His attempts to create state elementary schools, however, met with great opposition. William Cobbett rejected the supposed advantages of teaching the working classes to read and write:

> Education was the knowledge necessary for the situation in life in which a man was placed. Take two men – suppose one of them to be able to plough and the other able to plough and make hurdles and be a good shepherd. If the first man knew how to read as well as to plough, and the other man did not know how to read, even then he should say that the latter was the better. He pointed to the reports that stressed the growing immorality of the people in spite of increased educational provision and concluded that it tended to nothing but to increase the number of schoolmasters and schoolmistresses – that new race of idlers. (Hansard, 1833: 735)

The educational field ultimately had to be left to voluntary societies, supported with government grants, and largely to the Church of England, whose schools were also seen as a bastion against Nonconformity or Catholicism and outnumbered, by many times over, all the other types of schools in the country. In *Victorian Class Conflict,* the present author has analysed the variety of motivations articulated by the nineteenth-century clergymen. There were clear, religious aims for these schools, with Henry Newland telling teachers in 1856: 'When you have manufactured a steady, honest, God-fearing, Church-going population, then you have done your duty as Schoolmasters' (Smith, 2009: 1). Some clergy wrote of their schools as the most effective means of maintaining social order when village life was often boorish. John Sandford wrote in his clergy manual of 1845 that they would create 'habits of regular industry and self-control', while other writers used such phrases as 'the subordination of discipline', 'the contagion of obedience' and 'an instinct for order' (ibid.: 12).

By the mid-nineteenth century, the government was making large grants to voluntary schools and, reflecting Callaghan's words above, demanded to have value for money. Robert Lowe, the Vice-President of the Committee of the Council on Education, in 1862 insisted on the introduction of inspection and payment by results in the Revised Code. For the next thirty years the aims of schools were determined by the need to pass annual tests in the three Rs, which would determine the amount of public money allocated to schools and hence to teachers. Reading, writing and arithmetic were thus seen to be necessities for the developing workforce, and, particularly after the Parliamentary Reform Act of 1867, Lowe insisted in addition that they must educate those working classes who had been given the vote. He coined the phrase: 'We must educate our masters.' The utilitarian benefits of schooling were shown in W. E. Forster's words during the introduction of universal elementary schooling in 1870:

> We must not delay. Upon the speedy provision of elementary education depends our industrial prosperity. It is of no use trying to give technical teaching to our artisans without elementary education; uneducated labourers – and many of our labourers are utterly uneducated – are for the most part, unskilled labourers, and if we leave our workfolk any longer unskilled, notwithstanding their strong sinews and determined energy, they will become overmatched in the competition of the world. (Annual Register, 1871: 78)

Forster's schools supplemented the voluntary schools that had been created by church bodies. Attendance became compulsory in the 1880s. The continued emphasis on the three Rs (reading, writing and arithmetic), which were the grant-earning subjects, showed that the children were to be taught only what was needful. It was again argued that schooling induced the good habits of regular hours and submission to the demands of the bell and drill which were characteristic of the industrial system where most of them were destined to work.

This utilitarian concept of education for the working classes was challenged by Matthew Arnold, who condemned these emphases. He passionately argued that the fundamental purpose of even popular education should be to acquaint students with 'the best that has been known and said in the world, and thus with the history of the human spirit', from which they would derive insight and solace (Arnold, 1873: xiii). For Arnold, and all who followed him, there should not be a narrow system of pre-industrial instruction, as he believed a liberal education should be the prime aim of all schooling. His reasons have great contemporary relevance:

> The aim and office of instruction, say many people, is to make a man a good citizen, or a good Christian, or a gentleman; or it is to fit him to get on in the world, or it is to enable him to do his duty in that state of life to which he is called ... These are at best secondary and indirect aims of instruction; its prime direct aim is to enable a man to know himself and the world. Such knowledge is the only sure basis for action. (Arnold, 1868: 258)

By the start of the twentieth century there was indeed a relaxing of the curriculum, with the disappearance of 'payment by results' by 1891 and more freedom given to teachers to decide their own curriculum shown in the 1905 *Suggestions for Teachers*. Yet this was only thirty-eight years before the Norwood Report (quoted above) proposing a clear discrimination of aims in secondary education.

Current expectations

In interviews for their first teaching posts, trainee teachers are sometimes asked the question: 'What is your vision of education?' Business leaders have not been reticent in criticizing any failures in the delivery of instrumentalist aims. The Confederation of British Industry identified in 2009 'serious failings' in school leavers' abilities, claiming that over half of employers were dissatisfied with the basic literacy and numeracy of school leavers. There were similar complaints that some teenagers were 'unable to function in the workplace', claiming they could not make simple calculations in their heads, speak in an articulate manner or understand written instructions. This lack of basic skills was seen as threatening to lead to a significant fall in the country's competitiveness. Sir Terry Leaky, head of supermarket chain Tesco, in 2009 condemned the education system for its failures:

> As the largest private employer in the country, we depend on high standards in our schools. Sadly, despite all the money that has been spent, standards are still woefully low in too many schools … Employers like us are often left to pick up the pieces. (*Daily Telegraph*, 13 October 2009)

The British Chambers of Commerce reported in August 2011 that 'too many people [are] coming out with fairly useless degrees in non-serious subjects' and that small businesses were frustrated by the quality of applicants, who could barely concentrate or add up. Interestingly, the education secretary for over four years of the Conservative–Liberal Democrat Coalition government, Michael Gove, outlined before taking office that he accepted that a liberal education for all was 'a good in itself' and a central hallmark of a civilized society, 'the means by which societies ensure that everything which is best in our society is passed on to succeeding generations'. As shadow education secretary, Gove's speeches had reflected Arnold's conceptions that all children had a right to their inheritance of 'the best that has been thought and written' and he had questioned the accepted dogma of instrumentalism:

> There is a peculiar and to my mind quite indefensible assumption among some that the only cultural experiences to which the young are entitled, or even open, are those which have a direct, and contemporary, relevance to their lives … in making schools institutions which seek to cure every social ill and inculcate every possible worthwhile virtue – we are losing sight of the core purpose, and unique value, of education … the initiation of new generations into the amazing achievements of humankind. Because that is what education is for. (Gove, 2009)

Conversely, Tristram Hunt, the Labour shadow secretary of state for education, argued in 2014 that 'what our economy needs most [is] a high-quality, high-aspiration vocational education system' as 'economic strength in the twenty-first century will increasingly be defined by the quality of a nation's human capital rather than by its territorial endowments, natural resources or the sheer size of its labour force'. He added that a 'business as usual' approach, either economically or educationally, would be 'woefully inadequate at winning this race' (Hunt, 2014a). In a subsequent speech he proposed that education should foster the character traits of 'resilience, curiosity, discipline, self-control and grit' (Hunt, 2014b).

The present chapter began with reference to the idea that the aim of schooling might be to foster a joy of learning. Many inspirational teachers see this enjoyment of learning to be a destination rather than a vehicle for more instrumental aims. Henry Mayhew as early as 1842 penned the sentiments that 'reading, writing and arithmetic are no more education, than the possession of a knife and fork is a good dinner' (Mayhew, 1842: 44). For him, the great end of all education was 'to implant into a child such a spirit of inquiry as shall make him seek to increase the knowledge, respecting the order and harmony of the beautiful world without him, and also of the still more beautiful world of thought and feeling within him'. A century later, John Dewey saw the teaching of subjects and skills to be themselves only a means to the delivery of a much more important aim:

> Collateral learning in the way of forming enduring attitudes ... may be and often is much more important than the spelling lesson or lesson in geography or history that is learned. For these attitudes are fundamentally what count in the future. The most important attitude that can be formed is that of desire to go on learning. If impetus in this direction is weakened instead of being intensified, something much more than mere lack of preparation takes place. The pupil is actually robbed of natural capacities ... What avail is it to win prescribed amounts of information about geography and history, to win the ability to read and write, if in the process the individual loses his own soul? (Dewey, 1938: 49–50)

John Manson, a gifted schoolteacher in Belfast, who established what he termed a 'play-school', went so far as to suggest in 1762 that lessons might be 'an amusement' and that the teacher 'can make the course of education an entertainment to himself [sic] as well as to his children' (Manson 1762: 5). This is no secret to truly gifted teachers.

Points to consider:

- Why might it be argued that the sole duty of state schools is to prepare children for working life?
- Is there a canon of human knowledge which is the birthright of all children, and if so, what constitutes this canon?
- In what ways can it be said that society duplicates itself through schooling?

3

How far should the state interfere in education?

It is now assumed that the state will have a significant influence on schooling: determining curriculum, regulating compulsory attendance, organizing regular inspection regimens, setting the criteria for teacher and trainee performance and, not least, financing schools. This chapter investigates the historical background of state interference in education and shows how this influence increased throughout the nineteenth and twentieth centuries. It also counterposes the views of many, in the past and in the present, who feel for practical and philosophical reasons that such involvement should be limited and that much more should be left to parents and teachers themselves.

It is now rarely questioned in the UK that education is a legitimate area for state intervention. The government presumes the right by democratic mandate to involvement in schooling, with ministers ultimately accountable to electors. Among the many current responsibilities assumed by secretaries of state are the supply of buildings and employment of teachers, the funding of pupils (indirectly through local authorities), the specification of a national curriculum and assessment regimens, the laws compelling pupil attendance and the guarantee of quality assurance through school inspection. In the UK there is not a state monopoly, as there is still a significant independent sector, which does not receive government funding and which can determine its own curricula. However, discussion has been precipitated by the recent secretary of state for education, Michael Gove, about the limits to state involvement in schools. Gove initiated new academy schools and free schools directly funded by central government rather than through local authorities. They can determine their own management committees, can specialize in particular curriculum areas (science, arts, business and enterprise, computing, engineering, mathematics, modern foreign languages, performing arts, sport or technology) and are free to innovate. However, they must still follow a broad and balanced curriculum, delivering the core national curriculum subjects of Mathematics, English and Science, and they are subject to Ofsted inspection as are all other maintained schools. Indeed, by the end of 2015, four of the new free schools have already been declared inadequate by Ofsted and forced to close. The hand of the state is still therefore apparent even in such schools.

Harold Brighouse cogently argues the case in favour of the state's involvement in schooling, which in essence is to provide that educational opportunities are 'insulated from family background' (Brighouse, 1998: 140). Equal opportunity depends on the idea that 'for society to restrict someone's access to a rewarding life is to confer less value on her life than on that of those whose access is assisted' (ibid.: 146). This implies that, as far as possible, 'the quality of the education received by each child should be independent of the level of wealth, education, and wise choice-making ability of his or her parents'. He argues that parental rights, which are advocated by those who wish to reduce state involvement, are rights over others and that:

> To grant that parents have rights over their children prior to other social values is to treat children as chattel, rather than as individuals in their own right. Given other important values it may make good sense to allocate parents considerable discretion over their children's upbringings, but far less discretion than rights bearers usually have over their own lives. And whatever rights parents should be allocated are not fundamental (in the way that rights over oneself are), but are premised on their general benefit to the developmental interests of the child. (Brighouse, 1998: 149)

The alternative viewpoint, which was dominant before the Victorian era, is postulated by James Tooley, who rests at an extreme end of a continuum on state intervention. He argues that the state should be limited to compelling irresponsible parents to send their children to schools and to funding children of the very poorest parents, to provide in effect a minimum safety net. He thus advocates the priority of choice over other social values, claiming that parents have fundamental rights to control the education of their children. He feels that the natural concern that parents have for their children, coupled with the widespread knowledge that education provides valuable future opportunities, make government intervention 'unnecessary to achieve a minimum education for most, since all but the very poorest and most irresponsible parents would devote considerable personal resources to their children's education' (Tooley, 2000: 78). For Tooley, state involvement brings negative incentives to parents, reducing their involvement to the level that they abandon schooling completely to others outside the family. He feels that this abrogation of responsibility for their children can have a dangerous impact on society as a whole. In addition he questions the proposition that the state can indeed secure equality of opportunity as in any state system those parents who do maintain their interest of necessity increase the educational advantages for their own children and thereby mitigate against the delivery for equality of opportunity for all.

The laissez-faire philosophy of the pre-Victorian period maintained that all schooling should be left to private enterprise. This allowed no state provision, no state funding (except perhaps for targeted indirect funding for the poor), and minimal regulation. The nineteenth-century political agitator William Cobbett typified this view when he criticized government intervention in schools in the 1830s as offering 'Heddekashun' and posing the questions: 'What need had we of schools? What need of teachers? What need of scolding or force, to induce children to read and write and love books?' (Johnson, 1979: 90). He believed that there were ample resources within [working-class] communities themselves which did not need government schools in order to achieve education. He emphasized that the family, including the working-class family, was capable of schooling its own children in what was necessary to them, to the extent that the 1970s left-wing historian Richard Johnson saw him as the 'original de-schooler' (ibid.: 77). This poses a fundamental philosophical question for educational stakeholders as to who has primary responsibility for children, the parents or the state. Before the nineteenth century, the idea that the state should interfere in relationships between parents and their children was anathema. Respect for paternal authority remained everywhere with children recognized legally as the property particularly of their fathers, to be used by them to work or to be favourably married. For centuries the family structure and parental responsibility for children was held to be the will of God. More prosaically, it was felt by legislators that if the state attempted to supply what a father could not, it risked creating a welfare addicted underclass and this theme appeared in the concerns at proposed Poor Laws and ultimately the creation of the workhouses for paupers.

The growth of state involvement in education

Early nineteenth-century reformers were, however, contemplating some form of intervention, with a growing concern at the poor physical condition of children working in factories. An outbreak of fever in cotton factories in the 1780s made Lancashire doctors lay down the axiom that children under fourteen needed the 'active recreations of childhood and youth' for 'growth, the vigour and the right conformation of the human body'. There began to be revulsion at child labour. Sarah Trimmer at the start of the nineteenth century said she could not think about children in factories without 'the utmost commiseration'. They, like the climbing boys, began to be seen as 'white slaves' (as S. T. Coleridge phrased it). The 1802 Factory Act for the first time regulated the use of pauper apprentices. Legislators were beginning to lose confidence in the ability of parents to bring up their children and were beginning to question the sanctity of the family. Investigations into juvenile delinquency in London in 1816 outlined the role of parental neglect in encouraging criminal behaviour. In 1833, Richard Oastler wrote:

> It is notorious that the health of the Negro slave, of the adult felon, of the horse, of the ass, of the hare, of the rabbit, of the partridge, of the pheasant, of the cabbage and of the strawberry is protected by law, but at the same time, the children of the poor are unprotected by the law. (Cunningham, 2005: 142)

A Royal Commission recommended an act limiting the work of the young, although the period of childhood ended at fourteen when they ceased to be under the complete control of their parents. The state was therefore contemplating intervention in the rights of parents. Young people were prohibited from employment as chimney sweeps (1840, 1864 and 1875), in brickmaking (1875) and farming (1867 and 1876). Laws regulating how a father could employ his child lagged behind those regulating the conduct of a master outside the children's family and even Lord Shaftesbury expressed concerns at undermining parental responsibility, and thereby family stability and ultimately the stability of society. He was totally opposed to *compulsory* education in schools as an infringement of this parental right to bring up children as they saw fit (Pinchbeck, 1973: 357–8).

Before 1833 the government undertook no role in education. Three main areas however fell under government scrutiny in the following half-century: financing, curriculum and compulsion. The building of schools remained the preserve of the churches, through the National Society and the British and Foreign School Society, for most of the century. In 1833 the government made its first move into involvement with a grant of £20,000 exclusively for building purposes to these two societies. Grants were made on condition that schools should receive ten shillings from voluntary societies for each child for whom accommodation was provided and that the parish contribution towards the building of a school had to equal that given by the state. The state did not wish to create its own schools, but Althorp, the Chancellor of the Exchequer who introduced the measure, found that many local efforts were prevented 'from the want of means to make a beginning'. Schools still had to finance themselves on a day to day basis, as the government had no intention to make grants for the upkeep of the school or the salary of the teacher once it was running. The first true maintenance grants, as opposed to building grants, came in 1847, with the creation of the pupil-teacher system introduced by Kay Shuttleworth. The government promised a grant of ten pounds to thirty pounds a year to headteachers if they undertook to train, out of school hours, pupil-teachers in the art of teaching. The pupil-teacher was apprenticed to a headteacher at thirteen years of age and served for five years. In order to ensure accountability for the financial outlay, a new class of Her Majesty's Inspectors (HMI) examined the pupil-teachers annually and specified the requirements of their training. Parents still did not have free education and only in 1891 were parents finally given the right to demand the abolition of the school pence paid by their children. Such payments did not disappear completely until 1918 – another indication that the state expected parents to take some responsibility for their children's education.

The government began to interfere directly in the second major area of day schooling, the curriculum, in 1862. The Parliamentary Newcastle Commission had examined elementary education throughout Britain and its report of 1861 implied that all children should acquire at school the 'power of reading, writing and cyphering in an intelligent manner'. However, it saw irregular attendance and poor teaching as the greatest obstacles to the attainment of that goal. The Commissioners concluded:

> There is only one way of securing this result, which is to institute a searching examination by competent authority of every child in every school to which grants are paid, with a view to ascertaining whether these indispensable elements of knowledge are thoroughly acquired and to make the prospects and the position of the teacher dependent to a considerable extent on the results of this examination. (PP, 1861a: 157)

A minority of the commissioners continued to express their objections to state interference per se. They accepted that government might be enlarged in special circumstances, when 'the natural progress of society' was curtailed (as in war), but could not accept that educational duties were within its purview, except towards those in 'destitution, vagrancy or crime'. The government interference since 1833 had, they complained, caused financial waste, the sharpening of religious divisions over education and deteriorating relations between class and class. It was also seen to stifle the parental duty to educate their own children and the work of philanthropists (PP, 1861a: 298–9).

The government under the guidance of Robert Lowe implemented the new inspection regime in 1862 with the Revised Code. All grants were to be paid to school managers on the principle of 'payment by results' after examinations of all pupils in the three Rs. This had profound effects on both the curriculum of elementary schools and on teaching styles, which continued for the rest of the century. There were two conditions for the grants: attendance and results. Attendance was reckoned as a two-hour session in the morning or afternoon, with a grant of four shillings per scholar based on the average number in attendance throughout the year. Every scholar who attended more than 200 morning or afternoon sessions and passed the examination would earn a grant of eight shillings, although a third was deducted for each failure in reading, writing or arithmetic. The children were to be grouped in six standards and no child could be examined twice in the same standard. All girls had to receive tuition in needlework and the school buildings had to be maintained in a satisfactory condition to receive the grant. Thus the state had begun to dictate the standard of buildings, the curriculum and also assert pressure on teachers to enforce attendance.

However, in defining so precisely the acceptable curriculum, 'payment by results' caused a rigidity in teaching methods which went on into the present century. The teachers had to gear their teaching to the visit by the HMI. Their salaries were tied to the success of their pupils in examination and there was an increase in rote learning to ensure these successes. In the 1860s, HMI Sir Joshua Fitch criticized the mechanical spirit which had already been introduced into school work and Matthew Arnold, also a HMI, reported in 1867:

> I cannot say that the impression made upon me by the English schools … has been a hopeful one. I find in them, in general, if I compare them with their former selves, a deadness, a slackness, and a discouragement which are not the accompaniments of progress. If I compare them with the schools of the Continent, I find in them a lack of intelligent life much more striking now than it was when I returned from the Continent in 1859. This change is certainly to be attributed to the school legislation of 1862. (Arnold, 1908: 112)

Arnold felt that government interference had fostered a reliance on 'mechanical processes' and too little on the 'intelligence, spirit, and inventiveness of teachers'. This mechanical turn to inspection was seen to be 'trying to the intellectual life of the school'. Further central interference in the curriculum brought a new range of grants for history, geography and needlework to encourage the teaching of subjects other than the three Rs, but Arnold commented in 1869 that history, geography and language teaching had fallen into such decay that the tiny grants for these were little encouragement for schools to adopt them (Arnold, 1908: 115). He called for more 'free play' for the HMI and more free play in consequence for the teacher. In 1869 Arnold wrote:

Unless a rigorous effort is made to infuse more intelligence into its teaching, government arithmetic will soon be remarkable for its meagreness and sterility ... School grants earned ... by a scholar performing a certain minimum expressly laid down beforehand must inevitably concentrate the teacher's attention on the means of producing this minimum, and not simply on the good instruction of his school. (Arnold, 1908: 125, 128)

He warned the Education Department:

In the game of mechanical contrivances the teachers will in the end beat us; and as it is now found possible, by ingenious preparation, to get children through the Revised Code examination in reading, writing and cyphering, without their really knowing how to read, write or cypher, so it will, with practice no doubt, be found possible to get three fourths of the one fifth of the children over six through the examination in history, geography and grammar without their really knowing any one of these matters. (Arnold, 1908: 115)

Rote learning and endless repetition became the normal methods of instruction adopted by teachers. Individual initiative was crushed and any tuition beyond the minimum needed for a pass was seen to be unnecessary. HMI Johnstone in 1877 found that teachers were no longer devoting special time and effort to reading, but were aiming exclusively at a pass, and that the children would never in future read for their own amusement. He found arithmetic to be a subject beyond the rural mind, being 'never, except in the rarest instances, mastered', and he concluded, 'whole classes fail entirely in it and often pass only by accomplishing the mechanical details of such simple sums as to require no exercise whatsoever of the intelligence' (PP, 1877: 504–5).

The 1870 Education Act was intended to create non-denominationalist schools for the first time. Local Boards were elected to create their own schools to fill the gaps in the denominationalist system of education and their schools were financed from local rates, although the denominational schools still had to rely on grants from central government. The curriculum was not laid down by the state, but was still influenced by the payment by results system, which remained in force until 1890, when its place was taken by capitation grants of seventeen shillings for each infant and twenty-two shillings for each other child. Gradually the curricula of elementary schools changed, although it took some time for the end of mechanical tuition. The teachers themselves had been trained in rigid methods and the chief inspector of the Board of Education, Edmond Holmes, wrote in 1911:

> The State, in prescribing a syllabus which was to be followed, in all the subjects of instruction … did all his thinking for the teacher. It told him in precise detail what he was to do each year in each Standard, how he was to handle each subject, and how far he was to go in it …What degree of accuracy was required for a pass … and it was inevitable that in his endeavour to adapt his teaching to the type of question which his experience led him to expect, he should gradually deliver himself, mind and soul, into the hands of the officials of the Education Department, who framed the yearly syllabus. (Holmes, 2008: 79)

There was indeed a relaxing of the diktats on the curriculum at the beginning of the twentieth century and the *Suggestions for Teachers* of 1905 recommended that teachers decide for themselves the best ways to teach and much of their syllabus content.

A third area of state involvement was that of compulsion. The 1870 Education Act also allowed local school boards to demand some form of compulsory attendance. Lord Sandon's Act of 1876 declared that it was the duty of every parent to see that their children received adequate instruction in the three Rs and employers were forbidden to employ children under ten years old. Children between ten and fourteen years were obliged to attend school at least half-time. By the Mundella Act of 1880, all school boards were finally compelled to frame by-laws to enforce attendance on all children. The school leaving age was raised to eleven in 1893 and to twelve in 1899. With post-First World War unemployment came the Fisher Act of 1918, which took the opportunity of raising the school leaving age further and abolishing all exemptions (thus ending the half-time system, which had allowed older children to work in factories in the mornings or afternoons). Employment of children under twelve was prohibited, and those between twelve and fourteen were restricted to a maximum of two hours per day.

Twentieth-century interference

The twentieth century saw increasing government intervention in the education system. The 1902 Education Act created Local Education Authorities (LEAs) which controlled the disbursement of finances, audited accounts and inspected the secular programme of church schools as well as 'council' schools. They had a veto over teacher appointments and dismissals and also had the right to designate two of the six managers of every voluntary school. However, these powers were given not to central but to local government. In 1918 the school leaving age was raised to fourteen years and in 1926 the influential Hadow Report specified that the primary phase of education should cease at eleven and that there should be separate provision of secondary education. The most significant intervention came with the Butler Act of 1944 which specified Local Education Funding for secondary education, payment of teachers by a nationally agreed scale, the requirement of schools to hold an act of collective worship, and the further raising of the school leaving age. The Act established secondary education for all in a bipartite system of grammar schools and secondary moderns. However, the curriculum was left to individual schools and LEAs. Labour's education minister, Ellen Wilkinson claimed later:

> It is important not to make plans that are too rigid ... The schools must have freedom to experiment, room to grow, variety for the sake of freshness, for the fun of it, even. Laughter in the classroom, self-confidence growing every day, eager interest instead of bored conformity. (Wilkinson, 1946)

Primary teachers were now left with much autonomy over what to teach and how to teach it. Secondary schools for the older classes had to follow national examination syllabuses, although the freedom to organize learning was still considered one of the most important elements of teachers' professional autonomy. Further reorganization was demanded by the Labour Government of the later 1960s, with the establishment of comprehensive secondary schools following claims that too many children were being written off at eleven years of age. Those who had failed their Eleven Plus examination and had gone to secondary modern schools had not been allowed to transfer or even to sit examinations. Local authorities were therefore instructed to draw up plans to introduce comprehensive schools by the government, which withheld funding for new school buildings from those that did not comply. Some authorities resisted such reorganization but were reprieved by the new Conservative government in 1970, which left the decision to local process.

While the liberty over the curriculum remained in schools, this in itself brought some discontent from those who mistrusted the resulting experiments in teaching methods. One school in particular, the William Tyndale Primary school in London, came to symbolize the problem of allowing teachers total autonomy over curriculum. The school was castigated by parents and in the press as endangering pupils' futures by its progressive methods. The Inner London Education Authority eventually held a public enquiry and dismissed the teachers involved. The affair intensified calls for an end to the teachers' influence on the curriculum and a corresponding increase in teacher accountability. The political Right in particular questioned modern methods in a series of Black Papers and mistrusted teacher autonomy. Moreover, the economic crisis of the 1970s led industry to demand a better-educated workforce and hence a more prescriptive curriculum of basic skills. The Labour prime minister, James Callaghan was persuaded to begin what he termed 'The Great Debate' on education in his Ruskin College speech in 1976, seeking to 'equip children to the best of their ability for a lively, constructive place in society and also to fit them to do a job of work'. It seemed to him that there was no virtue in producing 'socially well-adjusted members of society' who would be unemployed because they did not have the skills needed by industry, nor 'at the other extreme must they be technically efficient robots' (Callaghan, 1976). He pointed out that schools were responsible for £6 billion a year of public money and that they should be inspected by people from outside of education, especially from industry, to ensure their efficiency. Thus he expected teachers to be fully accountable as a profession. It was left to his Conservative successor, Margaret Thatcher, to implement these changes and to assume unprecedented powers over the educational system of the country.

Thatcher, who took office in 1979, passionately believed that the free market models of education would increase both accountability and efficiency. Her first education secretary, Keith Joseph, proposed a voucher system, whereby parents would carry their allocation of government educational grant with them to the school of their choice, thereby instituting a competitive market between schools and therefore greater efficiency in the delivery of standards. Such extreme changes never actually occurred, as Joseph found the difficulties of implementation to be insuperable. The Conservatives remained concerned that, with existing freedoms for schools, left-wing values were being taught in classrooms. Rhodes Boyson, a former headteacher turned education minister, claimed that London schools housed Marxist and Maoist teachers who were attempting to indoctrinate children. The culmination of all these fears came in 1988 with the Education Reform Act, designed by the then education secretary Kenneth Baker, which increased government interference incrementally. There would be a prescribed national curriculum for all state-funded schools, both primary and secondary; there would be formal Key Stage Tests of all pupils at the ages of seven, eleven and fourteen and there would be publication of results to ensure teacher accountability; teacher appraisal was anticipated, as was parental choice of school up to its physical capacity. (The Act also anticipated a Grant Maintained status, whereby schools could leave LEA control, to be funded directly from central government, although by 1992 only 422 out of 24,000 schools had chosen to follow this route.) There was much opposition to the unprecedented interference in the educational system, from teachers, councils, MPs and even a Conservative ex-prime minister, Edward Heath, who commented in the Commons:

The Secretary of State has taken more power under this Bill than any other member of the Cabinet. The extent of the Secretary of State's power will be overwhelming. Within the parliamentary system, no Secretary of State should ever be allowed to hold such a degree of power. (Hansard, 1988: 792)

Power was indeed removed from LEAs, apparently to individual schools and parents, with headteachers and governors responsible for the management of their own institutions. However, in reality, there was a centralization of power that has continued to the present. Many teachers were dismayed at the levels of prescription over content and assessment, and the removal of any influence from them on curriculum development. The secretary of state himself appointed subject working groups to devise the programmes of study and personally appointed the advisory bodies, the NCC and SEAC. He made final decisions on curriculum content, attainment targets and methods of assessment. Denis Lawton wrote at the time:

In the Baker version of the National Curriculum, there is much talk of balance. But what we are now offered is not a balanced diet but a kind of anti-scurvy curriculum: we have a list of ingredients that Mr Baker thinks will be good for us, without any justification for the list ... it is a diet without consultation of a nutritionist – moreover a quack doctor. (Lawton, 1988: 32)

The reforms were carried further in 1993 with the creation of an independent inspectorate, the Office for Standards in Education (Ofsted). All schools would have a four-yearly inspection, with inspectors reporting on the quality of education, the standards achieved, financial management and the spiritual, moral, social and cultural development of the pupils.

The involvement of the state increased further in the twenty-first century under the New Labour government of Tony Blair, who in the 1997 election campaign had claimed that his priority would be 'Education, Education, Education'. However, he retained the Conservative faith in market competition between schools, published league tables of results, school choice, specialist colleges and the naming and shaming of failing schools. One recent historian, Sally Tomlinson, has summarized the policies:

Much continuity derives from the acceptance and elaboration of Tory reforms post-1988; indeed a pursuit of some of these policies passed the point that Tory ministers had been willing to go ... There was a continued emphasis on state regulation and control of the curriculum, its assessment, teachers and their training and local authority activity. (Tomlinson, 2001: 85)

There was significant intervention in schools with changes to the curriculum, the introduction of Citizenship as a compulsory subject for all secondary children, and the prescription of 'synthetic phonics' (a system based on teaching children letter sounds so they recognize the different components in a word) for teaching literacy. In 2005 the Department of Education and Skills introduced the 'pupil achievement tracker' that enabled schools to compare pupil performance data against national data with the expectation of analysis of value-added for individual pupils. Nursery places were made available to all four-year-olds, although childminders were expected to have learning plans for their charges and were subject to inspection by Ofsted. The secretary of state also specified that all children were to stay in some form of education or training until the age of eighteen. Similar interventions, not least in teacher training, occurred under the Coalition government between 2010 and 2015, and are dealt with in subsequent chapters.

For 150 years, governments have taken a deep interest in educational provision, not least because of the considerable national expenditure involved. In the projected 2015 budget, £33 billion was anticipated for primary and secondary schools in Britain and the state understandably expects schools to be accountable for such high outlay. The result of state involvement has been an enormous increase in educational provision since the 1860s, although this has come at the cost of increasing constraints on teachers' opportunities to exercise professional judgement. In January 2015, David Bell, the former Chief Inspector of Schools, questioned this situation, claiming that education had been too much at the whim of changing ministers and that governments in general had assumed too much power over schooling. He felt the amount of change, with over thirty Education Acts in thirty years, had not always been in the best interests of teachers and children, that innovations had never been given sufficient time to become embedded before new changes had been imposed, and that this demonstrated the unproven view of politicians that legislation 'must and can improve education'. Education policy was still being driven by 'short-term firefighting, ministerial personalities and electoral politics', which was particularly ridiculous when ministers 'have never taught a class of children or young people in their life' (Bell, 2015). Such increasing state interference also bears witness to a declining trust in teachers and a declining confidence that families can raise their children appropriately. For those parents who opt out of the system and the financial backing of the government by home-schooling, there were even plans in 2009 (admittedly dropped) to extend Ofsted inspections into such homes. The provision of free school meals for infant pupils in 2014 is in itself a continuation of the state's appropriation of parental responsibilities. There is clearly now a conception in all political parties that the rearing of children can no longer be left solely to families, nor indeed to teachers. As Bell concluded in his consideration of the curriculum, examinations and assessment: 'I think we can trust more those who know first-hand the experience of children, those who work with them, to give better advice so that we do not just rely on politicians and civil servants.'

Points to consider:

- How can the state ensure that the quality of the education received by children is independent of the level of wealth, education and choice-making ability of parents? Indeed, should it do so?
- The state now contributes £33 billion a year to educational provision. Does this alone justify state involvement?
- What limitations should there be on parental, teacher and state influence on the education of children?
- How valid are the arguments made by Tooley and Brighouse over the rationale for government interference in education?

4

How much influence should religion have in schools?

… no boy or girl can be counted as properly educated unless he or she has been made aware of the fact of the existence of a religious interpretation of life.

(SPENS, 1938: 208)

Faith-based institutions, statutory religious education and compulsory worship in schools are still features of the UK educational system, yet many feel that these are relics of the nineteenth and early twentieth centuries that no longer have a place in the new millennium. This chapter investigates the currently very contentious issue of religion in schools. It analyses its continuing influence in general, tracing its origins and showing the heated debates which were intensified by recent claims of the infiltration of fundamentalist views into Muslim state-supported schools in Birmingham. It also shows the arguments of those who feel that the subject is crucial in helping children to challenge an increasingly materialistic and secular society.

There are few more controversial issues in education than the role of religion in schools. In spite of falling church attendance and growing concerns about a society divided along religious lines, the number of faith schools grew under the Coalition government between 2010 and 2015. Almost a third of all state-funded schools are schools with 'a religious character' and supporters claim that the religious ethos, respect for authority, moral values and high academic achievement explain their popularity. Critics, however, argue that the prominence of religion in schools contributes to the fracturing of a multicultural society. Following on from events in Birmingham in 2014, with claims of the infiltration of fundamentalist views into Muslim state-supported schools, the place of religion in the English state school system is now being questioned more urgently than ever before, with even some clergy doubting its appropriateness in state-financed institutions.

Religious schools

There are many proponents of religious education and religious schools as an integral aspect of schooling. A 2012 survey commissioned by the Religious Education Council of England and Wales showed that 53 per cent of the 1,800 adults questioned believed that Religious Education (RE) should be compulsory in all state schools up to the age of sixteen. The cross-party parliamentary report of the same year, *RE and Good Community Relations*, claimed that religions were often portrayed inaccurately in society at large and that the teaching of RE could break down the prejudice that could develop as a consequence. However, there are many opponents of both RE and faith schools. One of the most vociferous, Richard Dawkins, claimed in an open letter to the prime minister in the *New Statesman* of 19 December 2011 that faith schools were 'the most obvious and serious case of government-imposed religion' which 'don't so much teach about religion as indoctrinate in the particular religion that runs the school'. He felt that modern society required 'a truly secular state', which meant state neutrality 'in all matters pertaining to religion, the recognition that faith is personal and no business of the state'. In his book *The God Delusion* Dawkins posits that faith can be very dangerous, and 'deliberately to implant it into the vulnerable mind of an innocent child is a grievous wrong' (Dawkins, 2006: 346). The British Humanist Association (BHA) have long agitated for an inclusive secular state system, maintaining that:

> Parents have an explicit right in the European Convention of Human Rights to bring up their children in the religion or belief of their choice without interference from the state. However, they do not have a right to state funding for confessional religious teaching or 'faith' schools ... the proliferation of state-funded religious schools will make for a more segregated future, especially as religions whose believers tend to come from particular ethnic groups gain more state-funded schools. (BHA, 2014)

A particular concern is that faith schools are permitted to teach their own syllabus of RE, unlike community schools which must follow a locally agreed syllabus. The teaching of RE in these schools is moreover not specifically inspected by Ofsted, but by diocesan (or faith) inspectors. The result, the BHA argues, is that it is often 'confessional' in nature, with the aim of instructing children in the doctrine and practices of a particular religion, and fails to give a fair account of non-religious views. Ethical issues such as abortion or assisted dying are approached from an explicitly religious perspective, and after the recent creation of 'free' state-supported schools, fears about the teaching of creationism and fundamentalism have increased.

Church control of education has been a basic feature of English history for centuries. Initially all schools were related to the church. Monastic song schools educated novices and taught plainchant. Grammar schools taught Latin and often were the training ground of parish clergy. The religious upheavals of the early sixteenth century culminated in Henry VIII breaking from the Roman Catholic Church and ultimately the dissolution of all monastic foundations, which had serious implications for education in the country. His son, Edward VI, compensated for their loss by re-establishing grammar schools in 1547. The issue of religious education continued to be contentious under Queen Elizabeth I, and in order secure her own position and that of Protestantism in 1559 she ordered that no man would be allowed to teach without a bishop's licence. All teachers had to submit to the Thirty Nine Articles of the Church of England and had to teach approved English or Latin Catechisms, to hold daily prayers in the school and to attend church with their scholars on sermon days. This was later re-enforced after the English Civil War by the Act of Uniformity of 1662, which required all teachers and clergy to subscribe to a declaration of conformity to the Church of England's liturgy. The subsequent Five Mile Act of 1665 barred nonconformists from teaching in any private or public school. A number of judicial decisions later established that at common law the church had no control over non-grammar schools, although bishops continued to claim rights of visitation and to license all teachers. Only in 1689, with the Toleration Act, were penalties against unlicensed teachers removed.

The Church of England dominated the educational landscape in the eighteenth century when the dearth of elementary schooling throughout the country encouraged action from many benefactors motivated by religious aims. The SPCK began charity schools, with the aim of propagating Christianity, and specifically Anglicanism, among the poorest children. Reading, writing, some accounts for boys and sewing for girls were taught, but the essential object for all was moral and religious discipline and an emphasis on their duties in society. At the end of the century, the Sunday school movement was trying to fill the gaps in the education system, which had left a third of all children still unschooled. In 1791, the children in the Sunday schools in Lincoln, for example, were taught to read, although they were obliged to say the church catechism daily and attend morning and evening prayers. Writing was not usually taught as it was regarded as an unsuitable occupation for the Sabbath. The provision of elementary day schools was largely initiated by the Church of England in 1811, with the creation of the National Society, and, as outlined in its first report, the religious purpose was paramount:

> The sole object in view being to communicate to the poor generally, by means of a summary mode of education lately brought into practice, such knowledge and habits as are sufficient to guide them through life in their proper stations, especially to teach them the doctrine of religion according to the principles of the Established Church and to train them to the performance of their religious duties by an early discipline. (National Society, 1812: 9)

Religious knowledge was also the primary aim of the rival, non-denominational British and Foreign School Society which began building schools in 1814, with the stated object of 'instructing them in the duties of civil life and in the principles of Christianity as professed by their parents' (BFSS, 1815: 3). The Church of England also assumed the responsibility for training teachers. By the early 1850s there were forty colleges in England and Wales with thirty-four of these belonging to the church. The resulting teachers were steeped in religious training and most had, in any case, been taught themselves in denominational schools and acted as Sunday school teachers. Even as late as 1922, fifty of the seventy-two training colleges belonged to the churches.

From the 1840s, the Anglican Church was bitterly resented by its rivals; it had established many more schools than all other denominations combined and was determined to maintain its hegemony. Archdeacon Dennison told a Parliamentary Commission in 1855 that the rule in all his schools was that a child would not be admitted unless she had been baptized in the Church of England, or whose parents were prepared to accept such baptism. All scholars had to attend the Church of England on Sundays with their teacher and had to learn the Anglican Catechism and Liturgy. In many villages no other school existed and unless children were prepared to accept such conditions, they would receive no education. The discontent and also the gaps in the existing denominational system led Forster, the president of the committee of council on education, in 1870 to begin the establishment of non-denominational schools, built by locally elected school boards. Denominational schools remained in this new dual system and continued to be given state grants based on passes in the three Rs, although they soon felt the competition from the much richer school board schools. By the beginning of the twentieth century, church schools suffered serious financial difficulties and Prime Minister Balfour accepted that they were under 'intolerable strain'. Their numbers still made them a significant and indispensable part of the

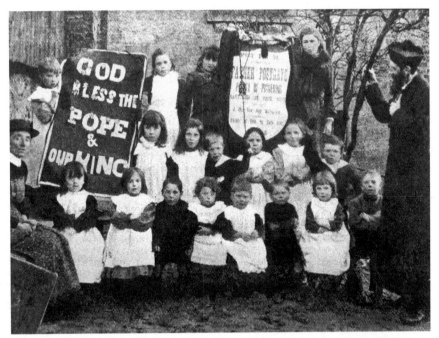

Fig. 3: St Joseph's RC Elementary School, Pickering, 1901 under the local priest, Father Bryan, The school banner, dedicated to the RC martyr, Nicholas Postgate, supports his legend 'I die for my religion.' Courtesy of St Joseph's School, Pickering

educational system and, as a result, the Education Act of 1902 extended rate aid to voluntary schools to cover their running costs completely. The cost of building remained the responsibility of the churches but the local authorities would make a grant for fair wear and tear. The Local Education Authority did undermine the religious influence somewhat by taking a third of all seats on the management bodies and had a veto on the appointment of teachers. Nevertheless, the church retained a two-thirds majority on the management bodies of the 12,000 National schools which it owned. The next major Education Act of 1944 gave voluntary (church) schools the option of accepting *controlled* status, under which the local authority would meet all the school's expenses and would appoint two-thirds of the management committee. The controlled school had to commit to undenominational religious worship and instruction. Schools might otherwise opt for *aided* status, under which the authority would pay the running costs and half the capital cost of adapting the school buildings to meet the requirements of the Act. The denominational atmosphere here remained completely intact and the church retained two-thirds of the managers. (In 1959 support increased for the latter to 75 per cent of the costs of adaptation.) In 1979, when Margaret Thatcher became prime minister, 28 per cent of primary pupils were still in voluntary schools, as were 17 per cent of secondary pupils.

Under Labour from 1997, Tony Blair encouraged the expansion in the provision of faith schools. The capital contribution for voluntary aided schools was cut from 15 per cent to 10 per cent of new building costs and the White Paper *Schools Achieving Success* of 2001 supported new schools to 'add to the inclusiveness and diversity of the system'. Blair's policies were highly controversial. The discussions in the Commons saw a rebellion from forty-five of his own MPs, who demanded that all faith schools should accept 25 per cent of their pupils from other faiths or none, but this was defeated. The motivations for such support have been categorized by Walford as Blair's own Christian faith, and his belief that faith schools fostered the integration of minority communities into the democratic life of the state (Walford, 2010: 59). As Blair himself put it, they were providing 'a high quality of education', their special ethos facilitated the development of morality, and they could promote tolerance and understanding between faith groups. His critics, by contrast, argued that the segregation of minority faith pupils into separate schools would lead to greater ethnic tensions in the future, and gave pupils a restricted view of their religion. Many Roman Catholic and some Church of England schools were criticized for indirectly selecting students according to social class, with their Christian ethos acting to exclude some ethnic minority students. There was also increasing concern that some faith schools inculcated bigoted views and allied to this was the abhorrence of the teaching of creationism (Walford, 2010: 52). The objections centred on the fact that state finance was supporting such teaching, which in some cases might be seen as proselytism or indoctrination. Terence Copley, however, articulated an alternative argument about such indoctrination:

> None of these commentators, interestingly, raises the question of whether indoctrination by omission is also possible. A child from a home in which religion and God are never mentioned and encountering a curriculum in which they do not occur, except perhaps en passant in history lessons, may not only have no belief in God, but may view the entire question of God as unnecessary and irrelevant, even incomprehensible. How much 'choice' has such a child had in forming this view? ... Surely this too is indoctrination, as it has very effectively fixed habits and dispositions without engaging the child's active power. (Copley, 2005: 5)

Until the 1990s, the UK had funded only Christian and Jewish faith schools, but by this time there were sixty independent Muslim schools, supported by first generation communities and keen to pass on their cultural heritage to their children. They particularly favoured single-sex schooling at secondary level for their girls, which for many was a cultural imperative. Formal application was made to the Department of Education and Science in 1986 for funding of such schools, but this was rejected a number of times over the next ten years. In 1992 Muslim school managers appealed to the High Court for a judicial review of the secretary of state's decision, but their applications were again rejected in 1993 on the grounds that there were surplus places in local schools, school buildings were deemed inadequate and there were concerns about their curriculum. Two primary schools were finally awarded grant-maintained status in 1998, thereby receiving state funding for the first time. In granting this, education minister David Blunkett confirmed that the schools had demonstrated that they would 'comply with the statutory provisions governing all maintained schools, such as delivering the national curriculum and offering equal access to boys and girls'. Ibrahim Hewitt, the development officer for Muslim schools, saw it as an important victory for civil rights, claiming that Muslims had been thereby recognized as equal citizens. By 2014, twelve of the existing 140 Muslim schools had been granted state funding. However, even as early as 2005, David Bell, the head of Ofsted, expressed concerns that 'Faith should not be blind ... many young people are being educated in faith-based schools, with little appreciation of their wider responsibilities and obligations to British society' (Bell, 2005). He called for the careful but sensitive monitoring of this growth in faith schools by government, to ensure that pupils received an understanding of not only their own faith but of other faiths and 'the wider tenets of British society'.

The marked expansion of faith schools continued under the Conservative–Liberal Democrat coalition between 2010 and 2015. Secretary of State for Education Michael Gove began free schools as part of the government's Big Society initiative to make it possible for parents, teachers, charities and businesses to set up their own schools. More than 400 such schools were approved for opening in England, representing more than 230,000 school places across the country, and 25 per cent of these were faith schools. (The Catholic Education Service was reluctant to be involved in these, as new admission rules allowed them to reserve only 50 per cent of places for children from Catholic families, unlike voluntary aided schools which can select all places using faith criteria.) Critics, however, saw the new danger of fundamentalist agendas, even though government guidelines specified that their curriculum had to be 'broad and balanced' and that creationism could not be taught as a valid scientific theory.

The Birmingham 'Trojan Horse controversy' of July 2014 triggered renewed discussion. Education secretary Michael Gove told MPs that hard-line Muslim governors had been conducting an organized campaign to change the character of their state schools. Parents had been encouraged to object to a school's leadership if they felt it was 'corrupting' their children with sex education, teaching about homosexuality, making their children pray Christian prayers or carrying out mixed swimming and sport. The aim was to secure a greater emphasis on religious studies, with girls and boys taught separately. Gove claimed that external speakers were not properly vetted, including those who 'spoke to students as part of a programme of Islamic-themed assemblies'. As a result of snap Ofsted inspections in 2014, five Birmingham schools were placed in special measures and Gove insisted that the government would in future require all schools to promote 'British values' of democracy, the rule of law, individual liberty and mutual respect and tolerance of those with different faiths and beliefs. Ofsted's chief inspector Sir Michael Wilshaw went further, calling for mandatory training for all school governors and an end to the exemption of free schools and academies from the national curriculum.

The final report of the independent Social Integration Commission (SIC) in 2015 criticized the fact that the drive to open free schools had led to increased numbers of children being educated in peer groups dominated by a single faith group or community and expressed concern that 'the small number of Muslim faith schools in the UK are experiencing particular difficulties in ensuring their pupils are able to meet and mix with children from different backgrounds'. The Commission called on the Department for Education only to approve applications for new faith schools when they had a clear plan for pupils to meet and mix with children from different faith backgrounds and communities (SIC, 2015: 12). The commission even suggested the building of new facilities or even full campuses for shared use by schools catering to different religious communities and encouraged initiatives for pupils to mix with and study religious practices and ethical questions alongside children of different faiths. In an interview with the *Independent,* the chair, Matthew Taylor singled out Muslim schools as being much more monocultural than Catholic or Church of England schools. In particular, the SIC commented on the danger of state-funded faith schools being free to teach their pupils exclusively about their own religion, although they accepted that most faith schools did indeed teach children about different religious beliefs and traditions.

Religious education

By the middle of the nineteenth century, the issue under contention was not – as now – whether there should be religious training in schools, but over the form of Protestant Christianity to be taught. The complaints of the nonconformists, who resented Anglican dominance, were heeded by the government in 1870. The new locally financed (Board) schools were still expected to teach the Bible, although, as mollification for a religious diverse society, parents were granted the right (by a Conscience Clause) of withdrawal from religious instruction and from religious observance. Section 7 of the 1870 Elementary Education Act stated:

> It shall not be required, as a condition of any child being admitted into or continuing in the school, that he shall attend or abstain from attending any Sunday school, or any place of religious worship, or that he shall attend any religious observance or any instruction in religious subjects in the school or elsewhere, from which observance or instruction he may be withdrawn by his parent.

To facilitate withdrawals, the period of religious instruction was restricted to the beginning or end of the day, thus giving withdrawn pupils the opportunity to remove themselves from the classroom. The nature of the religious instruction was also restricted within the board schools by a clause introduced by Francis Cowper-Temple, that 'No religious catechism or religious formulary which is distinctive of any religious denomination shall be taught in the school'. The Christian instruction would therefore have to be in a broad, non-denominational form. Controversies followed in many board schools and the instruction was sometimes reduced to the mere reading of the Bible.

School boards did have the right to forbid all religious instruction in normal school hours, and this was done in Birmingham board schools from 1873 to 1879. Under the influence of Dr R. W. Dale and Joseph Chamberlain, the National Education League in 1872 set upon a policy of entire separation of religious from secular education and this was adopted by the Birmingham School Board in 1873. Dale believed that religious teaching should be left outside normal school times, although he did not deny that they should receive religious education. The board therefore permitted religious instruction to be given only outside school hours by clergymen or others who were not concerned with the secular instruction and who even had to pay to use the classrooms. Joseph Chamberlain was keen to assert that he was not against the teaching of Christianity *per se*, but was against the sectarian bigotry that had emerged. His aim was that in Birmingham they would uphold 'the great principles of religious freedom and religious equality' that had made the nation strong:

> Ours, then, is no mere fight between the Dissenters on the one hand and a rival Church upon the other; ours is the cause of the nation against sectarianism, the cause of the people against the priests ... the hands are moving swiftly round the dial, and the knell of priestly domination and sectarian rule has already rung. (Boyd, 1914: 21)

This 'secular' solution received little support elsewhere and, according to parliamentary returns, in 1875 only fifteen school boards in England and twenty-six in Wales followed the Birmingham example. The policy failed partly because of objections by some nonconformists, especially Wesleyans, to the total exclusion of Bible in schools and partly because of the refusal of Anglicans to cooperate in extracurricular religious teaching. Moreover, from a practical point of view there were insufficient people available to give the religious instruction, and some of these untrained instructors had proven to have difficulty in keeping order. From 1879, Bible reading by the headteacher without note or comment was again permitted in Birmingham. The failure of the Birmingham secular experiment was a continued disincentive for future boards.

The dominance of the church and the resilience of religious education remained throughout the new century. The importance of the subject was reiterated in 1938 by the Spens Report, which claimed 'no boy or girl can be counted as properly educated unless he or she has been made aware of the fact of the existence of a religious interpretation of life' (Spens, 1938: 208). The report found that there was no large body of public opinion favourable to an entirely secular education, although it did criticize the casual nature of its delivery in some schools. The first syllabus conference was set up in 1923, when teachers and church representatives in the West Riding met to agree a syllabus for their local areas. The Archbishop of Canterbury wrote to *The Times* in 1941 that it was time to end the controversies over education and that the need was so urgent 'that former denominational and professional suspicions and misunderstandings must be laid aside, and that all who care for the place of Christianity in our common life should stand together'. As the future of schooling was being discussed during the Second World War, the archbishop called for an act of worship to be held in all schools at the start of the school day (*The Times*, 13 February 1941). The Methodist Church too claimed that the deficiencies in religious education were so grave that 'a united Christian front' was needed. *The Times* expressed shock at the large number of evacuated urban children who had no religious knowledge at all (a clear indictment of the schooling they had received), with one country parson writing that two-thirds of those who had arrived in his village did not even know who had been born on Christmas Day (*The Times*, 17 February 1940: 7). The two Anglican archbishops and the moderator of the Free Church Federal Council lobbied the minister of education, R. A. Butler, himself a committed churchman, who assured them of the importance of 'instilling the citizen of the future with a (proper) code of Christian ethics', to make the old faiths 'vivid to the next generation', particularly at a time when the war had unleashed 'frankly materialistic opinion' (Butler, 1943: 2). The church lobbying was persuasive enough to secure the introduction of compulsory religious

"AND WHAT IS YOUR RELIGION?"
"WELL, MISS, I'M CHURCH AND ME 'USBAND'S CHAPEL; BUT LITTLE MAUDIE'S COUNTY COUNCIL."

Fig. 4: 'And which religion are you?' Punch, 4 May 1921, lampooning the vapid religious instruction in schools. Courtesy of the Punch Archive

instruction and worship in all schools within the statutory system – council schools as well as denominational ones. The 1944 Education Act did not specify Christianity to be the basis of religious instruction, but this was taken for granted by politicians and teachers. The 1870 Cowper-Temple clause was re-enacted to ensure that religious education was uncontroversial and as inclusive as possible in council schools. Voluntary aided schools could still provide religious instruction in a form appropriate to the beliefs and interests of the founding church.

A review of the provision of religious education by the Institute of Christian Education *Religious Education in Schools* (1954: 27) summarized the resulting confessional nature of the religious education that followed:

> The agreed syllabuses from 1940 onwards reveal a great change of emphasis. Increasing attention is paid in them to worship and the aim of the teaching is declared to be that children should understand and accept the Christian faith and follow the Christian way of life ... the hope is expressed that school worship and religious instruction will in the words of the Introduction to the Lindsey syllabus, 'increasingly lead pupils to become and remain full members of a worshipping community outside the school'. (Institute of Christian Education, 1954: 27)

The content of the agreed syllabuses was chiefly Bible-based, comprising passages from the Old and New Testaments, biblical history and the history of Christianity in Britain, often with a particular focus on the coming of Christianity and on saints connected to the region. Furthermore, up until the 1960s there were few dissenting voices with regard to the 'confessional' character of religious education in schools. The syllabuses reflected the thinking of the time, which was that Britain was a Christian country and that the school had an important role to play in the replication of Christian culture.

Significant changes in the format of RE in schools did not come until the 1970s. Church attendance, church weddings, baptism and confirmation all declined dramatically in the 1960s and 1970s and there was a growth in those who professed agnosticism or atheism. As Barnes has recently concluded, a secular mentality came to prevail according to which religion was 'a private or individual affair' with the 'silent' majority remaining religious 'in an indeterminate way that combined beliefs from different sources without insti-tutional commitment' (Barnes, 2014: 32–3). The religious decline throughout the Western world from the 1960s led one commentator to claim that this was not merely a religious crisis but of 'total culture', of the relevance of 'long-standing patterns of thought and institutions of all sorts in a time of intense ... modernisation' (Hastings, 1986: 580). Moreover, as a result of post-war immigration from former colonies, there was a growing awareness of the multifaith nature of modern Britain. The new direction was signalled in 1971 with *Working Paper 36: Religious Education in the Secondary School*, produced by the Schools Council. The document did not question the impor-tance of the subject which was shown to address 'the element of mystery in life, particularly that created by the awareness of death', which could not be ignored 'without some damage to the personality' (Schools Council 1971: 40). The subject was also said to appeal to a need in children who 'have a deep sense of wonder and awe' and if this side of their personality was ignored they would be 'stunted in one direction'. For older children, there was 'a genuine search for meaning in life' and a sensitivity to the 'deeper aspects of human experience of which religion speaks' (ibid.: 16). Moreover, unless periods were set apart for the subject, it was feared that a larger proportion of the school week would be spent 'in adjusting people to a society whose aims are at best virtuous materialism' (ibid.: 20). However, confessional education was condemned on the grounds that it was indoctrinatory and inappropriate in a secular and pluralist society. The 'dogmatic' approach was said to begin 'with the assumption that the aim of religious education is intellectual and cultic indoctrination' (ibid.: 21):

Pupils belonging to minority faiths need to feel that their way of life is understood and its true worth appreciated. We believe that in a multi-racial and pluralistic society there must be dialogue between those holding different beliefs and growth in mutual understanding, not the widening of inherited divisions. (Schools Council 1971: 64–5)

Working Paper 36 suggested that the study of a number of different religions would further the aim of advancing religious tolerance and mutual understanding. In 1985 an official government inquiry into the 'Education of Children from Ethnic Minority Groups', chaired by Lord Swann, similarly concluded that this 'phenomenological' approach provided the 'best and only means of enabling all pupils, from whatever religious background, to understand the nature of religious belief, the religious dimension of human experience and the plurality of faiths in contemporary Britain' (Swann, 1985: 518). The inquiry concluded that the approach, increasingly called multifaith religious education, was an ideal vehicle for advancing tolerance and harmony between different religious groups and communities in society.

There was, however, a backlash from those who were concerned that children were failing to understand their Christian cultural and religious heritage, and there was strong lobbying by religious pressure groups before the 1988 Education Act. The compulsory nature of religious instruction and worship was maintained as part of this legislation, with the stipulation that all teaching should have within it a moral and spiritual dimension. The Act specified that any RE syllabus 'shall reflect the fact that the religious traditions in Great Britain are in the main Christian, whilst taking account of the teaching and practices of the other principal religions represented in Great Britain'. Oversight of religious teaching was also strengthened.

The 1944 Act had given each LEA the power to set up a Standing Advisory Council on Religious Matters, to monitor RE and collective worship, but the authority had not been compelled to do so. The 1988 Act prescribed that a Standing Advisory Council on Religious Education (SACRE) be set up in every authority, composed of four groups to represent the Church of England (in England only), other principal religious traditions in the area, the LEA and the teachers. The subject was now designated to be religious education, rather than religious instruction and the government reinforced the idea that Agreed Syllabuses must not be designed to convert pupils or urge a particular religion or religious belief on pupils. Each local SACRE determined its own aims and objectives for RE; voluntary aided schools were not obliged to follow these syllabi and their religious curriculum was determined by the school.

In spite of these concessions granted in 1988 to the churches, there were within their ranks many critics of the new direction of national education. The Church of England, Roman Catholics and Methodists had for some time been working together to forward the views of Christians to the government and the reactions of the three churches towards the national curriculum showed a common approach in defending the position of religious education *per se*. They also considered the act to be a serious threat to the spiritual dimension of education in the nation's schools as a whole, 'dominated by a secularist viewpoint, indicative of an increasingly utilitarian and materialistic approach to education in which market economics would become the overriding ethos of schools' (Chadwick, 1997: 90). Dr Graham Leonard, the Bishop of London, commented in an open letter to Kenneth Baker in September 1987: 'The main point we want to raise concerns the overall vision of education which inspires the government's plans.' Similarly, the Roman Catholic Archbishop of Westminster, Cardinal Hume, wrote at the time:

> I come reluctantly to the conclusion that in its obsession with technology and economic prosperity, society is in danger of losing its vision and its soul. Certainly this bill as it stands offers us an educational system and curriculum at the heart of which is spiritual emptiness. (*The Times*, 13 January 1988)

At the North of England Educational Conference in 1990, Cardinal Hume expressed the hope that his audience would not accept the view that 'the purpose of education is primarily to sustain economic prosperity, to promote industry and commerce, to produce competent technicians and managers'. While recognizing the importance of these aims, he still felt that 'training for a job or a profession and education are not co-extensive ... Education is broader and greater and does not always have to serve a utilitarian purpose ... The heart and the human spirit have needs as well as the mind and body' (*Tablet*,

6 January 1990). The Free Church Federal Council Education Committee report of 1995 commended the church schools, including the many Church of England ones, for their part 'in countering the increasing materialism or hedonism in what is sometimes called a post-Christian society' (Methodist Conference, 1997: 37). The Anglican *Way Ahead* Report of 2001 was also keen to assert that interdenominational rivalry had disappeared, and that the churches, working together 'in an increasingly secular world', would ensure 'the long-term continuity of a strong Christian presence' (Church of England, 2001: 30–1). The report put forward an alternative vision for society:

> Globalization and the ascendancy of consumerism have emphasized personal choice, but have not so far generated a balancing sense of community or a coherent sense of responsibility for sustaining the earth's own well-being or for the quality of our civilization. In a world of shifting sands, many parents have welcomed the stability offered by schools that offer an enduring alternative to the growingly secular values of society ... It is about forming people who, however academically and technically skilful, are not reduced to inarticulate embarrassment by the great questions of life and death, meaning and truth. (Church of England, 2001: 14)

The QCA review of 2000 stressed the continuing importance of RE within the curriculum, although with the caveat that it 'does not seek to urge religious beliefs on pupils nor compromise the integrity of their own beliefs by promoting one religion over another' (QCA, 2000: i). The non-statutory national framework for RE described learning *about* religion and learning *from* religion, the former signifying a factual base and the latter implying a form of experience from the pupils. This was reconfirmed in the 2007 Ofsted Report *Making Sense of Religion,* which stated clearly that it should 'engage pupils' feelings and emotions', as well as promote 'respect for the commitments of others while retaining the right to question, criticize and evaluate different viewpoints is not just an academic exercise: it involves creating opportunities for children and young people to meet those with different viewpoints' (Ofsted, 2007: 41). The non-statutory guidance on Religious Education in English Schools of 2010 stressed the growing consensus on its value:

> The UK has a rich heritage of culture and diversity ... Religion and belief for many people forms a crucial part of the culture and identity. The impact of religion on society and public life is constantly brought to public attention through extensive media coverage ... Religious education provokes challenging questions about the ultimate meaning and purpose of life, beliefs about God, the self and nature of reality, issues of right and wrong, and what it means to be human. (DCSF, 2010: 6–7)

The nature of current religious education lessons has, however, been criticized from many quarters. The objection for many agnostic critics is that religion presumes a belief in God and they cannot accept this god-focusing or even the idea of spiritual transcendence. One of the most enduring criticisms of multifaith religious education has been the accusation that it fundamentally perplexes pupils, because the content of different religions is presented thematically, under various headings such as sacred places, festivals, and rites of passage. Such thematic teaching became the norm from the 1970s to emphasize the similarities between religions. In parliamentary debates in 1988 this approach was particularly criticized for both confusing pupils and failing to respect the integrity of the different religions, especially Christianity. Many MPs felt that no recognition was being given to Christianity's unique role in shaping the history and social institutions of Britain. Multifaith thematic religious education was disparagingly characterized as 'a cocktail of faith', 'a value-free hotch-potch' and 'a mishmash of beliefs and practices' (Hull, 1991). In 1994 David Hargreaves, Professor of Education at Cambridge and subsequently chief executive of the QCA, advocated the replacement of RE in non-religious schools with citizenship lessons, as he depicted multi-faith RE as 'a pick n mix tour of religion' that 'trivialises each faith's claim to truth' (Hargreaves, 1994: 34). Terence Copley (2005: 119–20) strongly condemned as 'conceptual nonsense' the belief that one could understand a religion by seeing one slice of it alongside slices of other religions, and argued that thematic teaching unintentionally encouraged 'a dangerous concept of equivalence' – that the Christian Bible is the equivalent of the Quran to Muslims, the Guru Granth Sahib to Sikhs, or the Upanishads to Hindus, or that a rabbi is a 'Jewish vicar', a gurdwara is a 'Sikh church'. In his work in schools, Copley found that themes selected were nearly always secular. Units of work rarely appeared on God, revelation, sin, mysticism or prayer. He also complained that Christian confessionalism in schools had largely been replaced by secular confessionalism, whereby pupils were effectively indoctrinated into secular beliefs and values. Copley gives examples from religious education lessons that illustrate how familiar religious material such as the stories of Joseph, David and Goliath and the Prodigal Son are divested of their original religious meaning and reinterpreted to serve moral and social education: 'Be faithful to yourself', 'Stand up to bullies', and 'Always forgive'. He argued that religious belief and the religious context of the stories were overlooked, yet the lessons purported to provide *religious* education.

Ofsted similarly concluded in their 2013 report on the subject (which was based on evidence from 185 schools) that RE teaching was often failing to explore fundamental questions about human life and belief. Inspectors recognized it as a valuable part of the curriculum, fostering reasoned argument and promoting respect in a diverse society, but they highlighted teachers' uncertainty about its rationale, aims and purposes. They condemned in particular the superficial nature of pupils' subject knowledge and comprehension and reiterated their previous concerns from 2010 that too many pupils were leaving school with a very limited understanding of Christianity. They also highlighted the effect of major policy changes which had conveyed the message that, even though still a statutory subject, RE was of less value than other subjects. RE had, for example, been excluded from the list of EBacc subjects, there had been a reduction in teacher training places and the withdrawal of bursaries for RE trainees, and the DfE had decided not to fund an RE subject review within its review of the national curriculum. Within schools themselves, the teaching of RE is often given to non-experts, to fill up their timetables. Moreover, expansion of the academies programme meant that a growing number of schools were moving outside local authority control and were no longer required to follow the locally agreed syllabus (Ofsted 2013a). RE, one way or another, was being sidelined in education.

Collective worship

A daily act of collective worship had been a requirement for all council and voluntary schools since the passing of the 1944 Act, although parents are still allowed to withdraw a child from attendance. The collective worship specified in 1944 had to involve the whole school together and had to be at the beginning of the school day, although these specific requirements were withdrawn by the 1988 Education Act. The compulsory nature of religious worship remained. The arrangements for the act of worship now had to be made by the headteacher in consultation with the governors, although the Act reasserted that, in general, 'the worship must be *wholly or mainly* of a broad Christian character'. Most of the acts of worship during a school term had therefore to be Christian, and they were expected to reflect the broad traditions of Christian belief without being distinctive of any particular Christian denomination. The SACRE was given authority to allow this specification to be modified or removed in relation to a particular school at the request of the head and governors. Thus, where there was a significant minority of pupils from non-Christian traditions, there remained some flexibility and in all schools still the right of parents to withdraw pupils. The 1944 Act had stipulated that if a school did not have a sufficiently large hall, then the assembly need not take place, and many schools had used this to flout the demands, as shown by Swan's Report in 1986. The latter also suggested such a dereliction was understandable and that in a multicultural society it was inappropriate to conduct worship with a 50 per cent Christian bias. The legal requirement for compulsory daily act of worship in state schools has continued to be contentious, but perhaps less so because of the tendency for it to be largely ignored in secondary schools. In 2004, David Bell, the chief inspector of schools, admitted that 76 per cent of secondary schools were failing to provide for daily worship, blaming lack of space or free slots in the timetable. In a speech to mark the sixtieth anniversary of the Butler Act, he revealed that he had abandoned asking inspectors to take provision for worship into account in their reports, after running into 'a firestorm of protest' from schools over the issue, and he showed his own reservations on the requirement:

> How many people in this country, apart from school children, are required to attend daily worship? ... Are we right to be requiring from our young people levels of observance that are not matched even by the Christian faithful? ... I happen to believe that schools do not break the law lightly. So by making the requirement for collective worship weekly, or even monthly, rather than daily, we would immediately and significantly reduce current levels of non-compliance and in the process encourage all of those who participate to do so in a more meaningful way. (Bell, 2004)

During the passage of the 2011 Education Act, Lord Avebury put down an amendment which would have given schools with no religious character the freedom to decide for themselves whether or not to hold acts of religious worship. This was rejected in the House of Lords. The complaints have continued. The National Secular Society has described it as going beyond the legitimate function of the state and 'a violation of young people's rights' and points out that England is the only country in the Western world to enforce participation in daily worship. In 2014, the National Governors' Association, which represents governors across England, argued:

> If the 'act of worship' is not in your faith then it is meaningless as an act of worship ... schools are not places of worship, but places of education, and expecting the worship of a religion or religions in schools without a religious character should not be a compulsory part of education in England today. (*Daily Telegraph*, 14 June 2014)

Even church representatives are questioning its appropriateness. In July 2014, the chair of the Church of England's Board of Education, Bishop John Pritchard, admitted that compulsory participation in worship was more suited to the 1940s, could actively put people off religion and was meaningless to those who do not believe. While welcoming a time for 'spiritual reflection', he felt that worship was by definition a voluntary activity:

In the 1940s when all of this was put together it was possible to say that collective worship represented the mood of the nation but I do not think that is where we are now … There is a sense in which a compulsion about religion does a disservice to that which I think is most important, which is keeping the good news of the Christian faith alive in our culture. (*Daily Telegraph*, 7 July 2014)

The contemporary controversies

The Birmingham Trojan Horse controversy, mentioned above, has intensified concerns about the influence of religion in schools. The general secretary of the Association of Teachers and Lecturers, Mary Bousted complained in 2008 that in an increasingly multifaith and secular society it was hard to see why taxes should be used to fund schools which discriminate against the majority of children and potential staff because they are not of the same faith. The sentiment was reiterated in a letter to the *Daily Telegraph* in September 2014, the signatories – ranging from prominent atheists to Christian and Jewish clergy – claiming that parts of the education system were becoming insular and divisive and that basic questions about the place of religion in the classroom had not been properly debated for seventy years. The principles governing the place of belief in state schools were seen as no longer fit for contemporary society. They therefore demanded a royal commission to re-examine the issues of compulsory worship and the place of RE on the curriculum.

The present era does not have the moral certainties which pervaded the education of only sixty years ago, and many see any religious input as out of place in contemporary schools. Others accept it as no more than an aspect of cultural heritage, to be taught much as history is taught. Moreover, Britain has experienced a diversification of religious affiliations with significant rises in immigration. Figures released by the Office for National Statistics in December 2010 showed the number of people living in Britain who were born abroad had more than doubled in the previous three decades, rising from 3.4 million in 1981 to 6.9 million in 2009 (11 per cent of the total population). The Christian Church itself has witnessed enormous decline and yet it still has retained inordinate influence on the educational sector by owning so many of its own schools and by having powerful pressure groups. The Church of England still owns a quarter of all primary schools and one in sixteen of the secondary schools in England, and educates a million pupils in these schools. Islam, on the other hand, is of increasing importance in society, and yet some of its core, cultural tenets seem at variance with practices in schools. The debates are heated and appear not to be accessible to easy compromise. There are many who applaud the moral relativism of a post-Christian society, but in such a society the compulsory religious teaching of children might be removed from schools completely and left only to the families themselves. Alternatively, might it be argued that Copley was right to claim that religious education is essential to encourage children to question the mores, not to say the dogmas, of a secular and materialistic society, and thereby to avoid becoming their captives?

Points to consider:

- Is religious education a birthright?
- In a post-Christian society, how can the state justify the influence that the church continues to have in schools?
- Is the compulsory act of worship in schools an anachronism, or is there a value in its continuation?
- Does religious education act as a counterblast to the materialism in society and is this sufficient justification for its inclusion within the school curriculum?

5

Why do children misbehave?

Misbehaviour in schools is a persistent problem for teachers – so persistent that it appears to go back centuries. It occupies many column inches in contemporary newspapers and demands much attention from secretaries of state for education and Ofsted inspectors. The subject has been debated heatedly, with the innate proclivities of some children, the inequalities in society, poor parenting and poor teaching all held variously responsible. This chapter looks at the past and present examples of misbehaviour, under three interrelated themes: the nature and seriousness of misdemeanours; the sanctions thought appropriate in different ages; and the causes for poor behaviour in class and in society in general.

As seen in Chapter 1, the behaviour of children is a lively topic, generating much nostalgia for 'the good old days' when children were reputedly seen and not heard and when youth culture did not exist. Indiscipline in schools is, however, not a recent phenomenon. The issue of behaviour in schools, in its historical and present contexts, has for this discussion been itemized under three major headings: the changes in the nature of behaviour in schools; the forms of corrective action that have been attempted; and finally, the perceived origins of the unacceptable behaviour itself. All three show many similarities between past and present.

The nature of misbehaviour

In the thirteenth century the choir school of Westminster Abbey contained rules which give some indication that, even in monastic cloisters, the boys were apt to behave in a manner deemed inappropriate by the monks:

> After they have made up the beds properly, let them leave their room together quietly, without clattering and approach the church modestly with

washed hands, not running or skipping, or even chattering, or having a row with any person or animal; not carrying bow or staff, or stone in the hand … Whether they are standing or sitting in the choir, let them not have their eyes turned aside to the people, but rather toward the altar; not grinning, or chattering or laughing aloud; not making fun of another if he does not read or sing psalms well; not hitting one another secretly or openly, or answering rudely if they happen to be asked a question by their elders … Again, whoever at bedtime has torn to pieces the bed of his companions or hidden the bedclothes, or thrown shoes or pillows from corner to corner, or roused anger, or thrown the school into disorder, shall be severely punished in the morning. (Sylvester, 1970: 17–18)

At another monastery of the time, good manners were specified at mealtimes, with each youthful monk 'bidden to wash hands before meals', to 'keep his knife sharp' and say his grace. He was enjoined not to 'seize on the vegetables or dip his own spoon in the common dish or put gravy in his mouth with his knife'. The rules show similar pranks and the general exuberance which children display today.

Several centuries later, there were concerns that children did not behave as adults would wish. In 1707 James Talbott, while writing for Charity School teachers, listed the variety of misdemeanours in schools, with quarrelling and disobedience to parents or superiors given priority, alongside the religious failings: breaking the Ten Commandments by taking God's name in vain, profanation of the Lord's Day, unchaste and immodest behaviour, stealing and lying. Talbott also condemned 'loitering, truanting and a wilful neglect of their daily task' (Talbott, 1707). The monitorial system of the following century, developed by Joseph Lancaster and the Anglican clergyman Andrew Bell, outlined punishments for the common faults of talking, quarrelling, swearing, lying, coming to school dirty or late, playing truant, telling tales, disobedience or being absent from church. School log books, which were obligatory from 1862, and school punishment books of the start of the twentieth century show a surprising prevalence of the same low-level misdemeanours. They give an insight into the behaviour that was considered so serious as to warrant severe punishment in the Victorian era. The headteacher of the Kelvedon Hatch school in Essex, for example, described in detail in his log book of the 1880s the reasons for pupils being caned. In 1882 he struck a boy for passing round his slate 'with the most obscene drawing on it' and in the following year another boy was caned for writing 'very obscene words on a slate during the dinner hour'. A pupil was flogged for 'insulting an old man, as soon as he left the school premises' and 'Walter Malyon, a most audacious young scamp who will let no one or anything be at peace, had a good flogging this afternoon for bullying and fighting in the playground during the dinner time'. Two years later, two six-year-olds were punished for spending 'a portion of their school pence' (Kelvedon Hatch, n.d.). At the much bigger Carr Lane school in Bradford, the most frequent misdemeanour in the four years from 1901 was being persistently late for school (thirty-nine of the 178 canings reported in the punishment book), with truanting accounting for a further twelve cases. Three quarters of all incidents happened outside lessons – with children throwing stones or mud in the schoolyard (eleven cases), climbing on the school roof (eleven cases), fighting and bullying (sixteen cases, with ten of these involving boys hitting girls), trespassing in a field (two) and playing and splashing boys' collars in the 'closets' (six). Two more boys were castigated for 'continual playing in the girls' yard' and there were eight cases of swearing, again in the yard. In lessons themselves during these four years, there were only thirty-one incidents of disobedience (including eleven cases of speaking back to a young teacher or laughing when spoken to, and two girls who exhibited 'sulking'); laziness and persistent talking accounted for four more cases, and there was a single case of a boy lying to the teacher. No less than seven children were caned for 'persistent uncleanliness' and the punishment book records the caning of ten children on a single day for 'inability of answer a scripture question' (Carr Lane, n.d.). Interestingly in the following year, 1905, almost half of all canings happened because children were talking in class.

The persistence of such 'low-level misbehaviour' is echoed in more recent studies. Research on student lessons conducted by Ted Wragg and Pauline Dooley in 1984 found that the most common forms of misbehaviour in primary schools were associated with noise, with 'irrelevant talking' accounting for 61 per cent of teacher reprimands. Other incidents involved illicit eating (12 per cent) and movement at the wrong time (11 per cent). Physical aggression was involved in only 2 per cent of incidents, disobedience in only 1.5 per cent and insulting another pupil 1.5 per cent. Insults to the teacher were very rare (Wragg, 2006: 37–8). The more recent Ofsted Report, *Managing Challenging Behaviour*, analysed the types of behaviour that schools currently found challenging and again discovered the most common forms to be similar low-level disruption, such as talking out of turn, avoiding work, hindering others' work, being rowdy and making inopportune comments. Such disruption was nevertheless found to wear down staff and interrupt learning (Ofsted, 2005: 4). Acts of violence were again noted to be always rare, and mostly directed at other pupils, not teachers.

Punishments

The punishments meted out to miscreant pupils in the past have been the subject of much local myth. The use of physical punishment appeared to be the panacea for poor behaviour well into the twentieth century. In the monasteries noted above, if boys loitered after the rest, the rules suggested that they were to be 'smartly touched with the rod ... or to have their hair stoutly pulled', but the monks were also advised that boys should never 'be kicked or hit'. In order to pre-empt possible poor behaviour, when they sat in the cloister they were to have their own tree-trunk as a seat 'and so far apart that they cannot touch each other'. If one of them sang badly at Vespers because he was sleepy, he was given a large, heavy book to hold to wake him up (Sylvester, 1970). Corporal punishment did, though, remain the norm for centuries. It was rooted in the concept of 'original sin' and authority was obtained from the Bible to justify the practice. Proverbs contained such precepts as: 'He that spareth the rod hateth his son: but he that loveth him chasteneth him' (Prov. XIII.24) and 'Thou shalt beat him with the rod, and deliver his soul from hell' (Prov. XXIII.14). They became epitomized in the often-repeated maxim of 'spare the rod and spoil the child', quoted in William Langland's *Piers Plowman* of 1377 and again in Samuel Butler's poem *Hudibras*, first published in 1662. Such punishment was seen as morally necessary to ensure the salvation of the child. There were, though, many voices which deplored the practice even at this early stage. The inhumanity of corporal punishment was criticized in 1612 in the progressive ideas of James Brinsley, who recommended discipline by promotion and demotion according to merit and performance, not sarcasm and punishment. The master was advised to avoid argument with scholars which was demeaning and ineffective. Brinsley accepted that there would be times when corporal punishment was necessary as a disciplinary measure, although not as an aid to learning (Brinsley, 1917). Thomas Grantham, who had his own private school in London, deplored 'the misery that youth groans under in common schools, their pains great, the severity of the master intolerable, schools more like Bridewell than seminaries of learning' (Grantham, 1644). His contemporary George Snell, in his *The Right Teaching of Useful Knowledge* of 1649, condemned:

> slavish correction with the whip ... [which] breedeth in the corrected a base and abject spirit, a foul Bridewell face, bitter passions, a dogged ungentle disposition, a very hatred against the school, the teacher, and against learning, which hatred being once rooted is seldom afterwards removed from the heart ... the mind [is] stooped and broken by such

violent means ... many are the worse all their days for being under the discipline of intemperate choleric governors in their tender age. (Snell, 1649: 20)

Snell recommended 'sweet allurements' as the only means to 'breed good wits and good spirits'. In 1640, Ezekiah Woodward similarly disparaged 'reproachful, scorning words', which discouraged the weak child, who might be helped with the use of praise and commendation 'above his merit and proportion' (Woodward, 1649: 25).

Protests about the barbarity of school punishments continued to be made throughout the seventeenth century and there were attempts in 1669 and 1698 to check this by parliamentary legislation. John Locke, when advising on the education of upper-class boys, questioned the use of corporal punishment, believing 'great *severity* of punishment does but very little good; nay, great harm in Education' (Locke, 1693: 44). He believed that children should be allowed to do 'without punishment whatever is natural for them to do at their age; their learning should be made easy and pleasurable and based on curiosity and activity rather than rule and rote and that it should be inspired by affection, not fear'. Locke's book, *Some Thoughts on Education*, had great influence and went through fifteen English editions by 1777. He did not preclude beating, particularly when a situation became 'a contest of mastery' (Locke, 1693: 83), but he condemned the 'usual, lazy and short way' of chastisement which was 'the only instrument of government that tutors generally know, or ever think of' (ibid.: 48). The relationship with the teacher was seen as of greater importance and he felt that once this relationship had been established with pupils, 'a look will be sufficient in most cases' (ibid.: 89). He encouraged the use of praise for doing well, which was made doubly effective when this was given in public. Moreover, when a child had to be chastised, Locke believed it had to be with unpassionate words and in private. For him 'inadvertency, carelessness, and gaiety' was the natural character of the young and should not be dealt with severely. They must be allowed 'the foolish and childish actions suitable to their years, without taking notice of them' (ibid.: 89).

Locke's contemporary, James Talbott described in 1707 the need for both rewards and punishments, his stress on the former appearing very modern. These rewards might be 'commendation, advancement and promotion' and the punishments as 'reproof, degradation, corporal correction and expulsion':

'Tis very truly observed by a celebrated writer concerning education that children (earlier perhaps than we think) are very sensible of praise and commendation. They find a pleasure in being esteemed and valued, especially by their superiors, and in the presence of their fellows: And on the other side, they are so naturally apprehensive of shame, and of that state of disgrace and disesteem, which attends a just reproof from the same hands; that, I am confident, a discreet and seasonable use of these two methods of discipline, as occasion shall require, will in many cases supersede the rest. (Talbott, 1707: 96)

Talbott admitted that there were 'some dispositions' in children which demanded the rod, but this should be confined to the breaking of the Ten Commandments. If an offence was small, he stressed that the reproof should not be severe or public, although for serious misdemeanours a pupil 'should be rebuked before all ... that others also may fear to do the like'. He did caution that corporal punishment should not stem from 'the effect of passion or unkindness in his Master, but purely from his (the child's) own demerit' and the teacher had in all cases to convince the offender that the punishment was a remedy to prevent future misdemeanours rather than as a 'furious and passionate revenge for what is past'. Anger in the teacher was seen as ineffective, and Talbott describes the rod in any case as not as effective as the feeling of shame on 'modest and ingenuous tempers'. The teacher should act as a loving father.

Schoolmaster John Manson refused to use corporal punishment at all in his school in Belfast, and in 1762 he wrote of his methods of dealing with the low-order misbehaviour of noise, which he found 'extremely disagreeable and difficult to suppress'. In his classroom he used a clear assertion of expectations, a detention system (called the 'trifling club') and an innovative use of peer pressure. Pupils were encouraged to 'ba or hiss' when naughty children resumed their seats in the classroom (compelled to enter the room with one hand on their mouth and the other covering up their left eye), and those who refused to join in the general censure were seen to be their accomplices. Peer pressure was also used to prevent noisy behaviour:

One person only can be heard at once; the rest must therefore speak, spell or read below their breath. Whoever wants to speak to the teacher, must do it after one has done reading, and before another begins. The teacher calls NOISE, whenever he knows the author; upon which the offender marches to the trifling club: But if he neglect going till the teacher call him by his name, this is a double catch: therefore all who are noisy, generally march at the first call. Every scholar has the privilege of protecting those who sit next him, by putting his hand on the noisy person's head, before the teacher call NOISE, and warning him to speak below his breath. Those who make a noise, leave their seats, or misbehave in any respect when the teacher is absent, or before strangers, are to stand up in the trifling club, to learn manners after the rest are gone: They are left at liberty, as to what they read and dismissed after giving a specimen of good behaviour. (Manson, 1762: 11)

The expectations of the teacher and the routines in the classroom are quite apparent here.

The Lancastrian schools of the early nineteenth century stressed the necessity of discipline and punishments, which were set out in Bell's *An Experiment in Education made at the Male Asylum at Egremont, near Madras* (1797), and were used in Lancaster's school in Borough Road, Southwark from 1798. The 'system', which lasted over thirty years, required a single schoolroom and one teacher, assisted by monitors chosen from among the older and abler pupils. Bell claimed that this new 'intellectual and moral engine' would produce better Christians, better scholars, better men and women, and better workers. Children were taught 'to act their part and perform their duty in future life with punctuality, diligence, impartiality and justice' and 'to take an early and well directed interest in the welfare of one another'. There were both rewards and punishments. At the school at Usk in Monmouthshire, the best boy of the class in each week was rewarded with 1/2d; the best catechism boy of the day was given a medal with a ribbon and occasionally 1/2d; promotion earned 1/2d and monitors could earn 1/2d, 1d, or even 2d for good results. An elaborate system of rewards was devised by Lancaster, with merit tickets which could be exchanged for prizes, tops, balls, kites, and even silver pens and watches, according to the value of tickets collected. All rewards were forfeited by neglect to attend church on Sunday. Lancaster conceived that most classroom misbehaviour was the result of exuberance rather than malevolence and his own range of punishments was designed to isolate offenders and to expose them to the ridicule of their classmates. The sanctions included confinement in a closet, suspension in a basket or sack from the ceiling, a pillory, having their hands cuffed behind them, wearing a dunce's cap and ultimately expulsion. Alternatively miscreants were detained after school hours. Public washing was given to those who came to school dirty, and an over-exuberant boy might have to parade around the room with a heavy log fixed around his neck. There was rarely corporal punishment.

At the beginning of the twentieth century there was little challenge to the dominant view that some corporal punishment was necessary in the rearing of children, whether in the home or the school. A 'lover of my country' wrote in 1908:

If we would maintain our position in the world as an imperial race, we must insist upon a virile training both in the home and the school, which shall raise up a people hardy, bold, accustomed to concentration of thought,

Fig.5: Father Christmas visiting the 'good' children at Pickering elementary school in 1905. Courtesy of Beck Isle Museum, Pickering

firm of purpose and not afraid of struggle and difficulty. Such a people cannot be raised without discipline. (Cunningham, 2006: 201)

However, in the 1920s the idea began to spread that a child's behavioural problems might stem from his or her individual background or psychological make-up. The solution to the poor behaviour might not therefore be strict routines and rules. Such thinking led to the setting up of Child Guidance Clinics in the 1920s. By the 1930s educational psychologists were almost universally of the opinion that corporal punishment was more likely to do harm than good, although schools were far from abandoning the practice. The courts continued to accept the principle of reasonable punishment by a teacher acting *in loco parentis* as a defence in cases of physical punishment. They did, though, adjudicate that the punishment should be reasonable and given 'in good faith', be consistent with school policy and such as the parent might expect if their child did wrong. Kenneth Hopkins described in the 1930s three forms of punishment in contemporary use: explanation, public disgrace and caning. He was concerned that there had been a too rapid tendency to diminish the severity of punishments under the increasing knowledge of childhood psychology and particularly the Freudian doctrine of repression and he felt that the reduction in punishments might seem to some children as merely exhibitions of weakness (Hopkins, 1939: 10). He conducted research to discover children's own perceptions of the punishments in their schools and reported that corporal punishment was resented by the oldest pupils, but surprisingly was thought effective by pupils below the age of twelve. They accepted it as a justifiable punishment for bullying and lying at all ages, although it was felt that it should be administered rarely and only by the headteacher, who, by virtue of his office, was 'aloof from the society of all but the oldest pupils'.

The Inner London Education Authority banned corporal punishment in primary schools in 1973 and in all its secondary schools in 1981. The European Convention on Human Rights, which was conceived after the Second World War, had over thirty cases in the 1980s from British parents claiming the punishment breached human rights of both children and their parents. In 1982 the Courts ruled on the Campbell and Cosans case that it constituted 'degrading punishment' and had contravened parents' philosophical convictions. Moreover, exclusion from school for refusing to accept the sanction was held to be a denial of the right to education. The ruling was used by the pressure group, the Society of Teachers Opposed to Physical Punishment (STOPP), set up in the UK in 1968, which argued that such punishment caused serious physical and psychological harm to children. The society also claimed that it implied that violence was an acceptable strategy for resolving conflict, thereby encouraging children to use it themselves to get people to do what they wanted them to do. Parliamentary legislation ensued after the court cases and corporal punishment was finally removed from British state schools in 1986 and all private schools in 1998.

There has been a growing literature on school sanctions since this time. In America, Lee and Marlene Canter found in the 1970s that many teachers were struggling to manage the undesirable behaviour of their pupils and developed the approach known as 'assertive discipline'. The approach expected teachers to establish several clearly stated classroom rules defining the limits of acceptable and unacceptable behaviour, which were explained, practiced, and enforced consistently. The key for teachers was then to catch students being good, with the belief that students obeyed the rules because they get something out of it (positive feedback from the teacher). To maintain acceptable behaviour, teachers needed to act assertively, as opposed to aggressively or non-assertively. In the UK, Bill Rogers popularized the idea of the assertive teacher who expected compliance but acted with respect, keeping the aims of discipline clearly in mind. In their research of 1984, Wragg and Dooley noted the sanctions used by teachers in primary schools, just before corporal punishment was removed. In the majority of cases (61 per cent) teachers used a verbal enjoinder for an activity to stop and in a further 25 per cent this became a verbal reprimand; threats were made in 10 per cent of cases and pupils were moved in 3 per cent of cases and other punishment given in only 1 per cent (Wragg, 2006).

The Department for Children, Schools and Families interfered directly in school discipline in 2007 with non-statutory guidance to heads that advised them not to 'over-discipline' unruly pupils persistently for fear of alienating them (DCSF, 2007). Instead they were enjoined to hand out praise five times more often than punishments. Teachers were also advised not to repeatedly praise only the same good pupils, but that rewards might be given to persistent miscreants who showed an improvement in behaviour. Positive reinforcement was expected to be the policy of the classroom, with 'good news' postcards sent home to reward the pupil and help to improve relations with those parents who had become tired of receiving letters and phone calls when things went wrong. Teachers were also advised to show respect to children from racial or religious backgrounds who saw public humiliation as particularly shameful. The advice was condemned by teacher organizations as little more than repeating commonly accepted practice, with Alan Smithers claiming that pupils were quick to pick up on false praise and discount it and the shadow education secretary, David Willetts feeling its overuse would be resented by pupils who might see bad behaviour bringing rewards. The department guidelines under the Coalition government in February 2014 specified what was deemed appropriate punishment for bad behaviour. It did not give detailed sanctions and teachers subsequently expressed uncertainty about the measures allowed. Michael Gove, the education secretary, felt it necessary to give a number of media interviews which attempted to reassure teachers that they had a full range of sanctions and were allowed to use 'appropriate physical intervention' to separate fighting students or to restrain unruly pupils.' Much to the disgust of teacher unions, Gove suggested as novel some commonly used sanctions, such as community service projects, litter-picking and dining hall clearing (Gove, 2014). The guidance itself was described as no more than a public relations exercise by the National Association of Head Teachers general secretary, Russell Hobby, who asserted that teaching had always been about finding a balance between rewards and punishments.

The causes of misbehaviour

The causes of poor behaviour, as Elton observed in 1989, are complex. As mentioned above, the first schools saw children tainted with original sin and it was this that was seen as the root of all misbehaviour. There were a few voices that suggested other causes. Ezekiah Woodward in 1649 called for better teachers and that teaching should not be the business of 'the worst and unworthiest of men'. His words show at least the beginning of the apportionment of blame to others than the child itself. The root of poor behaviour is no longer seen to be solely a child's natural proclivity to disobedience. However, there is still today an accepted role in misbehaviour for the individual characteristics of the child. As John Weisz claims in his text on psychotherapy:

> Child characteristics, many largely inborn give some youngsters a predilection for disruptive behaviour. Such characteristics may include attentional problems, impulsivity, or irritability that shows up as early as infancy in the form of difficult temperament. Beyond these factors, children with a predisposition to developmental delay or even thought disorder may also have difficulty complying with parental directives. (Weisz, 2004: 180–1)

The nature–nurture debate is longstanding and Weisz describes how the characteristics of an individual are magnified by their interaction with other factors, such as parental characteristics, family stressors and environmental conditions. In addition, as they separate themselves from parental and adult influence, older children fall more under the influence of peers, media examples and popular culture. Steer admitted in 2009 that a significant number of pupils who behaved badly in schools were likely to be suffering from what he termed 'mental illness' and that this had not been sufficiently recognized in the past, 'with the result that children's needs have been neglected' (Steer, 2009: 65). He also suggested that for all children it was in the nature of childhood that 'it is a period when mistakes are made and lessons learned' (ibid.: 16). In its extensive survey of 2012, the DfE accepted that psychiatric morbidity surveys had estimated that 5–6 per cent of children and young people in the UK had clinically significant conduct disorders, characterized by 'awkward, troublesome, aggressive and antisocial behaviours' (DfE, 2012: 22).

In addition to these inherent causes for misbehaviour, Sue Palmer in *Toxic Childhood* claims that modern society is also responsible for current behavioural problems. Teachers have been pointing out for many years that children were becoming more difficult to teach, that they found it more difficult to pay attention, and they were more 'distractible, impulsive, egocentric and difficult to manage' (Palmer, 2007: 147). Palmer claims that children were being raised in a 'morally relative society', where modern life had eroded good manners. The problem was for her a by-product of increased the pace of life, the breakdown of family and the influence of modern technology. Researchers from Loughborough University concurred; after surveying 500 parents in 2006, they perceived that lack of sleep impaired children's academic performance and behaviour. Two-thirds of all children were found to be getting insufficient sleep. The poor diet of pupils was drawn into sharp focus by

Jamie Oliver, the celebrity chef, who urged parents to replace junk foods, fizzy drinks and sweets with healthier alternatives.

Parents themselves have been seen as a root cause for poor behaviour in schools. The Steer Report of 2009 apportioned the prime responsibility for bringing up children to parents and that schools were 'rarely responsible for causing bad behaviour among the young and are good at helping to ameliorate the problems of society' (Steer, 2009: 17). The report signposted concerns that some parents were abrogating their responsibilities and that they failed to 'model good behaviour for the child to learn', to help their children 'to acquire the social skills necessary for them to be harmonious members of the community' and to give the schools support, even in difficult circumstances (ibid.: 39). Teacher unions themselves are not slow in apportioning responsibility to parents. In 2010, Mary Bousted, general secretary of the Association of Teachers and Lecturers, claimed in the *Daily Telegraph* that some parents were failing in their duties to help children to understand how to behave in school, to respect authority and to respect the right of other pupils in the class to learn and 'the right of the teacher to teach' (*Daily Telegraph*, 22 March 2010). In 2012, an ATL survey of 814 teachers and support staff reported that low-level disruption was still the biggest problem in schools, with 87 per cent of teachers complaining of failing pupil attention, 85 per cent of disrespect and 63 per cent suffering verbal assaults. Teachers blamed a lack of parental support as one of the main reasons for such declining behaviour standards, although the problems were seen to stem from a minority of students (*Daily Telegraph*, 30 March 2012). An NASUWT survey of more than 13,000 teachers in 2013 similarly held parents to account. Many teachers also felt a lack of support from their headteachers, with some even claiming that pupils were filling in questionnaires for the heads which rated their teachers' performance. Chris Keates concluded that there was more focus on monitoring the behaviour of teachers than monitoring the behaviour of pupils and that this was dramatically undermining the teachers' authority (*Daily Telegraph*, 29 March 2013).

Teachers have also been held responsible for poor behaviour within their own classrooms. Canter believed in the 1980s that, of three types of teachers, the non-assertive and hostile types created problems in their lessons either by their passive, inconsistent, timid, non-directive manner, or alternatively by their aggressive approach. He popularized the notion that assertive teachers succeeded because they did not view students as adversaries and did not use an abrasive, sarcastic or hostile style. Bill Rogers similarly criticized the 'indecisive' teacher, who hoped for compliance but did not insist on this and proved to be timid in the face of challenge. He also condemned the autocratic teacher, who used power relationships to demand compliance without any room for choice. The Elton Report, *Discipline in Schools*, identified 80 per cent of disruption in schools as being 'directly attributable to poor classroom organisation, planning and teaching' (Elton, 1986: 25). Just months after his appointment as Chief Inspector of Schools in 1993, Chris Woodhead singled out teachers for the poor behaviour in classes, claiming that 15,000 of them were so incompetent that they should be sacked. After his departure from the inspectorate, he continued to castigate teachers for their incompetent management of ill discipline. In a major report of 2005, *Managing Challenging Behaviour*, Ofsted again found that behaviour in lessons was strongly associated with the quality of teaching, with teachers condemned for 'lack of consistency of expectation, failure to plan lessons satisfactorily to meet wide ranges of need and lack of variety in strategies to engage pupils in learning' (Ofsted, 2005: 15). Teachers were blamed for intensifying discipline problems by poor classroom organization, starting lessons late, having low expectations and setting tasks which were unimaginative and 'too simple or too difficult, especially in relation to pupils' capability in literacy'. They often gave 'too many oral instructions so pupils become confused'. They failed to intervene quickly, diverting pupils' attention and 'did not use a variety of strategies to engage and hold pupils' interest'. In a small number of the schools, some staff were reported to show a lack of respect by shouting at pupils, making fun of them, making personal, derogatory remarks or using sarcasm, which antagonized further some disruptive pupils (ibid.: 16). Pupils themselves felt disruption was caused by the fact that teachers did not explain things well, shouted too much, seldom gave praise and that different teachers had 'inconsistent expectations' (ibid.: 27). Parents similarly told the Ofsted researchers that 'concentration was difficult when lessons were boring and restrictive'. The criticism of teachers continues to the present day. The Ofsted report *Below the Radar* of 2014 claimed that:

> In some schools, teachers blur the boundaries between friendliness and familiarity, for example by allowing the use of their first names. In these circumstances, pupils too often demonstrate a lack of respect for staff by talking across them or taking too long to respond to instructions. (Ofsted, 2014: 6)

Responses from teachers have been predictably antagonistic to this wave of criticism. The *Teaching Times* echoes the historical interpretations above which place misbehaviour squarely back onto the inherent naughtiness of children:

> Students are not automatons, where they respond automatically to certain input and produce a correspondingly unavoidable reaction to the stimuli. The reality is that one also has to consider 'deliberate choice' as

a reason to misbehave, and put aside the false assumption that the input students get from their teachers is far more important than the input they get from their peers ... Students coordinate their behaviour. They behave badly when their peers behave badly. They behave badly when their peers expect them to behave badly. They behave badly when it will increase their standing with their peers. (*Teaching Times*, October 2014)

With all these competing influences, one might conclude that it has never been easy to be a child, nor indeed to be a teacher.

Points to consider:

- Who is responsible for poor behaviour in schools?
- Has the nature of misbehaviour altered to any great degree over the centuries and if so, why?
- How can poor behaviour be managed effectively by schools and by teachers?

6

How are children to be taught?

In 2014, there was enormous controversy over Ofsted's actions in promoting certain pedagogies and castigating schools and teachers for not using child-centred methods in class. Some branded the inspectorate as a child-centred inquisition, a far cry from the more formal didactic methods used previously in history. This chapter describes the development of these two incarnations of teachers who have been categorized as the 'sage on a stage' or the 'guide on the side'. It shows the origins of child-centred and cooperative pedagogies and how their dominance is now being challenged once more.

In 1993, a minor article entitled 'From Sage on the Stage to Guide on the Side' by Alison King appeared in the American journal *College Teaching*, criticising college professors for having only one style of teaching: the lecture. King argued that students needed to use their existing experience to understand new material and when engaged in actively reconstructing information in personally meaningful ways, they were more likely to remember it (King, 1993: 30). Her title became a rallying call for those who disapproved of the didactic method of teaching *per se*.

In its most elemental form, teaching 'method' can be divided into two basic categories: whole-class teaching, where the teacher takes centre stage in explaining, demonstrating and directing a lesson; and group work activity, where pupils are set tasks and the teacher's role is to monitor, support and facilitate learning. The tasks might range from small group activities, individualized tasks, projects, experiential learning, role-play activities and ICT-based tasks. Adherents of the latter cite Piaget's, and later Vygotsky's, constructivist theories of learning (popularized in the 1960s), which see children as active learners, needing to compare and contrast new experiences with current understandings (schema), either confirming them or challenging them. Piaget argued that it was through continuous cycles of assimilation and accommodation in the light of new experiences that the child's understanding develops.

Jerome Bruner and Helen Haste also claimed in 1987 that there had been a quiet revolution in developmental psychology, with a renewed appreciation that learning is 'a social process', that 'through social life, the child acquires a framework for integrating experience, and learning how to negotiate meaning' (Bruner et al., 1987: 1). Related to this, the competitive nature of schooling was challenged as early as 1899 by Dewey, who condemned the prevailing ethos that for one child to help another in his task had become 'a school crime'. He therefore advocated a 'spirit of free communication, of interchange of ideas, suggestions, results, both successes and failures of previous experiences', that pupils help each other, which 'instead of being a form of charity which impoverishes the recipient, is simply an aid in setting free the powers and furthering the impulse of the one helped' (Dewey, 1915: 13). Group working was encouraged further with the development of cooperative learning, described in 1984 by Elizabeth Cohen as small groups on a collective task 'without direct and immediate supervision of the teacher' (Hallinan, 2013: 157). Such interdependence was seen to result in positive interaction as pupils 'encourage and facilitate each other's efforts to learn' (Johnson and Johnson, 1999: 187); Topping and others have justified the practice as 'a participant might never have truly grasped a concept until having to explain it to another, thereby embodying and crystallising thought into language' (Topping, 2005: 637).

Throughout history, it was taken for granted that teachers were best qualified to decide how to teach their lessons. Their results were under scrutiny, particularly after the 1862 Revised Code, but choice of teaching method was invariably the preserve of individual teachers. However, since 1997 there have been attempts to encroach on this preserve by both governments and inspectors. The introduction of the National Literacy and Numeracy Strategies in 2002 defined the precise timing and format of three-part lessons. Although the framework was 'non-statutory' (and thus not obligatory), the pressure brought to bear on teachers through the Ofsted inspection process meant that the content and methods of the framework were effectively prescribed. This was followed by the specification in September 2006 that synthetic phonics must be used in the teaching of literacy. The teachers' preserve in this area had been jealously guarded and the unions objected not to the phonics programme per se but to its legal imposition.

In more recent years, pressure to conform to a particular style of teaching has come through the widespread belief that Ofsted favoured a certain style of lesson and was issuing critical reports to those teachers judged to be using too traditional a method. Outstanding lessons had to promote independent learning and foster group work. After the appointment of Christine Gilbert as chief inspector of schools in 2007, the *Guardian* judged that her central mission was to make Ofsted 'the national leader in what continentals call pedagogy, pinpointing exactly what works and what doesn't' (*Guardian*, 27 November 2007). In the following years, Ofsted was criticized as a 'child-centred inquisition', after becoming increasingly vocal about the form of teaching inspectors wanted to see. Like the DSCF, there was an expectation that there would be the promotion of independent learning, which the department defined in 2008 as requiring 'a new role for teachers, which is based not on the traditional transmission of information, but on process-oriented teaching, which ensures that pupils are actively involved in the learning process' (Meyer, 2008: 4). The Ofsted lesson observation guidance of September 2010 made it explicit that inspectors should investigate whether pupils were working independently:

> Are they self-reliant – do they make the most of the choices they are given or do they find it difficult to make choices? To what extent do pupils take responsibility for their own learning? ... How well do pupils collaborate with others? Do they ask questions, of each other, of the teacher or other adults, about what they are learning? (Ofsted, 2010)

This led to growing concern within the teaching profession that Ofsted was promoting a pedagogical orthodoxy, often termed the 'Ofsted style', which showed an aversion to direct teacher instruction.

There was, however, a culture shift with the appointment as chief inspector of Sir Michael Wilshaw in 2012. Shortly after his appointment he stressed to inspectors that it was not Ofsted's remit to define acceptable pedagogy. He told the Royal Society of Arts in April 2012 that Ofsted should be celebrating 'diversity, ingenuity and imagination in teaching' and that, as every class was different, one size rarely fits all:

> We, and in that word 'we' I include Ofsted, should be wary of trying to prescribe a particular style of teaching, whether it be a three part lesson; an insistence that there should be a balance between teacher led activities and independent learning, or that the lesson should start with aims and objectives with a plenary at the end and so on and so forth. We should be wary of too much prescription. In my experience a formulaic approach pushed out by a school or rigidly prescribed in an inspection evaluation schedule traps too many teachers into a stultifying and stifling mould which doesn't demand that they use their imagination, initiative and common sense. Too much direction is as bad as too little. (Wilshaw, 2012a)

In the following November, at the London Festival of Education, he reasserted that Ofsted did not have a preferred style of teaching and that inspectors would simply judge teaching on whether children were 'engaged, focused, learning, and making progress, and in the best and most outstanding lessons, being inspired by the person in front of them' (Wilshaw, 2012b). From 2012 to 2013, he made numerous alterations to the Ofsted inspection guidance, reinforcing the message that Ofsted should not penalize any style of teaching. The subsidiary guidance for inspectors was altered in December 2013, with a new section specifically detailing the teaching methods for which inspectors were *not* to show a preference:

> inspectors must not give the impression that Ofsted favours a particular teaching style ... For example, they should not criticise teacher talk for being overlong or bemoan a lack of opportunity for different activities in lessons ... Do not expect to see 'independent learning' in all lessons and do not make the assumption that this is always necessary or desirable. On occasions, too, pupils are rightly passive rather than active recipients of learning. (Ofsted, 2013b)

This was followed up on 22 January 2014 with a letter to all inspectors, in which Wilshaw condemned inspection reports which persisted in praising 'independent learning' and 'collaborative learning' and criticizing 'teachers talking too much'. He informed them that a number of these reports had been removed from the Ofsted website and had been rewritten to extract phrases that might suggest a preference for a particular teaching style. He ended the letter by stating that inspectors should report on the outcomes of teaching rather than its style and he pleaded: 'so please, please, please think carefully before criticising a lesson because it doesn't conform to a particular view of how children should be taught' (Vaughan, 2014). These sentiments were echoed by the secretary of state, Michael Gove in a speech of September 2013 which criticized Ofsted inspectors who marked teachers down for 'such heinous crimes as "talking too much", "telling pupils things" or "dominating the discussion"' (Gove, 2013). He complained that 'direct instruction has been held up to criticism and ridicule' and told his audience that he wanted a system 'which believes, right from the early years, in the importance of teaching' and that too much emphasis had been given to group work and discovery learning. The issue is by no means yet resolved. In her recent book *Seven Myths About Education* (2014), Daisy Christodoulou studied 228 lesson reports from recent Ofsted inspections, discovering that those lessons which were praised almost exclusively focused on skill development over knowledge acquisition, and had placed pupils in control of their own learning. She concludes that for Ofsted 'teacher-led fact-learning is highly problematic ... The alternatives they promote involve very little learning of facts, and very much more time spent discussing issues with limited teacher involvement' (Christodoulou, 2013: 35). Wilshaw himself in May 2014 yet again provided lead inspectors with a list of phrases which would not be allowed in their reports, such as 'teacher talk dominates too many lessons' and 'children do not have enough opportunities to be engaged in independent learning (Peal, 2014: vi).

The era of didactic teaching

Before the nineteenth century, the pedogogic orthodoxy, as far as teaching literacy was concerned, was to teach reading phonically. Letters were first memorized in order, and then used to spell words. By the fourteenth century this had been standardized as:

+A.a.b.c.d.e.f.g.h.i.k.
l.m.n.o.p.q.r. .f.s.t.
v.u.x.y.z.&.9.:.est amen

Various devices were used to show children the shapes of letters. They were at times written in large letters on the whitewashed wall of the church vestry which was used as the schoolroom, and three Tudor ABCs survive on the vestry wall of the church at North Cadbury. By the thirteenth century hand-held wooden tablets were used, some covered with horn for protection, and thus nicknamed 'horn-books'. Children might be given a primer – a small book with the alphabet, the Lord's Prayer, creed and the Ten Commandments. Some contained a syllable table. There was also the 'musical' chanting of the alphabet and Nicholas Orme shows evidence that they were taught three or four letters each day – the possible origin of the abbreviation, the ABC (the beginners' lesson). In the nineteenth century, Flora Thompson recalled the infants in a village school in the 1880s still chanting the ABC forwards, then backwards, in a metrical form, over and over again. She claimed: 'once started, they were like a watch wound up and went on alone for hours' (Orme, 2003: 260). In 1538, injunctions stipulated that the recitation of the Lord's Prayer, the Creed and the Ave Maria in English were necessary before a child could be admitted to communion, and chanting was customarily used to teach the children in church. Catechisms were an important aspect of education, with a repetition of set questions and set answers and memory playing a major role.

The most popular teaching manual of reading instruction in the seventeenth century was *The English Schoolmaster*, written in 1596 by Edmund Coote, a teacher in the free school at Bury St Edmunds. It went through twenty-six editions in the next sixty years and was still in use in 1704. Its method involved the child being first introduced to the upper and lower case alphabets, then taught vowels and consonants, before proceeding to graded vocabulary exercises of one, two then three syllables. They used verses to help memory. The pupil was then taught to syllabify using a catechistical form:

Scholar: Sir, I do not un-der-stand what you mean by a syllable?
Master: A syl-la-ble is a per-fect sound, made of so ma-ny letters, as we spell to-ge-ther; as in di-vi-si-on you see few-er syl-la-bles
Scholar: How ma-ny let-ters may be in a syl-la-ble? (O'Day, 1982: 47)

The formality of lessons was clear in *The Christian Schoolmaster*, written in 1707 by James Talbott, Rector of Spofforth to help teachers employed in charity schools. On reading, he instructs systematically the learning of the alphabet from a primer or horn-book and then teaching spelling and syllables from a spelling book. Only then would pupils proceed to reading full words as they are joined together in a sentence. He cautioned that great care had to be taken from the beginning that each syllable and every word should be pronounced 'plainly, distinctly, and audibly without muttering or stammering (where the defect is not natural and incurable) and without any disagreeable tone, which all children are very apt to learn from one another'. The pupils would be taught punctuation, which was seen as important in order to read intelligibly, and their first reading was expected to be from the church catechism (Talbott, 1707: 79).

Writing was not accepted as part of the elementary school curriculum, although it might be taught by a peripatetic scrivener for a fee. The formal nature of tuition is evident. John Brinsley complained in 1612 that it needed constant practice and that children taught briefly by a scrivener soon lost the skill. He advocated one hour a day, with paper divided into squares to help the children to form letters. The lesson was yet another form of drill. Only when a pupil could form each letter separately were they allowed to create words (Brinsley, 1917). Talbott recognized that when pupils proceeded to writing lessons in the charity schools, they should not be castigated for large handwriting, 'it being generally observed, that everyone comes by degrees to write a smaller hand than he was taught at first, but never a bigger'. When they had become more competent, they were expected to spend their lesson transcribing sentences from Scripture, or Aesop's *Fables* (Talbott, 1707).

There was undoubtedly the imposition of a particular didactic 'method' in the Lancastrian schools of the early nineteenth century. In the monitorial system, the central area was filled with rows of benches for writing drill and the surrounding space, where the bulk of the time was spent, was occupied by 'drafts' of children standing for instruction by their monitor, usually with the aid of cards on the wall. Bell's system had the desks in the outer areas, facing the walls, and the central area was used by the classes of children standing in squares for instruction by their monitors. Each monitor, who was usually a boy of about eleven years old, had ten children, although in national schools it might be twenty. The work consisted of reading, writing and arithmetic in the boys' school, with needlework in the girls' schools. The monitor drilled his group in work in which he had previously been drilled by the master. General monitors supervised the overall work and the general discipline. The system is described by John Poole in 1813:

> Most of the children in the seventh class, and all, except the head child in the eighth class, take their turns for an hour at a time, as teachers to the other classes; and at the expiration of the hour, the children who have been acting as teachers are called back to their classes; and a new set is appointed ... the children of the first class, having to learn the alphabet, are seated at their desk, which is nearly horizontal, and contains a sort of shallow trough, formed by thin slips of wood nailed to the top of the desk, covered with dry sand. Before each child or pair of children, is placed a pasteboard or card, containing, in large character, the printed letter which the children are learning, and which, to ensure their attention to its form, and to impress it on their minds, they are directed by their teacher to imitate with their forefingers in the sand ... The capitals are taught in the following order: I,H,T,L,E,F,V,W,M,N,Z,K,Y,X,O,U,C,G,J,D,P,B,R,Q,S, the small letters according to the order of the alphabet. (Gosden, 1969: 4)

The pupils were called out three times an hour to a large board of the whole alphabet hung on the wall, and in a semi-circular group had to name the letter the monitor pointed to, or to find the letter called out. 'The teacher himself in no case corrects an error, until the whole class have been applied to.' When they had mastered the alphabet, they proceeded in the second class to copying words on slates and finally to copying dictation from the monitor. Even the commands to be used in the school were clearly laid out in mechanical precision.

The Revised Code of 1862 further fostered drill in lessons because of the annual tests in the three Rs conducted by HMI. Matthew Arnold was one inspector who consistently opposed the system as 'a game of mechanical contrivance in which the teachers will and must more and more learn how to beat us' (Gosden, 1969: 36). He described in 1869 how a book might be selected at the beginning of the year for the children of a certain standard and that 'all the year, the children read the book over and over again'. When the inspector came, they were examined on this book and could read their sentences fluently, but they had in effect learned it by heart and could not read any other book. Even the writing test for the third standard was to write from dictation a sentence from their own reading book. After the 1870 Education Act it was possible to earn grants in other subjects, but this led writers of both history and geography books to use the catechism form to enable pupils to memorize the questions likely to be asked by the HMI. One book, and indeed one lesson, posed these questions:

> *Who was Henry VIII?*
> Son of Henry VII.
> *What was his character?*
> As a young man, he was bluff, generous, right royal, and very handsome.
> *How was he when he grew older?*
> He was bloated, vain, cruel, and selfish.
> *What title did the Pope give him?*
> 'Defender of the Faith'.
> *Why did he so call him?*
> Because Henry wrote a book to defend the Roman Catholic Religion.
> (Gosden, 1969: 50)

After inspecting history lessons in 1870, HMI J. Lomax claimed:

> If a teacher has succeeded in cramming into the minds of his children a host of dates and historical facts having no relation whatever to each other, he appears to think that he has established a claim to a grant; and I have examined children who could tell me readily enough that Julius Caesar landed on the coast of Kent and the date of his invasion, or the dates and circumstances of the battles of Crecy, Poitiers and Agincourt, who never-theless were wholly ignorant of the geographical position of these places, ignorant. (PP, 1870: 110)

W. Scott Coward found 'a hasty cram' and in numerous cases he found answers were so absurd or intelligible that he could not understand why the children had ever been presented for examination, 'fragments of knowledge presented with no connexion to render them useful are not worthy of the name of knowledge' (PP, 1874: 91). There was little improvement by 1877, when H. F. Codd commented: 'the history presented is very poor stuff; it is only the committing to memory of some cram-book of outline' (PP, 1876: 458) and Rowan condemned 'the dry bones of dates and events' which required 'abundant clothing', rather than the customary rote teaching (PP, 1876: 513).

However, lessons in this early period of schooling were not all didactic; there were examples of more child-centred methods. As early as 1612,

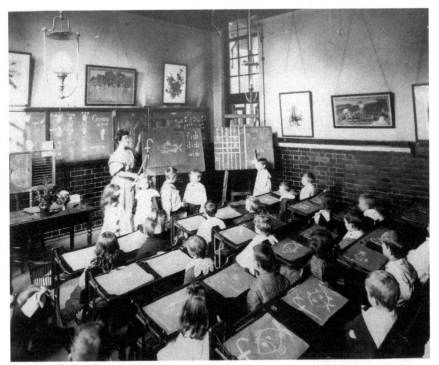

Fig. 6: A phonics lesson at Shrivenham elementary school in 1900. Courtesy of Shrivenham Heritage Society

Brinsley felt learning should be a form of play, specifically for the affluent boys who might afford education at the time. He had the children reciting the alphabet front to back and back to front, and then showing the teacher which was a, b and c. They played at finding them first in the alphabet and then in 'any other place'. The child was to learn to spell using competitive games. Mulcaster's *Elementary* also recommended that material given to children should be modified to suit their interests and abilities and felt that children would learn better if the material was entertaining. With the availability of printed books, visual aids became more frequent. John Hart's *Method* of 1570 used a combined pictorial and phonetic approach (O'Day, 1982: 54). The years 1640–60 saw educational theorists proposing radical educational changes. In the education of young children the importance of sensory perception instead of oral rote learning was emphasized by Comenius, whose *Orbis Pictus* of 1657 used pictures of common objects to facilitate a look-and-say method. Charles Hoole in 1659 brought out an English edition, and recommended game-like visual aids of various kinds for teaching reading in the petty schools. They used picture alphabets, flash cards, illustrated books, religious pictures and counting frames.

Recent research by the present author (Smith, 2014) has shown that the later nineteenth century saw teachers and textbook writers giving much thought to what they were trying to achieve through teaching, and experimenting with different approaches and teaching styles. The over-use of dull and repetitive textbooks was condemned by almost all late Victorian writers, with Sir Joshua Fitch as early as 1881 recommending the vivid and picturesque, which kindled a strong interest in the subject, rather than the 'dry-bones of the text-book' (Fitch, 1880: 381). Archer believed drawing, colour work and clay and cardboard modelling were essential (Archer, 1916: 95–6). Landon had observed the use of a clay model battlefield, with strips of coloured paper to represent troops, which left 'a lasting impression upon the mind of the child' (Landon, 1908: 403). Adamson pleaded in 1907 for the children to do something 'physically' to kindle curiosity (Adamson, 1907: 270). The education secretary, Lord Sandford did not interfere with such methods. His instructions to inspectors in 1872 had specified that they were to look at results and not techniques of teaching, with Education Circular 44 stipulating that, if satisfactory results were obtained, 'no adverse criticism should be made on method ... if the results are good, he need not be urgent for changes ... which would be a hindrance in the case of a teacher trained under another system' (Gosden, 1969: 54). A. J. Church included extensive dialogues in his textbook *Stories from English History* of 1894, for example to tell the story of the murder of Thomas Becket, and he devoted forty-eight pages to imagined dialogues with an old grandfather, telling the stories of Julius Caesar, Caractacus and Boadicea (Church, 1894: 159–64). Harriet Finlay Johnson, teaching in elementary schools in Sussex in the 1890s, pioneered the 'dramatic' method, publishing her ideas after her retirement in 1910. Her aim was to get children to learn for themselves, writing and enacting their own plays about historical events and personalities. She identified the need for activity, recognizing that it was not in keeping with children's nature to sit constantly 'as a passive bucket to be pumped into'. She emphasized that her first priority was to 'arouse the desire to know' and when her pupils began to dramatize their lessons, they 'at once developed a keen desire to know many things which hitherto had been matters of pure indifference to them'. Moreover, her children showed 'by instinct how to get ideas into their companions' minds', coming almost always from the same neighbourhood and 'limited to the same vocabulary' and therefore able to find in their impro-vised school plays 'the correct terms of expression to convey the necessary intelligence to their hearers' (Finlay-Johnson 1912: 15, 18, 27).

Science also became more widely taught, often by visiting teachers, with Birmingham having eight science demonstrators in schools by 1900. One of the more popular types of lesson was the object lesson, ranging from simple demonstrations in science with the class drawing objects, to concrete examples in number work. By 1896 object lessons were added to the compulsory subjects, along with drawing for the boys. In explaining the 'method' in the early 1890s, George Ricks outlined the ideas that children needed to be taught through the senses, which were for him 'so many doors and windows by which knowledge enters the mind', and he asserted that the object lessons should assist the child to discover knowledge for himself 'rather than to pour information into his mind like wheat into a sack' (Ricks, 1895: 1–2). He stressed that being a passive recipient of information gave no pleasure to a child and he preferred to use the children's natural curiosity and their desire to 'handle, and examine, and, if possible, to take to pieces, or otherwise experiment upon, anything they see'. The object lesson provided 'something for the children to do to satisfy their innate activity, something to examine and discover to arouse their curiosity, and something to copy to gratify their desire for imitation' (ibid.: 3–4). His aim was thus to cultivate observation, comparison and contrast and that children should be led to 'make their own investigations and to draw their own inferences'. They should be told as little as possible, and 'induced to discover as much as possible':

> The conversations, however, should not take a desultory form; but should have a definite object and serve a definite purpose ... the object should be placed as far as possible in the hands of all the children ... whatever may require to be done by way of experiment, such as feeling, tasting, etc., should be done by the pupils themselves. It is what the child does, that it learns to know. (Ricks, 1895: 6)

The highest form of teaching was, for Ricks, when the teacher 'by skilful questioning leads her scholars to imagine that they have discovered something new for themselves' (ibid.: 7). The theory was not always followed in practice, and a number of textbooks for teachers outlined, in almost catechetical form, the leading questions, and expected answers, to be posed by the teachers.

There was a growing emphasis from 1900 on child-centredness. The government's *Handbook of Suggestions for the Consideration of Teachers* encouraged a new spirit of independence within the elementary school, declaring that 'the only uniformity of practice that the Board of Education desires to see in the teaching of Public Elementary Schools is that each teacher shall think for himself [sic], and work out for himself such methods of teaching as may use his powers to the best advantage and be best suited to the particular needs and conditions of the school' (PP, 1905). This freedom in curriculum was further highlighted in 1911 when Edmond Holmes, former chief inspector of the Board of Education, in *What Is and What Might Be*, called for a revolution inside the elementary school. In the first part of the book, subtitled 'The Path of Mechanical Obedience', he deplored what had been the prevailing system of class teaching which assumed children to be inherently sinful and directed their every thought, word and deed. In many schools, he found 'children engaged either in laboriously doing nothing – in listening, for example, with ill-concealed yawns, to *lectures* on history, geography, nature-study, and the rest; or in doing what is only one degree removed from nothing – working mechanical sums, transcribing lists, of spellings or pieces of composition, drawing diagrams which have no meaning for them'. Holmes contrasted this in his second part, 'The Path of Self-Realisation', with his ideal school with 'the ceaseless activity of the children' and 'the bright and happy look on every face' (Holmes, 2008: 114). This book inspired a generation of child-centred teachers and went through four impressions in only seven months.

The ascension of child-centred learning

In the inter-war years the cause of child-centred education became the intel- lectual orthodoxy of the primary school. The second Hadow Report of 1931 saw the aims of schooling in an early industrial society as no longer adequate, and schools 'whose first intention was to teach children how to read' had to broaden their aims 'until it might now be said that they have to teach children how to live' (Lawson, 1973: 387). It advised that younger children be taught less through subjects and more through hands-on and aesthetic experience, integrated schemes and topic work, 'activity and experience rather than of knowledge to be acquired and facts to be stored' (Board of Education, 1931: 91–104). The report did, however, stress that it was essential that provision should be made for an adequate amount of 'drill' in reading, writing and arithmetic (Lawson, 1973). The Education Act of 1944 confirmed these basic ideas, although there was the new pressure on primary schools to succeed in the Eleven Plus examinations, which resulted in streaming according to academic ability even being extended into the infant school.

The Plowden Committee, which reported in 1967, again advocated child- centred teaching and this intensified the debate over formal versus informal methods of instruction. For Plowden, schools should allow children to be themselves and to live 'as children and not as future adults'. Schools were to lay 'special stress on individual discovery' and teach 'that knowledge does not fall into neatly separate compartments' (Plowden, 1967: 187). A political backlash quickly followed, with the 'Black Papers' and critical press coverage of radical teaching practices at London's William Tyndale primary school during the mid-1970s. Ministers expressed a dissatisfaction that schools were too free to do as they pleased. Some were critical in particular of the supposedly unstructured 'child-centred approach'. A survey of thirty-seven primary school teachers and their pupils in 1973 and 1974 by Neville Bennett purported to show that children taught by formal methods were several months ahead in Maths and English, and the 1975 Black Papers argued that the best way to help children in deprived areas was to help them to be literate and numerate and not to subject them to social engineering experiments. This criticism culminated in the speech by Prime Minister James Callaghan in 1976 (see Chapter 2) in which the schools' role in preparing the future generation to contribute to the country's economic success was re-articulated.

The national curriculum of 1988 created by the Conservative government of Margaret Thatcher was intended to address some of these failings in educational achievement, and inspection and publication of results focused the teaching of schools. It did not specify pedagogy per se, but in 1990 the QCA brought in Standard Assessment Tests (SATs) at the end of key stages, to provide formative and diagnostic information to guide teachers' practice and provide summative information about the levels of attainment reached by children. The tests soon became accountability tools, enabling the government to compare children, schools and teachers in published league tables. The 1992 DES report *Curriculum Organization and Classroom Practice in Primary Schools* by Chris Woodhead, Jim Rose and Robin Alexander (nicknamed the Three Wise Men) recommended more subject-based lessons and whole-class teaching. The authors stressed that the three basic strategies – whole-class, group and individual – were not in practice mutually exclusive, and that many teachers used all three; and they encouraged teachers to judge for themselves the strengths and weaknesses of different approaches 'in the interests of effective teaching and learning' (DES, 1992: 27). However, whole-class teaching was undoubtedly encouraged as providing the benefits of order, purpose and concentration, while topic work was seen to lead to 'fragmentary and superficial teaching and learning':

Whole class teaching is associated with higher-order questioning, explanations and statements, and these in turn correlate with higher levels of pupil performance. The potential weaknesses of whole class teaching need, however, to be acknowledged. There is a tendency for the teaching to be pitched too much towards the middle of the ability range, and thus to risk losing the less able and boring the brightest. Observational studies show that pupils pay attention and remain on task when being taught as a class, but may, in fact, slow down their rate of working to meet the teacher's norm, thus narrowing the challenge of what is taught to an extent which advocates of whole class teaching might well find uncomfortable. (DES, 1992: 28)

The Three Wise Men condemned the 'persistent and damaging belief that pupils should never be told things, only asked', and they stressed how important it was for teachers to be able to explain ideas to their pupils (ibid.: 31).

Government direction of pedagogy was most evident in 1998 and 1999 when New Labour introduced the National Literacy and Numeracy Strategies in England. These were centrally devised plans to increase the focus on basic literacy and numeracy. The Primary National Strategy of 2003 claimed a purported commitment to increasing the autonomy of teachers:

> Teachers have the freedom to decide how to teach – the programmes of study state what is to be taught but not how it is to be taught ... the National Literacy and Numeracy Strategies, though they are supported strongly, are not statutory ... Ofsted will recognise and welcome good practice ... teachers and schools can decide which aspects of a subject pupils will study in depth ... how long to spend on each subject ... QCA guidance suggesting how much time should be allocated to each subject is not statutory ... Our aim is to encourage all schools to ... take control of their curriculum, and to be innovative. (DfES, 2003: 16)

However, at the time, Robin Alexander scorned this ostensible offer of autonomy, as there remained testing, targets and performance tables and 'the creeping hegemonisation of the curriculum by the Literacy and Numeracy Strategies, with three-part lessons, interactive whole class teaching and plenaries soon to become a template for the teaching of everything'. These lessons had 'closed questions, brief answers, phatic praise', and an emphasis on recalling information rather than on speculating and problem-solving. His conclusion was that the strategies were 'ambiguous to the point of dishonesty about the government's true intentions towards primary education' (Alexander, 2004a: 28). In their survey of literature on the effects of the strategies, Wyse and Torrance (2009) showed the limiting of opportunities for pupils to question or explore ideas, with teachers using more directive forms of teaching. The Ofsted inspection regime also fostered a climate of compliance to QCA-prepared materials, which had been published to advise teachers on the very format of lessons. Many schools and hard-pressed teachers used QCA exemplar schemes of work, which carried official approval through appearance on government websites, for every subject, as a quick, effective solution to lesson planning needs. The constant surveillance, prescriptive and centrally didactic curricula and assessment were seen by Wyse to be demoralizing and deskilling teachers.

A new and very different pedagogical orthodoxy for both primary and secondary schools was generated by New Labour and Ofsted in the second half of the 2000s, based on 'personalizing' learning. This was defined by the chief inspector of schools, Christine Gilbert in 2006 as 'learner-centred and knowledge-centred' and expected learners to be 'active and curious: they create their own hypotheses, ask their own questions, coach one another, set goals for themselves, monitor their progress and experiment with ideas for taking risks, knowing that mistakes and being stuck are part of learning' (DES, 2006: 6). Gilbert expressed concern that many pupils reported that their experience of school was still marked by long periods of time 'listening to teachers or copying from the board or a book' and that personalizing learning had to involve 'changing, and challenging, such routines' (ibid.: 13). Ofsted therefore proposed the encouragement of dialogue between teachers and pupils and expected pupils to 'explore their ideas through talk, to ask and answer questions, to listen to their teachers and peers, to build on the ideas of others and to reflect on what they have learnt'. Collaborative relationships were promoted to enable all pupils to participate. The Department gave clear advice in 2008 which criticized the old practices of teachers who helped pupils individually when they were stuck during the 'heads down' period of the lesson:

> This emergency model still has applications, but it does spread the teacher very thinly and focuses efforts on a small number of children. Guided work offers an alternative approach and a fair distribution of time for all children. Working systematically with groups makes good use of teacher time, and those who have a teaching assistant to deploy can delegate the 'surveillance' of the other pupils. (DCSF, 2008: 10)

The new advocacy was 'quality first teaching', which demanded 'pupil involvement and engagement with their learning', 'high levels of interaction for all pupils', 'appropriate use of teacher questioning, modelling and explaining', 'an emphasis on learning through dialogue, with regular opportunities for pupils to talk both individually and in groups', 'an expectation that pupils will accept responsibility for their own learning and work independently (ibid.: 12). It also advocated cooperative learning, which was seen as playing 'a crucial role in building teams and developing community cohesion' (ibid.: 31). A range of grouping options were recommended for the collaborative techniques of 'jigsawing', 'rainbow groups' and 'envoys', with paired working to facilitate discussion (ibid.: 32). In cooperative learning small groups of students were said to work together to maximize their own and each other's learning, sharing information, evaluating each other's ideas and monitoring each other's work. The teacher's role thus had to change from giving information to facilitating student learning by formulating objectives, assigning students to groups and arranging materials. The Rose Review of the primary curriculum in 2009 did not explicitly refer to pedagogy, although its author again pointed out that children 'relish learning independently and co-operatively' and love to be engaged in practical activities, readily empathizing with others through working together (DfES, 2009: 10). These sentiments show the context of the pedagogical demands of Ofsted inspectors noted above, which were found so objectionable by teachers and by the new secretary of state from 2010.

The phrases 'sage on a stage' and 'guide on the side' present something of a false dichotomy and educationalists have at times mistakenly assumed the two to be incompatible. Some schools have indeed adopted cooperative pedagogy to such an extent that more formal classroom practices are prohibited. It is this exclusivity that Ofsted was applauding in recent years and which is now being questioned by the chief inspector. In practice, teachers have disciplinary and teaching expertise to select the approach that works best for their particular pupils, for themselves, and for the content that they are teaching. It has been argued that the reduction of teachers to the role of nothing more than a guide has undervalued their position, with a consequent disempowerment and challenge to their authority – a disempowerment hastened by the explicit or implicit directives of the government. One corrective claims that the teacher is not just a facilitator of learning but that 'she is more like an orchestral conductor who knows both the nature of the music and the styles and abilities of the performers' (Carlile, 2009).

The Three Wise Men concluded their report in 1992 with a plea:

> The debate about standards and classroom practice is all too often conducted in terms of a simplistic dichotomy between 'traditional' and 'progressive', or 'formal' and 'informal'. The move to a more mature and balanced discussion of the issues is long overdue. (DfE, 1992: 5)

Perhaps pupils need both a sage and a guide, and the balanced and mature discussion proposed almost a quarter of a century ago is still, it seems, far off.

Points to consider:

- Should Ofsted or the Department for Education have a preferred learning and teaching style and is it acceptable that this should be imposed upon schools?
- What are the major issues which underlie the two phrases, 'sage on a stage' and 'guide on the side'?
- One observer has commented that pupils do not know what they do not know. Does this show the importance of the teacher's role as a director and not simply a facilitator of learning?

7

Why have girls (and boys) underachieved in education?

If you give a girl too much to do she breaks down;
if you give a boy too much to do, he doesn't do it.

(HADOW, 1923: 62)

For many years there was much concern that girls were not succeeding in school. Measures were taken to encourage achievement, which appear to have been incredibly successful, to the extent that the concern of the last fifteen years has been about the comparative underachievement of boys. This chapter looks at the educational experiences of both boys and girls, currently and historically, to discern any patterns and causes for these problems for schools and to analyse the many remedies proposed to encourage boys now to excel.

For centuries girls had been underprivileged in schooling in the UK. By the millennium, there had been four decades of attempts to increase gender rights given to girls, but Holland felt in 1998 that the 'gender see-saw' had tipped too far (Holland, 1998: 174). Ted Wragg predicted in 1997 that the underachievement of boys would become one of the biggest challenges facing society in the new millennium (*TES*, 16 May 1997). Failing boys were similarly described by the chief inspector of schools, Chris Woodhead as 'one of the most disturbing problems facing the educational system' (*TES*, 5 March 1996). The sentiments unleashed a barrage of complaints that the schools were now failing boys. The present concerns about their underachievement were initially precipitated by publication of comparative tables in the late 1980s showing the relative percentages of boys and girls achieving five or more A* to C grades at GCSE, the government's preferred criterion for judging successful schools.

The initial statistics showed that girls had achieved more of these 'benchmark grades', and the gender gap has steadily increased. In 2013 figures showed that 24.8 per cent of the GCSE examinations sat by girls were graded A* or A, compared with just 17.6 per cent of those taken by boys; 72.3 per cent of all examinations sat by girls were graded C or higher, while just 63.7 per cent of boys reached these grades. Girls had outperformed at C grade or higher in every subject other than Maths. In 2014, there was a similar disparity in the numbers achieving five GCSEs at A to C grade, with over 69 per cent of girls reaching this benchmark and only 57 per cent of boys. The gulf in achievement is now also shown across phase. At primary level, the 2014 Key Stage 2 SAT results showed girls continuing to outperform boys: 82 per cent achieved level four or above compared to 76 per cent of boys; 27 per cent of girls achieved level five or above compared to 20 per cent of boys. In 2000 girls also outperformed boys in the highest grades at A level for the first time, although their overall pass rate had continued to be higher since 1992 (Arnot, 1998: 11). In higher education, in 2010–11 there were 10 per cent more female than male full-time undergraduates enrolled at university and in 2013, 55 per cent of all new graduates were women. It might be argued that a definition of achievement solely in terms of grades awarded is a narrow one, but the data exposed a cause for concern, which has attracted the continuing attention of the media and a plethora of government initiatives to counteract this supposed gender disparity.

This imbalance is rare in the history of schooling. For centuries it was the girls who underperformed – or rather were prevented from performing – in the educational field. Formal education for girls in the Middle Ages was fragmentary. From the fourteenth century nunneries, like monasteries, educated their own novices, but many also boarded and educated a few girls and even small boys to help the convent's finances. The bishops frowned on this as it tended to disrupt the religious life and what the nuns taught was determined by their own personal accomplishments, which were often not high. Book education was not considered important even for rich women and most girls could be taught what was needed for their future life at their mother's knee: sewing, cooking, medicine, housewifery, and agricultural skills. Even Renaissance educationalists noted for their liberal ideas on female education accepted the common conception of women's family vocation. Vives, for example, when writing of the upper class, devoted a large part of his *Instruction of a Christian Woman* to the importance of the maintenance of chastity. A woman's domestic vocation dictated the limits of her educational needs, and Vives emphasized correct social behaviour rather than the cultivating of the intellect. Reading was a means for protecting the female mind from idleness and sin, although their reading matter was censored and women were not expected to indulge in conversation with men outside the family. By the sixteenth century, co-education did exist in some elementary schools, as witnessed by Richard Mulcaster in 1581 (Mulcaster, 1888: 180), but extensive education was not demanded even by richer parents. It was thought not necessary for women to acquire more than a smattering of formal academic learning. Many families could not afford to release their daughters for what was perceived as useless and expensive schooling. Moreover, schooling alongside boys was regarded as dangerous for the preservation of a girl's most precious commodity: her chastity. There were some changes in attitude, though only for the upper classes. Some Tudor aristocratic ladies were educated well, able to read Latin and Greek and to speak French and Italian. Thomas Becon, for example, asked why girls' schools should not be built, as well as boys', and claimed 'is not the woman the creature of God as well as the man? And as dear unto God as the man?' (Becon, 1844: 377). He wanted girls' schools under 'honest, sage, wise, discreet, sober, grave and learned matrons ... with honest and liberal stipends'. This would enable a woman to govern her household in a godly fashion. Neither he nor Mulcaster saw this as appropriate for the poor, although some educational theorists of the time, such as Comenius, Hartlib, Dury and Petty, were proposing radical educational changes, which included elementary schooling for all, boys and girls alike.

The fight for female academic achievement

From the seventeenth century, private boarding schools for girls were established in some rural villages, teaching reading, writing, music, dancing, needlework, household skills and sometimes French and Latin, although John Locke questioned their quality. He believed that it was the mother who could educate children for the first eight to ten years of life and that it was thus imperative that women should receive a better and more appropriate schooling themselves. Reflecting twenty-first-century concerns, he did suggest that many middle-class girls could learn French quickly, while gentlemen often found their sons 'more dull or incapable than their daughters' (Locke, 1696: 196). Daniel Defoe and Jonathan Swift also believed that women should be well educated and not merely ornamental, but only so that they could be better companions for their husbands. The idea of a vocational or even intellectual choice for women simply did not exist. Between 1580 and 1700, women appear to have been the most illiterate group in society. Of female deponents sampled in East Anglia between 1580 and 1640, only 5 per cent could sign their names, and there were eight literate males to every literate female. Between 1660 and 1700, female literacy seems to have risen, but to only 18 per cent. David Cressy has written that East Anglian women were no more literate, or perceived to be in need of literacy, than 'building workers and rural labourers'. In London, literacy rates were higher. The gender gap closed in the eighteenth century, and a sampling of marriage registers in 1754 showed that 60 per cent of men and 35 per cent of women could sign their names, which by 1800 had narrowed to 60 per cent and 45 per cent respectively. Female literacy was clearly rising faster than that of males over all social classes, although not necessarily because of increased schooling. Few gentry, let alone the poorer classes, could afford to support their daughters through an indefinite period of spinsterhood. It was also ironic that many educated women themselves deplored the exaltation of intellectual gifts over housewifery and motherhood, with Mary Evelyn, for example, seeing a conflict between learning and housewifery.

In the 1850s, the education of even affluent girls had been regarded as superfluous. In the upper- and middle-class drawing rooms, women were expected to be decorative, not intellectual; even the dresses of the period were too cumbersome to be utilitarian and it was seen to be more important for a young lady to play the piano and to sing well than to be erudite. Education came through private governesses and even the boarding schools which had developed concentrated on the domestic arts. Moreover, most commentators accepted the view that nature had ordained women to devote their energies to these (with the exception of the fifteen Quaker boarding schools, which maintained that both sexes were equally deserving of education, based on simplicity of manner and a religious improvement of the minds of youth).

The 1850s and 1860s saw a growing interest in middle-class female education, with three women in particular in the forefront of the movement: Frances Buss, Dorothea Beale and Emily Davies. Together they exploded the myth that a girl's intellect and physique were too feeble to withstand the assault of a full school training. Beale was principal of the new Cheltenham Ladies College, which she revitalized into a large day school and boarding school. Even she attempted to discover 'the right means of training girls, so that they may best perform that subordinate part in the world to which … they have been called' (Kamm, 1958: 72). Slowly she widened the curriculum and employed better teachers and by 1877 the school was teaching 470 girls. Buss began the North Collegiate School for girls in her own home, believing that intelligent girls made the best wives and mothers, but also wishing to equip them intellectually for careers. She was keen to show that girls could match boys in intellectual prowess and totally repudiated the usual course for girls, which paid too much attention to 'showy accomplishments'. By 1870 the small college had been transformed into a large school in new premises, with 500 girls in the upper school and 400 in the lower school. The curriculum was wide: Scripture, English, history, geography, arithmetic, French, Latin, drawing, singing and sewing. As soon as the opportunity became available in

1863, Buss entered girls for the Cambridge public examinations, but it was 1878 before London University opened its degrees to women.

Another major contribution to girls' education came with the Taunton (School Enquiry) Commission of 1864, the first Royal Commission to deal with secondary education as a whole. Owing to the insistence of Emily Davies, it undertook to investigate female education. The findings estimated that the average middle-class girl spent a quarter of her time on music and only 1/13th on arithmetic, and that in English, history, geography and general knowledge there was a slavish dependence on the question-and-answer methods of popular teaching manuals, from which girls learnt a string of words without understanding their meaning. Female education in general was condemned for 'want of thoroughness and foundation; want of system; slovenliness and showy superficiality; inattention to rudiments'. The Commission concluded: 'it is no exaggeration to say that in the mass of girls' schools the intellectual aims are very low and the attainments lower than the aims.' Bryce on the Taunton Commission advocated considerable changes in instruction so that more stress should be laid on arithmetic. He recognized that girls had great potential:

Although the world has existed several thousand years, the notion that women have minds as cultivable and as well worth cultivating as men's minds, is still regarded by the ordinary British parent as an offensive, not to say revolutionary paradox ... There is mighty evidence to the effect that the essential capacity is the same, or nearly the same, in the two sexes. This is the universal and undoubting belief ... throughout the U.S. (PP, 1868: 792)

The Commissioners refuted the 'long-standing tradition that girls were less capable of mental effort and less in need of it than boys'. The Endowed Schools Act of 1869 addressed something of these concerns and the number of middle-class girls' colleges increased from a mere twelve in 1864 to eighty in 1890.

The education of working-class girls, like that of working-class boys at the start of the nineteenth century, was scanty. As shown above, the common view of the eighteenth century was that children of the poor should be 'brought up to labour not to learning'. By the early nineteenth century, poorer girls did often learn to read in the Sunday schools, although in all the day elementary schools it was common that girls should be given sewing or cleaning to accustom them to their future domestic role. Even after the Factory Acts had required children between eight and thirteen to attend school on a part-time basis, inspectors still found that girls acquired little except sewing practice. As one Mr Winder reported to the Newcastle Commission in 1861:

Mixed schools devote usually an hour and a half, girls' schools about an hour and three quarters to this purpose daily; and as in the majority of cases, by a stupid arrangement, needlework is given only in the afternoon, a mill girl may, during her afternoon turn, lasting a week or a month ... have not more than an hour a day for intellectual instruction (PP, 1861b: 228)

In some schools needlework took up the whole afternoon, so that a girl might not have a reading lesson for a month. Even the needlework was of dubious value. The girls were not allowed to make dresses, but merely to sew the seams or turn up hems. Kay-Shuttleworth, from 1839, had called for education for boys and girls alike to provide a useful training and a general education, with 'the theory and practice' of domestic economy for all elementary school-girls. He had also facilitated the continuation of their studies by allowing them (along with the boys) to become pupil-teachers, apprentices for the job of teaching. Girls' elementary education was condemned in 1861 by the Newcastle Commission, which found both sexes poorly trained, with girls leaving school who could 'scarcely read or write and certainly not spell and few can cast up a simple sum'. They had no skill in needlework and 'darning stockings is an unknown science'.

The Revised Code of 1862, which began payment by results, demanded compulsory needlework for all girls, but it did perform an enormous service to female education in that teachers were rewarded for the passes of all their pupils in the three Rs. Passes by girls were as valuable as those for boys and the teacher would no longer see any distinction in the sex of his or her pupils. There was at last equality for females. Schooling for girls in the 1860s broadened and this was shown in improving literacy figures. Greater opportunities for female education came from the 1870 Education Act, which established a system of mass state schooling for all children. The Bryce Commission of 1894 recognized the changes in public opinion on female education, claiming that the increase in the supply of good public secondary schools for girls had been both an effect and the cause of the widening acceptance of 'the idea that a girl, like a boy, may be fitted by education to earn a livelihood' (PP, 1895: 75).

By 1905, half of elementary schools and a quarter of secondary schools in England and Wales were mixed. There were still inequalities in the education sphere, however. The new 1904 Board of Education Regulations for Secondary Schools (the new grammar schools for girls) insisted on compulsory housewifery for girls, while boys studied extra science. They also stipulated: 'in a girls' school in which the total number of hours of instruction is less than twenty-two per week, the time given to science and mathematics may be reduced to one-third of that total' (PP, 1904: 18). The curriculum of the Higher Elementary Schools in the 1909 Code had as one of its two objects the 'provision of special instruction bearing on the future occupations of scholars, whether boys or girls. Manual work for boys and domestic subjects for girls.' The assumption was that girls' occupation was to be domestic.

The employment of women during the First World War again affected their status, as they assumed jobs vacated by the men who had volunteered or been conscripted into the army. Lloyd George's Committee of the War Cabinet on Women in Industry pronounced that 'good training' was the factor which came next to good health in increasing the value of women in industry. The removal of all educational disabilities for women and the provision of equal facilities for technical training and apprenticeship was encouraged. After the war, the Hadow Report of 1923 looked in detail at the different achievements of the two sexes at secondary school level. It rejected the few 'facile generalisations about the mental differences between boys and girls', and was convinced that 'one boy differed from another, and one girl from another, even more than boys differed from girls' (Hadow, 1923: xiv). The pre-1860 era was condemned for its assumption that girls were a weaker sex and therefore in need of more limited schooling. The post-1860 ethos was characterized by Hadow as an equality in schooling, with only additional needlework and housecraft for girls. He did, however, feel that the time had come to allow some differentiation once more, as many girls were expected to do 'a considerable amount of fairly heavy house work in their homes' and in cases of sickness to act as nurses, with the result that they were 'often seriously overworked physically and mentally' (ibid.: 60). Different personal attitudes to schoolwork were seen to place even greater pressure on girls, who were generally more industrious, while boys were characterized as having 'a habit of healthy idleness' and living from day to day; as one witness expressed it: 'If you give a girl too much to do she breaks down; if you give a boy too much to do, he doesn't do it' (ibid.: 62). Hadow thus recommended a reduction of pressure in girls' schools by delaying examinations, positing that 'dissimilars are not necessarily unequals' (ibid.: xiii). Cyril Burt's evidence saw differentiation in schooling to derive from future roles in society and no longer in any biological difference:

There are important physical differences, there are also important differences in temperament and emotion; there are too fairly broad differences due to training and tradition. But in the higher intellectual levels, at any rate before adolescence is completed, inherent sex differences seem undoubtedly small. The bearing of psychological conclusions upon sex differentiation in the curriculum is thus comparatively slight. Whether the training offered in Secondary Schools to girls should differ from that given to boys is a question to be decided on other than psychological considerations, by our views both as to the ideals to be aimed at in all education and to the parts which men and women should (or in practice will) play in a civilised community. (Hadow, 1923: 90)

The clear assumption was that there were no intellectual disabilities in gender, but that the social constructions of gender roles were the predominant reason for any differences in educational provision.

There was a commonly accepted assumption that girls did mature earlier than boys, but that boys would catch up in the secondary schools. This, alongside the assumed gender roles in future careers, led to girls suffering discrimination once again in the Eleven Plus examination for grammar school places throughout the 1940s and 1950s. There were more boys' grammar schools than girls' and local authorities adjusted boys' scores upwards or added new tests to skew boys' results. For many years, a quota system was operated, with girls who should have passed the Eleven Plus based on their scores having to go to secondary modern schools. If quotas had not been imposed in the mixed grammar schools, then two-thirds of all grammar school pupils would have been female. The Crowther Report as late as 1959 affirmed that there should be 'different but equal' education, with boys educated for careers and girls for 'a different relevance'. Crowther presumed that it was natural that the vocational test of future work should be more frequent in boys than in girls, 'for a good many of whom wage earning is likely to seem a more temporary preoccupation' (Crowther, 1959: 112). The report

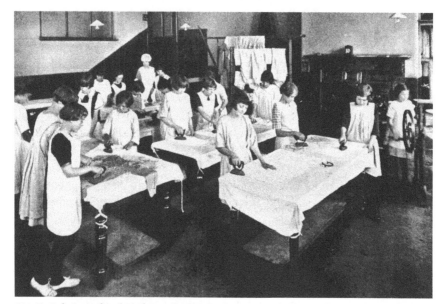

Fig. 7: Saltaire school in the early 1920s. Courtesy of The Archive of Saltaire Stories: Past, Present and Future, Shipley College

did, however, recommend that the tendency to regard physics and maths as masculine empires, and biology and literature as feminine, was a mistake and ought to be corrected. It also criticized the tendency for certain subject areas to be taught solely by men or women and thus to become gender-linked.

The social construction of educational variance was still apparent in 1963 when the Newsom Report again saw marriage as the vocational aim of most girls:

> For all girls too, there is a group of interests relating to what many, perhaps most of them, would regard as their most important vocational concern – marriage. It is true that at the age of 14 or 15, this may appear chiefly as preoccupation with personal appearance and boy friends, but many girls are ready to respond to work relating to the wider aspects of home making and family life and the care and upbringing of children ... Boys in boys' schools spend on average the equivalent of half a morning a week more in the maths and science field than do girls in the girls' schools, who in turn spend a correspondingly greater amount of time on the practical subjects ... To some extent these variations are caused by a differing diagnosis of needs of pupils. (Ministry of Education, 1963: 37, 234)

The campaign for true equality of access went on. The Plowden Report, which investigated primary schools in 1966, found increasing change, with girls and boys undertaking similar tasks in craft and modelling. The distinction between what was done by boys and girls was seen to have 'partly disappeared' and Plowden concluded: 'except possibly for the older children, it is quite artificial and unhelpful: boys enjoy stitchery and girls can benefit from work in wood and metal' (Plowden, 1967: 249). At the end of the decade, Hunt's survey for the HMI of fifteen-year-old girls showed a significant change in their own perceptions, with most seeing marriage and motherhood 'not as a full-time vocation but as an interruption of their working lives'. The report concluded that they might be encouraged to accept that skills and qualifications obtained early in life would not be wasted (Hunt, 1975). The introduction of coeducational, comprehensive secondary schools by the Labour government in the late 1960s was a fillip for female education. The removal of the Eleven Plus and the barriers to female success benefitted many who would have been denied a grammar school place.

Few comprehensive schools at first offered a common curriculum. Home economics, metalwork, needlework and woodwork were still 'gendered' subjects. The Sex Discrimination Act of 1976 pronounced that equal meant the same in employment, advertising, careers guidance and training for employment, but the DES Circular 2/76 used the Act's phrase 'not less favourable treatment' to claim that this did not imply identical classroom

Fig. 8: Girls' needlework at Saltaire in 1924. Courtesy of The Archive of Saltaire Stories: Past, Present and Future, Shipley College

provision for girls and boys. HMI continued to complain that schools were still formalizing 'different expectations' of boys and girls when they entered the junior school at seven years old, and that this was still widespread for the nine-to eleven-year-olds (DES, 1975: 3). Career expectations and subject choices were still structured along traditional gender lines, to the disadvantage of girls, and aspects of the hidden curriculum contributed to the reinforcement of gender roles. Nevertheless, in 1976, 23 per cent of girls compared to 22 per cent of boys achieved five or more higher grades at O level or grade one in the CSE examination. Girls were beginning to achieve in spite of the hurdles placed in their way.

Younger and Warrington have described how during the 1970s and 1980s the focus of equal opportunities was crucially to improve girls' performance. In the classroom, for example, teachers had been seen to respond more readily to boys who 'monopolized linguistic and physical space and teacher attention'. Equal opportunity initiatives focused on confronting these issues, on producing new textbooks and language conventions to reduce gender bias, and on a common curriculum to attract more girls into science, technology and mathematics (Younger, 2005: 16). The DES pamphlet *Education in Schools* of 1977 again stressed that 'schools should not by their assumptions, decisions or choice of teaching materials, limit educational opportunities offered to girls' (DES, 1977: 7). The HMI report *Curriculum 11-16* of the same year saw the role of men and women continuing to change, with both contributing 'to the care and upbringing of children'. Society was seen as needing young people 'who have acquired certain essential skills, who have learned to work on their own, who have been encouraged to think for themselves and to discriminate, and whose earlier education will enable them to benefit from further education and training' (HMI, 1977: 10). HMI stressed that this was 'as true of the education of girls as of boys', since women were assuming their place alongside men in working life. The country was committed to equal opportunity in education, which, the report concluded, 'must lead to some redistribution of responsibilities within the home as well as in the world of work'. The 1988 Education Act and the ensuing National Curriculum was a further fillip to female educational opportunity, in that all state pupils, regardless of gender, had to study the same curriculum at both primary and secondary level. The start of GCSE examinations, with a greater emphasis on coursework, was also seen as a benefit to girls, who were thought to perform better in this than in written examinations. By 1990 the statistics were beginning to tell the surprising story of the success of girls in schooling, with almost 40 per cent attaining five A to C GCSE passes, as compared with 30 per cent of boys. The gender imbalance was repeated in every subsequent year, with a difference of over ten percentage points in each year from 1996 to 2007.

Why are boys now the underachievers?

Many theories have been put forward to explain the new disparity in performance. Ofsted reviewed the issue in 1998, concluding that there were no simple explanations. It did point to the introduction of GCSEs, the national curriculum, and the moving away from a focus on facts to applying knowledge in different contexts, all of which favoured girls:

> Girls are more attentive in class and more willing to learn. They do better on sustained tasks that are open-ended, process-based, relate to realistic situations and require thinking for oneself. Girls may over-rate the difficulty of particular subjects. Girls find timed end-of-course examinations less congenial. Teachers believe that coursework favours girls ... Boys show greater adaptability to traditional approaches which require memorizing abstract, unambiguous facts which have to be acquired quickly. They are more willing to sacrifice deep understanding for correct answers achieved at speed. Boys do better on multiple-choice papers whatever the subject. (Arnot, 1998)

The then schools standards minister, Stephen Byers blamed the 'laddish anti-learning culture', which was impeding boys' achievement. He lamented the failure to raise their educational achievements, which would lead them to 'a bleak future' in which a lack of qualifications and basic skills would mean unemployment and little hope of finding work (*Guardian*, 6 January 1998). Local authorities were therefore required to draw up development plans to address the issue. The gender debate has also been switched on its head, as biological imperatives began to be blamed for boys' failures in school, unlike the previous concerns at the supposed intellectual weaknesses of girls. It is now argued that the physiology of males produces more aggressive behaviour, logical patterns of thinking and linear communication, while that of females makes them more peaceful, emotional, intuitive and nurturing. Ofsted's 2003 report on the issue suggested there were clear brain differences between girls and boys, intensified by boys' increasing testosterone and their 'natural' development (Ofsted, 2003: 9). The representation of boys as naturally more boisterous remains salient, as does the notion that boys' and girls' mental development occurs at different rates. Boys' brains are purported to struggle with intuitive work, while girls work best with exploratory and reflective tasks. Hence, contemporary practice in classrooms that encourages dialogue and reflection is said to disadvantage boys.

Some commentators have proposed that the differences in attainment originate from socially constructed, gender-specific identities. Boys are seen to be influenced by media concepts of masculinity, which depict males as strong, aggressive and independent. These characteristics appear unhelpful in giving boys a sense of direction in schooling. Numerous studies have found that boys display aggressive behaviour to maintain a 'masculine' identity. Ofsted in 2003 quoted research which found that:

> The most important factor that prevents the motivation of boys identified by the pupils and teachers alike was the boys' peer group culture. The presence of friends in the group made the boys work less hard. The peer group observed in school was not an anti-work but a pro-social group ... Within the peer group the boys worked to establish their self-esteem through social interaction not academic performance. (Ofsted, 2003: 10)

Ofsted cited Australian research which showed that pressure for gender conformity was far stronger on boys than on girls and that, even at primary level, boys seek to construct a form of masculinity through which they can acquire popularity and status within their peer groups (ibid.: 102). Many boys seem to crave acceptance by other boys and thus have to act in line with peer group norms to stress this belonging. Some boys do manage to become part of a group where hard work is accepted and others are able to ignore taunts from their peers, but 'for many boys, being "one of the lads", being "real hard", "having a laugh sometimes", "not showing your emotions" and "having to win" embody the essence of the all-important macho image' (ibid.: 18). Teachers also report that girls are academically successful because of their industriousness. Susan Jones has suggested that girls are more likely to lack confidence, and that their successes point to compensatory hard work on their part. Conversely, the underachieving boy is often over-confident, and 'misjudges his own ability, failing to appreciate how much work is needed to achieve the results of which he is capable' (Jones, 2005: 279).

It has also been argued that there is a gender bias in contemporary schools in favour of girls in terms of classroom dynamics, teaching methods and resources. There is a widely held belief that boys and girls tend to have different learning styles. Tony Sewell has written that boys are being failed by schools because lessons themselves have become too 'feminized' and he has called for more nurturing of traditional 'male' traits, such as competitiveness and leadership. He told a NASUWT Conference in 2006:

> We are often frightened by the traditional idea of the male, where we think it's wrong to be overtly competitive, and boys often lack an outlet for their emotions ... the girls seem more able to adapt to more theory-only learning, while boys want more action. (NASUWT, 2006)

For Sewell, boys have an action-oriented and competitive disposition, which is not valued in current school practices. Their learning preferences are being ignored, as is their preference for factual teaching to project work. School culture and increased emphasis on coursework is seen to similarly disadvantage them, although recent reversals of the trend has not made any significant fall-back of girls' performance.

Allied to these conceptions is the belief that boys no longer have appropriate male role models in school or in the home. There is increasingly – particularly in primary schools – a vast preponderance of female teachers. This imbalance was taken seriously by the Teacher Training Agency, who in 2001 specified a 15 per cent recruitment target for male primary teachers. It has been argued that pupils respond better to teachers of the same gender and that female teachers are less likely to teach in a way that reflects the needs of boys. Male teachers are thought to be more capable of dealing effectively with boys' 'laddish' behaviour. However, there is recent research evidence to show that matching teachers and pupils by gender does not significantly improve male performance (Carrington, 2008). Commentators have also pointed to the decline in motivation caused by the increasing difficulty for boys to find employment after school. Holland described the demoralizing effects of unemployment on communities, which serve as a disincentive to young boys to strive at all in school; they appeared to be predicting the futility of their work situation and this disaffection prevented them from 'picking up' in the later years of compulsory schooling (Holland, 1998: 175).

There is no uncontested evidence that learning styles are gender-specific. The binary portrayal of males as logical and rational and females as emotional and irrational has itself been challenged as too crude and simplistic. Masculinity and femininity have been simplistically construed as mutually exclusive opposites, rather than a continuum. Treating boys and girls as homogenous groups ignores the significant differences within gender categories, and it has been posited (as it was by Hadow in 1923) that achievement gaps within gender groups are larger than those between boys and girls. Social class, ethnicity and parental attitude to learning all contribute to academic success. Epstein stressed in 1998 that social class and the level of parents' education remain the 'most reliable predictors of a child's success in school examinations' and this situation still prevails for boys (Epstein, 1998: 11).

While boys' relative underachievement is obvious, it is important to see the statistics in the context of an ongoing improvement in standards. The media headlines that appear year on year give the distorted impression that all boys are failing to reach their potential and all girls are successful, whereas in reality the results achieved at the end of all key stages show that attainment levels have risen for both boys and girls. Boys are not 'failing', although girls' results are improving much more dramatically. Some researchers are concerned that the focus on 'failing' boys has sidelined other gender issues, and that underachieving girls are being ignored. Jones, for example, has shown from her survey of both teachers and pupils that girls' problems frequently go unrecognized because girls are perceived as more cooperative, more quietly diligent, and less intolerant of poor teaching (Jones, 2005). They tend to hide their underperformance. Frequently too, off-task behaviour of such girls is subtle and disguised, carefully cloaked under a mask of normal working and participation in learning, and far less likely to be confrontational. The underachieving girl remains 'a shadowy figure, rendered invisible and rarely challenged in terms of work level or achievement' (Younger, 2007: 228). The difference in achievement of girls from high and low socioeconomic backgrounds remains greater than that between boys and girls, yet these underachieving girls appear to be a lost group demanding little attention. Some feel that there has been an exaggerated response by male politicians at an apparent loss of patriarchal power. Warrington and Younger, for example, argue that the attention given to boys' underachievement is disproportionate and shows society's bias towards males. This was shown by public reaction in the UK to the 2001 A level results, when the fact that girls had outperformed boys for the first time was viewed as a cause for concern rather than an achievement to celebrate (Younger, 2007).

The simplistic view of gender differences in schooling in the past was that girls could not and need not achieve academically. The simplistic view today assumes conversely the intellectual superiority of females and suggests that boys lack motivation, and that 'masculine' culture derides academic achievement. Although many studies over twenty years have shown that there are typical patterns of behaviour, not all boys in any sense are underachievers and some boys clearly devise coping strategies which enable them to be most successful within this supposed male culture. Many girls have been very successful academically over the last two decades, but not all girls are high achievers who conform to the conscientious, hard-working and well-motivated stereotype. The attention must be focused rather on the individual child's strengths, weaknesses and motivations.

Points to consider:

- Do boys perform poorly in schools and if so, what are the fundamental reasons for this underachievement?
- 'Equal but different' – how could this be a solution to the inequality in achievement in schools?
- Does the emphasis on failing boys detract from the hidden issue of failing girls in schools?

8

Why has citizenship education within the national curriculum been so contentious?

Citizenship, which became compulsory in secondary schools and optional in primary schools in 2002, faced extinction in the national curriculum review of 2013. This chapter traces both its origins and its current incarnation, with comparisons and contrasts between the moral training and nationalistic teaching of the early twentieth century and the current inclusion of Britishness into the statutory coverage of the subject. It shows the enduring aim of instructing children in their responsibilities in society and the continuing attempt to use schooling to foster good order and stability.

The rationale for citizenship education was argued vehemently in 2011 when a major review of the curriculum was launched. It was thought that Michael Gove, the new secretary of state, would demote citizenship to an optional subject after saying that the curriculum 'must not cover every conceivable area of human knowledge or endeavour and should not become a vehicle for imposing passing political fads' (*Guardian*, 20 January 2011). Gove had told his party two years before that he doubted its efficacy, questioning 'why is it that we imagine a particular subject put on the National Curriculum can address these deep and long standing challenges?' (*Daily Telegraph*, 10 April 2009). The Association for Citizenship Teaching (ACT) reacted immediately, arguing that England would be unique in the developed world in depriving teenagers of lessons on politics and democracy and the corresponding encouragement to participate in society. David Blunkett was instrumental in lobbying the government not to scrap citizenship, arguing: 'We could not have a civilised, well-informed and participatory democracy if it didn't have young people who understood the world around them and their role as active citizens.' Citizenship was ultimately reconfirmed as a statutory subject for eleven to sixteen-year-olds, with a revised curriculum taught from September 2014. Blunkett himself welcomed the cross-party assurance of its continuation, which sent a message to schools about its importance. He felt that it would ensure that pupils would gain the skills to debate political questions and become actively involved in their own communities. Andy Thornton, CEO of the Citizenship Foundation celebrated that, in spite of the secretary of state's reactionary reputation,

> Michael Gove's curriculum isn't about Land of Hope and Glory Britain. It is about giving teachers the responsibility of opening students' eyes to the politics that is everywhere around them. Not only has he flagged up the importance of citizenship education, he's nailed his party's colours to the mast. (Thornton, 2014)

The revised statutory programme of study for citizenship from 2014 reaffirms the optional nature of the subject for primary schools, merely stating that they 'often also teach citizenship' but with no advice. At Key Stages 3 and 4, the subject remains compulsory but without the former emphasis on moral education. At KS 3 pupils need 'a sound knowledge' of how the UK is governed, the political system and participation in democratic systems, the role of the law, volunteering, thinking critically about political questions, and, as an addition, tuition in the importance and practice of budgeting and how to manage money 'on a day to day basis and plan for future needs'. At KS 4 the electoral and legal systems have to be covered, along with 'UK relations with Europe, the Commonwealth, the UN and the wider world' (DfE, 2013). The new incarnation also, as before, stresses coverage of 'the diverse national, regional, religious and ethnic identities in the UK and the need for mutual respect and understanding'. More controversially, pupils should learn about financial products and services, savings and pensions, credit and debit, and 'how public money is raised and spent'. There is a further emphasis on community volunteering and responsible activity.

Citizenship lessons had been originally introduced as a compulsory element of the national curriculum in September 2002. At the time DfES advice, taken directly from the report by Sir Bernard Crick, explained the rationale for such lessons in three strands: social and moral responsibility, community involvement, and political literacy. The first involved pupils learning about socially and morally responsible behaviour in and beyond the classroom, 'towards those in authority and each other'; the second was to discuss how children might become involved in the concerns of their communities; the third strand consti- tuted information about the institutions, issues, problems and practices of democracy and how citizens could make themselves effective in public life.

Fig. 9: The dilemma of citizenship in practice, in a Cartoon published in The Times Educational Supplement, *15 November 2002. Courtesy of Grizelda*

Historical antecedents to citizenship lessons

Early citizenship education – at least as far as the first two strands above are concerned – could be discerned in eighteenth-century Sunday schools, with their emphases on moral and good behaviour. However, as far as political literacy was concerned, significant segments of the governmental and industrial establishment had been convinced of the necessity for keeping the bulk of the populace ignorant and passive. This view was expressed most forcibly in an education debate in the Commons by one MP speaking in 1807 against parochial schools, which 'instead of teaching them subordination ... would render them fractious and refractory ... it would enable them to read seditious pamphlets'. One of the foremost exponents of a universal education system, Henry Brougham, Lord Chancellor from 1830 to 1834, equated citizenship education with a narrow version of moral training. In 1811, James Mill's article 'Schools for All' in Brougham's own periodical, *Philanthropist*, maintained that people became 'depraved from want of knowledge' and there was a great danger that 'social harmony be destroyed'. The aim was to teach morality and fixed principles of rectitude, and Mill concluded:

It is this flagrant neglect of the education of the poor that our gaols are thronged with criminals, and our legislature employed in framing new laws for the punishment of crimes, or vainly adding to the severity of old ones. (*Philanthropist*, 1811: 79)

Social unrest following the Napoleonic wars stimulated debate on how to control the poor and Brougham's solution was the school. He claimed in 1820 that the wisest governments held education as the 'best security for morals, subordination and the peace of countries' (De Montmorency, 1902: 283). In January 1828 he reiterated this belief in education to the Commons:

There have been periods when the country heard with dismay that 'The soldier is abroad.' That is not the case now. Let the soldier be abroad – in the present age he can do nothing. There is another person abroad – a less important person in the eyes of some, an insignificant person, whose labours have tended to produce this state of things. The SCHOOLMASTER IS ABROAD. And I trust more to him, armed with his primer, than I do to the soldier in full military array, for upholding and extending the liberties of his country. (*Hansard*, 1828: 58)

In 1835 Brougham delivered a long address to the Lords on schooling, which he still saw as an insurance against social convulsion. It would instil into the minds of the poor a respect for property and would do more to eradicate crime than 'the gallows, the convict ship or the treadmill' (*Hansard*, 1835: 1314), a sentiment endorsed by the Prime Minister, Lord Melbourne and the Archbishop of Canterbury (ibid: 1333). Bishop Blomfield argued in the Lords in 1839 that religious education was 'the cheapest, as well as the most effective measure of police which any government can adopt' (*Hansard*, 1839: 1302). The clergy handbooks from the mid-century constantly return to the duty of the school to be an agent of social control and a means of civilizing the parishioners. John Sandford wrote:

The owners of property will more and more be impressed with the conviction, that the best security for property, as well as life, is the early establishment of religion in the hearts of the people; that the best corrective of Chartism is Christianity and the best preventive of socialism, Church of England principles. (Sandford, 1845: 69)

Sanford felt that the children of the poor could not be taught too soon that 'they must avoid giving any trouble or disturbance to others, and that by neatness, order and arrangement this may be avoided'. He felt that this would create 'habits of regular industry and self-control; of kindness and forbearance; of personal and domestic cleanliness; of decency, and order' (ibid.: 111). Clergy handbook writers phrased their expectation variously as creating 'the subordination of discipline' (Best, 1849: 13), 'the contagion of obedience' (Jones, 1866: 177) and an 'instinct for order' (Blunt, 1856: 181). Robert Simpson emphasized the importance of rescuing the child from the pernicious domestic influence and that 'if no one interferes on their behalf these poor children will grow up in habits of lying, swearing, and theft, and familiarity with drunkenness, gluttony, and the grossest vice' (Simpson, 1842: 82). J. H. Blunt in 1864 saw the school as a means of social order. He recommends to clergy that 'a quasi-military salute should be required from the boys, and a gentle curtsey from the girls on meeting the clergyman, or the teacher, in the street as well as in the school ... all trifles in themselves, but all affecting the future social tone of the class trained in them' (Blunt, 1880: 290). M. C. Morris, diocesan inspector of the York district in the final quarter of the century, reported that:

> The main object of the clergy, and I am convinced of the church school teachers also, is not only to make good scholars of the children, but also good citizens; to teach them to be honest, truthful, obedient, industrious, well mannered; in fact, to humanise, and to Christianize them. (Morris, 1922: 103)

Even in 1904 the Board of Education defined the general purpose of the public elementary school as forming the character and developing the intelligence of the children entrusted to it. It was to assist both boys and girls 'to fit themselves, practically as well as intellectually, for the work of life'. Children were to be taught by parents and schools to become 'upright and useful members of the community in which they live, and worthy sons and daughters of the country to which they belong'. To this end, teachers were 'to implant in the children habits of industry, self-control, and courageous perseverance in the face of difficulties; they can teach them to reverence what is noble, to be ready for self-sacrifice, and to strive their utmost after purity and truth' (PP, 1904a: 8). Also reminiscent of current debates, the 1905 advice suggested that a 'branch of moral training for the advancement of which the elementary School offers special opportunities is the instruction of the child in the elements of thrift and economy' (PP, 1905: 159). Heater has recently concluded that even in 1949, the first official publication devoted to citizenship, the pamphlet *Citizens Growing Up*, contained such phrases as: 'there are forward looking minds in every section of the teaching profession ready to reinterpret the old and simple virtues of humility, service, restraint and respect for personality. If the schools can encourage qualities of this kind in their pupils, we may fulfil the conditions of a healthy democratic society' (Heater, 2001: 107).

However, the third strand of the twenty-first-century citizenship curriculum, political literacy, was largely ignored. Brougham's widely circulated *Practical Observations* of 1825, which ran to nineteen editions in three months, proposed the radical notion that even political works should be published cheaply. They might teach 'sounder views' to the working classes, explaining the 'mutual relations of population and wages ... and true principles of the constitution, ecclesiastical and civil'. He concluded that this would enhance the 'good order of society ... the peace of the country and the stability of the government' (Brougham, 1838: 109). Such an optimism was not held by many, and Brougham was lampooned for his attempts to propagandize the workers with Whig notions. It was not until the passage of the 1867 Second Reform Act that there was a serious necessity to educate the working classes in their responsibilities as voters. The ignorance of the time was epitomized by T. H. Huxley, who judged that:

The child learns absolutely nothing of the history or political organization of his own country. His general impression is that everything of much importance happened a very long while ago; and that the Queen and the gentlefolks govern the country much after the fashion of King David and the elders and nobles of Israel, his sole models. (Whale, 1882: 9)

After the passing of the 1867 Reform Bill, Robert Lowe's precise phrase (which became popularized as 'we must educate our masters') was that it would be 'absolutely necessary that you prevail upon our future masters that they learn their letters'. There is no hint here of political education. The need for effective elementary education was, he argued, 'a question of self-preservation, a question of existence, even of the existence of our Constitution' (Simon, 1974: 355). The same consideration was expressed by W. E. Forster when he introduced his Education Bill three years later to create elementary schools to 'fill the gaps' in the voluntary systems. He went so far as to declare that 'the safe working of our constitutional system' depended on this 'speedy provision'. However, few people in public life advocated the direct teaching of political matters. Basic literacy and a patriotic version of English history were the most frequently prescribed remedy. Sir John Seeley, Regius Professor of History at Cambridge, in the 1870s and 1880s condemned this lack of any 'systematic study of politics' as 'perverse'. In 1877, he saw nothing more ominous than 'that a nation which, like this, claims the most unlimited right of self-government, should entirely neglect to educate itself in politics'. In schools, he observed, 'the subject is avoided, for fear of giving bias, though it is precisely on this subject that, in after life, we have to decide and vote' (Whale, 1882: 9). Whale commented in 1882 that it was 'but now' that there was any encouragement in the study of history in elementary schools, and that there was 'scarcely an approach to training for political duties' even for the pupils in their final year.

A. H. D. Acland's lectures to the Cooperative Union in 1883 expressed his conviction that, with the development of local government in particular, it was most important that every citizen should have a sound knowledge of the affairs which concerned his locality:

> We shall all agree that there are few things more neglected than any systematic consideration of what our duties are as citizens of a great country, what that Government is which we help to create, what our relation to it should be, and how far we may further or retard that influence which the great machine of Government can exercise for good or for evil. (Acland, 1883: 27)

Unlike many who believed that cooperative societies could have nothing to do with politics, Acland propounded that 'subjects concerning the relation of the citizen to the state' could be taught 'without the introduction of party matters' (ibid.: 26). However, he saw such education to be only for adults, and not for the elementary school. His syllabus on citizenship, which was introduced for night schools in 1885, reflected closely the syllabus proposed for the year 2002, but it was not intended for children.

The most common form of citizenship coverage remained a jingoistic imperialism throughout the Victorian and Edwardian period, with the emphasis on children being the sons and daughters of Empire. During the Boer War, schools displayed wall maps with the military positions marked. Edmond Holmes, chief inspector of elementary schools wrote in 1899 of the village school having a 'national, not to say imperial role ... Its business is to turn out youthful *citizens* rather than hedgers and ditchers ... preparing children for the battle of life, a battle which will ... be fought in *all* parts of the British Empire' (PP, 1900: 254–6). Military drill was first introduced into the school curriculum in a minor way in 1871 and was extended at the time of the Boer War. The aim was to promote discipline and smartness among pupils. The *Model Course of Physical Training*, issued by the Board in 1902, was based on army training methods. These close military connections caused an outcry among some teachers. T. J. Macnamara, an MP who supported the NUET, condemned the move as an attempt to make elementary schools and the Board of Education 'a sort of ante-chamber to the War Office'. As a result of protests, modifications were made, although drill remained. The radical journal *Justice* carried an article in 1894 bewailing the fact that working-class children were being taught basically to 'honour the Queen, obey your superiors' (Lawson et al., 1976: 34). The widely used textbook, H. O. Arnold Foster's *Citizen Reader*, which sold a quarter of a million copies from 1885 to 1916, was decidedly jingoistic.

In its *Suggestions for Teachers* of 1905, the Board of Education limited its aims in citizenship teaching to creating and fostering 'the aptitude for work and for the intelligent use of leisure and to develop those features of character which are most readily influenced by school life, such as loyalty to comrades, loyalty to institutions, unselfishness and an orderly and disciplined habit of mind' (PP, 1905: 7). It recommended the value of history teaching, particularly for British children:

> all boys and girls in Great Britain have, by the mere fact of birth, certain rights and duties, which some day or other they will exercise; and it is the province of history to trace how these rights and duties arise ... the scholars are not too young to be taught what a debt they owe to their forefathers who won the Great Charter of British liberties and sowed the seeds from which our modern Parliament has sprung ... Such teaching, if it can be satisfactorily attempted, will lead the scholars to take an intelligent interest in current affair. (PP, 1905: 211, 214)

It recommended the use of songs and oral biographies of 'heroes and heroines', particularly the lives of great men and women 'from all stations in life' to furnish 'impressive examples of obedience, loyalty, courage, strenuous effort, serviceableness, indeed the qualities which make for good citizenship'. By 1906 the Board asserted 'lessons on citizenship may be given with advantage in the higher classes' (PP, 1906) and it provided thirty-five lessons in citizenship in the history syllabus. Nevertheless, the general expectation was still very much that of a passive citizenry. Schools were to inculcate habits of temperance and loyalty and history and geography textbooks contained lessons in imperialism. One commonly used book, *Highroads of History*, of 1907 claimed:

> No Briton can help being proud of the Union Jack. It flies over the greatest empire the world has ever known; and wherever it flies there are to be found at least justice and fair dealing for every man ... Men have fought to make it glorious, and have died to shield it from dishonour. Every British boy and girl will desire not merely to keep the flag unsullied, but to blazon it still further with the record of noble deed nobly done. (Horn, 1989: 58)

The *Oxford and Cambridge English History* of 1906 stressed the territorial expansion under Queen Victoria, that 'the British Empire ... is so vast in extent ... that for the protection of British interests, and ... for the preservation of the very integrity of the Empire itself, the British army has very often had to fight in many wars on its borders'. Chambers' *Geographical Readers of the Continents* of 1901 justified British rule in India as it had spread the blessings 'of peace, security, and justice throughout the length and breadth of the land'. Robert Roberts recalled his own schooldays in a Church of England school in the slums of Salford:

> Once instructed however the indigent remained staunchly patriotic. 'They didn't know', it was said, 'whether trade was good for the Empire, or the Empire was good for trade, but they knew the Empire was theirs and they were going to support it.' (Roberts, 1971: 112–13)

There was a sea change after the First World War, with a denigration of militarism and a fostering of reconciliation among nations. The *Suggestions for Teachers* of 1926 added new features in the study of history, which reflected the hopes for future peace. Teachers were encouraged to teach the history of the League of Nations to their pupils:

> In the modern industrial world the increased communication between nations, owing to improved methods of transport, the economic inter-dependence of nations upon one another, and above all the vast scale and terrible machinery of modern warfare, have made it necessary that the people of the world should combine with their natural sense of local patriotism a conception of their common interests and duties. (Board of Education, 1927: 126)

The unusual step was taken to include a whole chapter on the League to advise teachers. It included an analysis of the Covenant of the League, which called for efforts to secure fair and humane conditions of labour 'in their own countries and in all countries, to which their commercial and indus-trial relations extend'. Information on the World Court of Justice was added to the *Suggestions* in 1937 (Board of Education, 1937: 585). It also gave quotes from teachers, who had written that history lessons provided the best medium to develop 'the beginnings of training in intelligent citizenship' and that lessons on 'current economic, political and social problems ... in a historical setting, will do much to stimulate a thoughtful interest in current affairs and in the duties of citizenship' (ibid.: 428). Some teachers had chosen to teach separate lessons in civics, citizenship or 'current topics', although the Board of Education did not encourage this and recommended that this should always be taught in the historical context. There was hesitancy on the teaching of citizenship in a political sense. In the 1937 edition, teachers were to teach about the circumstances which 'have made it necessary that peoples of the world should combine with their natural sense of local patri-otism a conception of their common interests and duties'. But they were sternly warned to 'avoid troublesome details'.

With the threat to democracy posed by the 1930s totalitarian regimes of Hitler and Mussolini, the Spens Consultative Committee of the Board of Education in 1938 claimed that the future of democracy rested on the extent to which the youth of the country could be 'fitted to fulfil later their duties, and to take advantage of their opportunities, as citizens of a democratic state' (Spens, 1938: 37). However, its prevailing attitude remained the belief, shown among many of its members, that political matters were beyond the comprehension of school children under sixteen. There was a role recognized for history, which might help judgement, 'so that not only the reality of political differences but the measure of common ground may be fully recognised' (ibid.: 38). But the main thrust was that success would come largely through the 'unconscious influence of example', with the report praising the debt owed by boys and girls to a teacher 'who is able to combine with clear political opinions both wide sympathies and the habit of dispassionate criticism of political creeds'.

After the Second World War, the 1944 Education Act did contain the first ever statutory reference to education for citizenship, Section 43, although this was merely that county colleges might be built for those older children not in school to 'enable them to develop their various aptitudes and capacities and will prepare them for the responsibilities of citizenship'. The Act made no further definition of the requirement. The *New Secondary Education*, issued in 1947 continued to interpret the subject as no more than the descriptive studies of the machinery of constitutional government:

> The individual pupil needs to develop as a member of a community and he must learn to live with other people. The Secondary School can make a deliberate effort to include a leading feature of its syllabuses and training a study of what has come to be known as 'citizenship' or 'civics', that is the basic information about local and national government, rates and taxes, the judicial system and so on. It can lead the pupil to a wider conception of his status and responsibilities as a citizen of this country and of that of the relation between this country and the British Commonwealth and the United Nations. (Ministry of Education, 1947: 15)

Little more appeared for a further forty years. The Schools Council, when discussing the raising of the school leaving age in 1965, did recommend that the new fifteen to sixteen-year-olds in school might engage in discussions on various aspects of citizenship, but schools retained the right to teach as they saw fit:

> The rule of law, a sense of justice, a willingness to accept responsibility, an honourable carrying out of undertakings freely entered into, a sense of debt to the past and responsibility towards the future, government

by consent, respect for minority views, freedoms of speech and action, readiness to recognise that freedoms depend on trust, friendship and individual responsibility for the manner in which they are exercised. (Schools Council, 1965: para 65)

Official encouragement for education for citizenship continued to be weak and intermittent, even in 1970 when the voting age was lowered to eighteen. Speaker Bernard Weatherill's commission was initiated in 1988 to consider citizenship in schools and optional lessons on citizenship were finally introduced in 1989, as one of five non-statutory cross-curricular themes. It is interesting to discern the government's motivation for such a change. John MacGregor, secretary of state for education, spoke to the national conference of the Commission on Citizenship in Schools in Northampton in 1990, stressing that schools 'should teach children to value democracy, respect the law and be tolerant towards minorities and people with whom they disagreed'. Pupils should be taught strength of character to help them to resist evils 'such as crime, violence, drugs and "lurid" aspects of the media' (*Independent*, 17 February 1990). Jack Straw, the shadow education secretary, endorsed his strictures on violence on television. However, his words were challenged by some opposition MPs who saw it as no more than a continuation of the Thatcher government's efforts to persuade citizens to play a more active role in law and order through neighbourhood watch schemes. The *TES* Editorial of 23 February 1990 characterized the impulse towards encouraging good citizenship as based on 'not much more than a horror of lager louts and rubbish in the streets'. The 1980s had shown that, in the words of the editorial, 'freedom without a proper understanding of the responsibilities people have towards themselves and society breeds a selfish materialism, which undermines common bonds – as well as grosser manifestations such as drug addiction to football violence'. The newspaper questioned if the good citizen was 'simply one who avoids throwing litter and who travels meekly to work every morning on the 7.15 and does what he is told all his life' and also concluded 'pious platitudes from adults are not enough; teenagers can see straight through them – and if they can't, they ought to...'

Citizenship lessons of the new millennium

What of the renewed interest in the new millennium, after the existing non-statutory curriculum strands had been found to be ineffective? A compulsory citizenship curriculum was already being mooted before the devastating statistics of 2001 showed that only 59 per cent of those eligible troubled to vote in the general election and that the under-thirties had largely disenfranchised themselves. There was an obvious need to engage young voters. David Kerr also claimed that the Blair government's approach to citizenship was centred on a communitarian rhetoric with a particular emphasis on 'civic morality' and based on civic responsibilities of the individual in partnership with the state:

> The Labour Government is urging individuals to act as caring people aware of the needs and views of others and motivated to contribute positively to wider society. This is part of what is commonly referred to as the 'Third Way' ... a much-needed antidote to counter the harmful effects of the rampant individualism. (Kerr, 2000)

Kerr refers to the decline in traditional forms of civic cohesion, which had been defined as a 'democratic deficit', with the worrying signs of alienation and cynicism among young people. The political impetus came personally from the Labour secretary of state for education and employment, David Blunkett, who had long been passionate about the subject and had been guided by his mentor and old tutor, Bernard Crick. He proposed reinstating the political aspect of what T. H. Marshall had defined as a triumvirate: *the civil, the political and the social*, with children learning socially and morally responsible behaviour in and beyond the classroom towards both those in authority and each other. Blunkett's aspirations might be gleaned in a radio interview which he gave as home secretary on 12 July 2001 after the Bradford riots, in which he claimed that the citizenship lessons which he had introduced into the curriculum would help to end such disorders and would help to create a harmony in society (Blunkett, 2001). This appears again to be a continuation of the age-old tradition of attempting to pacify a disaffected and potentially dangerous generation.

Since its introduction as a compulsory curriculum subject for secondary pupils, there have been constant criticisms that social and moral responsibility and political engagement cannot and should not be taught by schools. Some argue that the premise of the curriculum is an unreflective reverence for established social institutions and values. The 2002 curriculum had specified that teachers show the 'importance of voting' to pupils, with a disregard for the view, typified by the stance of Russell Brand before the 2015 election, that not voting was a legitimate form of protest. The celebration of Britain's version of liberal democracy has been challenged, as has the preaching of equality and justice as essential British values at a time when many see society as characterized by inequalities (Curtis et al., 2009: 83). There are also many who caution that citizenship might be open to political manipulation. After the 2005 London bombings, perpetrated by British-born fundamentalists, the concern at the failures of citizenship motivated Prime Minister Gordon Brown to call for a review of the curriculum content to introduce an emphasis on British identity. He told the Fabian Society: 'We should not recoil from our national history … British history should be given much more prominence in our curriculum … a narrative that encompasses our history' (Brown, 2006). In the 2007 report on *Diversity and Citizenship* (DfES, 2007), Sir Keith Ajegbo asserted that this had been neglected in citizenship education, in part due to lack of teacher confidence and training, and a 'culture of avoidance', and Alan Johnson, as the secretary of state for education, similarly called for the mobilisation of the school curriculum to create community cohesion, 'so that pupils are taught more explicitly about why British values … prevail in society' (Johnson, 2007). The subsequent revision to the programme of study for England (QCA, 2007) made a greater emphasis on social cohesion, with a new Key Concept of *Identities and Diversity: Living together in the UK* which asserted that:

> Citizenship encourages respect for different national, religious and ethnic identities. It equips pupils to engage critically with and explore diverse ideas, beliefs, cultures and identities and the values we share as citizens in the UK. (QCA, 2007: 27)

This again opened the subject to criticism of its use as a vehicle to promote a contested version of Britishness.

Under the Coalition since 2010, academies and free schools (roughly half of all secondary schools) were given the right not to teach the subject at all. Routine Ofsted school inspections have recently not reviewed it systematically, although it was noticeable that, under the 'Trojan Horse' investigation, it came down heavily in judging that one recently demoted Birmingham academy (Park View) had 'not taught citizenship well enough'. One of the controversial additions in the 2014 guidance is the teaching of personal finance, an area that many feel belongs in PSHE rather than citizenship *per se*, and that the discussion of public finances was politically motivated to justify cuts in government expenditure. A second current major area of concern is the lack of progression from Key Stages 3 to 4, with what is seen by many as a most important topic, human rights, having been removed entirely from the KS 3 curriculum. More contentiously, in the light of the 'Trojan Horse' issue in Birmingham mentioned above, is the new requirement that pupils are taught the importance of 'the precious liberty enjoyed by the citizens of the United Kingdom', which educationalists find an obscure and contentious phrase. It has reopened the accusations that the curriculum might become the vehicle for the purveying of nationalistic views. The delivery of citizenship has still in many respects the same aims as the delivery of a general moral instruction or moral training in the late nineteenth and early twentieth centuries. There is still a desire, as in 1814, to instruct children in the duties of civil life and in particular to enhance the 'good order of society, the peace of the country and the stability of the government'. The threats might be different, but the underlying aims of current legislators seem very similar.

Points to consider:

- What are the major difficulties for teachers of citizenship in maintained schools?
- Should citizenship be a compulsory subject in all schools, including academies and primary schools?
- What should constitute citizenship education in twenty-first-century schools?
- Citizenship can be taught as cross-curricular themes, as a discreet subject or as particular citizenship days. What would you see as the advantages and disadvantages of each of these methods of delivery?

9

Should sex and relationships education be part of the school curriculum?

Who, in such cases, ought to answer the questions and in what circumstances?

(PLOWDEN, 1967: 260)

The compulsory teaching of SRE has been proposed by the House of Commons Select Committee on Education, citing the new and increasing threats to children from the internet, predatory adults and peer pressure. This chapter looks at the arguments for and against making this a statutory part of the curriculum, as articulated by current pressure groups and those of the early twentieth century, when the issue was similarly debated heatedly. It is indicative of the desire of the state to be involved in all aspects of pupil training and strikes at the very heart of parental rights.

In 1913, a sex education lesson was taught to thirty-six girls between the ages of eleven and thirteen at Dronfield Girls' Council School by the headmistress, Miss Outram. We would hardly recognize this as a 'sex education' lesson today, as it involved only answers to questions about the gestation and birth of babies, and nothing about sex *per se*. Yet it caused a furore among parents. They claimed that the sex education had caused mental deterioration in their children and undermined parental authority. The Derbyshire County Education Committee refused to dismiss the headteacher, but, supported by the school managers, the parents sent a petition to their MP and held a public meeting attended by over 500 people. One father was distressed that the school had told his daughter that mothers with large stomachs were 'in the family way' and that the old story of the doctor or nurse bringing the baby in their bag was 'all toffee'. He found it 'most disgusting and abominable' for an eleven-year-old girl to hear this and to know 'as much as midwives' (*The Times*, 4 February 1914: 5). The headmistress herself told the education committee that the mothers were raising their daughters in the same state of extreme sexual ignorance in which they themselves had been brought up. The National Board of Education also refused to dismiss the teacher, although she did have to give an undertaking that she would not go outside the syllabus in future (Cook, 2012). Over a century later, an MP expressed similar concerns about current sex education policies, when he announced to the Commons:

> I don't want my children to have the teacher's values instilled in them whether or not I like them or support them. These are things that should be done by parents and parents alone. Teachers should be there to teach people about things that parents are not capable of teaching about, not the things that parents should be teaching about if they were doing their job properly. (*Hansard*, 21 October 2014: col.768)

Sex and Relationships Education (SRE) in schools remains contentious and the current arguments reflect those of the past – encapsulated in this early conflict over the rights of parents, the appropriate age for instruction, and the values underpinning the teaching. As in 1913, there are still many who question if the subject should be addressed at all in schools.

Currently, primary schools do not have to provide SRE beyond the biological basics of the statutory science curriculum, while secondary schools also need to address the issues of sexually transmitted disease. Academies and free schools are under no obligation to offer the subject at all. Surveys consistently indicate that parents approve of school sex education, with a 2011 Mumsnet survey reporting 98 per cent of parents approving of such lessons and a 2013 survey by the National Association of Head Teachers indicating that 88 per cent of parents wanted SRE to be compulsory. There is, however, a vocal minority of parents who insist that SRE is the responsibility of parents rather than the state and a growing concern, particularly from Muslim and Roman Catholic parents, at the amoral framework adopted by state schools. The fears of the value-neutral approach in schools is evident in the joint statement of the Church of England Board of Education and the Catholic Education Service of 2000, which emphasized that marriage was the fundamental building block of society, of family life, and the proper context for the nurture of children. For them, sex education should show that 'any other physical sexual expression falls short to some degree of that ideal ... human sexuality is not fulfilled in self-gratification or in promiscuous or casual relationships' (Church of England, 2000). As long ago as 1989, a Muslim educational spokesman protested that a majority of Muslim parents would be happy if there was no sex education at all in schools (Sarwar, 1989: 17). His objections centred on 'the inevitable study of contraceptive methods' in sex education, which were accepted by society as 'the best way to allow young people to experiment with sexuality without the fear of unwanted pregnancy' (ibid.: 13). There was clearly a perceived cultural gap between attitudes in the West, where 'premarital love and intimacy are considered to be almost indispensable' and Islam, which prohibited pre- or extramarital sex (ibid.: 8). Equally objectionable was the practice of not separating boys and girls for their sex education classes.

What was the rationale for sex education in schools?

The Dronfield case shows that some teaching about sexual matters did actually take place at the start of the twentieth century, but there is little evidence to suggest that this practice was widespread. Many oral reminiscences show that children's only sex education came from friends and siblings. Maude Braby observed in 1908 that little if anything was ever said to girls, which gave them the impression that 'the subject of sex is a repulsive one, wholly unfit for their consideration, and the functions of sex are loathsome, though necessary'. She pleaded for honest sex education:

> Why cannot girls – and boys too, for that matter – be taught the plain truth (in suitable language of course) that sex is the pivot on which the world turns, that the instincts and emotions of sex are common to humanity, and in themselves not base or degrading, nor is there any cause for shame in possessing them, although it is necessary that they should be strenuously controlled. (Braby, 1908: 101–2)

In 1915, Norah March described children's natural and healthy curiosity, which, if not satisfied, led them to 'seek the information from other sources – sources often wholly undesirable, often vulgar and pernicious, at any rate less valuable and wholesome than the mother's loving instruction could provide'. She described how girls often had no advice and were 'totally unprepared for the onset of menstruation and experienced severe nervous shock'. Boys similarly had no guidance before experiencing their first seminal emissions and 'are frequently, through lack of a wise counsellor, driven to confide in companions or to seek aid from quacks, thereby being led to believe themselves in a condition of ill health' (March, 1915: 60–1). Marie Stopes claimed in 1921 that children had for centuries been learning from 'dirty-minded servants, other children and school fellows, such filthy nonsense about sex that their attitude towards the supreme act of life has been so debased' (Hall, 2012: 30). In the same year, Maude Royden, a preacher at the City Temple in London, similarly found that parental evasion encouraged children to seek answers from 'more grimy sources' and arrive at the conclusion that 'in the relations of men and women there is also something that is repulsive ... so base that even our own parents will not speak to us about it' (Royden, 1922: 119).

There was no compulsion on schools to cover the subject, with the Board of Education no longer prescribing a curriculum in the 1920s. Its issue of 'suggestions' in 1928, in the *Handbook on Health Education*, included no reference to sex education (though it was not coy about emphasizing the need for frequent bowel movements). As Pilcher has concluded, this laissez faire attitude placed no urgency on schools to provide programmes of sex education to pupils (Pilcher, 2004). Even when parents did try to explain the 'facts of life' to their children, confusion often resulted. In her recent survey of the evidence, Hall discovered that supposedly modern mothers who instructed their daughters in the facts of life by describing the pollination of flowers did not show the relevance to human reproduction (Hall, 2012: 32). Theodore Tucker and Muriel Pout reported adults deploring their own shyness and lack of knowledge and during the courses that they ran in Wales to instruct parents, the vast majority professed themselves 'unequal to the task' (ibid.: 22). However, Hall uses the Mass Observation surveys of the 1940s to show that many parents still considered it their duty, that 'the child should be instructed only by the same sex parent' and 'not before the age of thirteen'. Two women emphasized in 1942 that they felt it was up to them to teach the girls and up to the fathers to teach the boys and that this should never be done at school (ibid.: 22). However, a significant number of respondents commented that they had themselves been ignorant of sex even at the time of their marriage.

There was a clear deficiency in sex education for children when the Board of Education made its first official statement on the subject in 1943, in the pamphlet *Sex Education in Schools and Youth Organisations*. The motivations for the statement, issued surprisingly urgently at a time of wartime paper shortages, were major health concerns over venereal diseases and a perceived 'social dislocation', which had broken down 'restraints' and led to increasing numbers of young people falling victim to 'the special temptations and circumstances of wartime' (Board of Education, 1943: 1, 2). The document admitted that until that time sex instruction had not been given in one-third to two-thirds of all schools (ibid.: 13). Like so many subsequent documents, it stressed that the first responsibility rested on parents to deal with their children's questions, but that a substantial proportion of parents 'either have some reluctance to give this knowledge to their children, or feel the need of some guidance' (ibid.: 3). In addition, because of service in the forces and child evacuation from cities, many were separated from parental advice in any case. As a result, many schools felt it their duty to ensure that young people were not left 'in dangerous ignorance, nor alternatively left to acquire knowledge in ways which are likely to distort or degrade their outlook on sex and their sense of responsibility in regard to it' (ibid.: 22). Some teachers saw their responsibility to be simply to insist that parents themselves should address the subject, with one headteacher telling a father directly that it was 'his bounden duty to give the boy sound advice and be candid about it'. This same head did, though, give a final message to his boys when they left school about the dangers of venereal disease (ibid.: 15). The laxity of morals among young girls was of specific concern, with increasing incidence of venereal disease and the increase in illegitimate births (from 4 per cent of live births in 1940 to 9 per cent by 1945). Hence the underlying aim, stated at the end of the document, was clearly to encourage schools to 'protect young people in these unsettled times' (ibid.: 22).

Cyril Bibby's guidance of the following year showed the prevailing ignorance of pupils, with examples of questions put to teachers. They included, from thirteen-year-olds: 'Is it true that the baby comes out of the back passage? … Can conception happen when a man and woman kiss? … Is there only certain times when a male can fertilise a female as there is only certain times it happens in a female?' One ten-year-old asked: 'Does a baby have to be cut out?' (Bibby, 1948: 151–60). However, Bibby did not believe that sex education would be a panacea for society's ills. He shows the wellsprings of the wartime concerns in his judgement that many in society were hopelessly unrealistic in expecting sex education alone to 'wipe out prostitution and casual promiscuity, to make all marriages successful and all divorce disappear, to abolish adultery and to prevent all fornication'. He believed that the sexual ills of society were 'many and deep seated' and that 'education unaided will not eradicate them'. He did deplore 'those who use sex education as a euphemism for dilation on the horrors of venereal disease and hope to frighten young people into goodness' (ibid.: 6).

Three editions of government handbooks on health were issued in the next thirty years. The motivation for including sex education on the curriculum were clearly twofold: health motivations (to limit the spread of infections and reduce the numbers of illegitimate children born to young girls); and, more altruistically, to reassure children during the great changes involved in puberty. Both became more pressing with increases in the minimum school leaving age, which was raised from fourteen to fifteen years old in

1947 and to sixteen in 1972, thereby keeping young people in education well beyond puberty. The 1956 edition, in its coyly entitled chapter 'School the future parent', grounded the school role in preparing children for marriage and parenthood, noting that a lack of sensible guidance could lead to unhappiness and broken marriages. It warned against prostitution and extramarital births, which had begun to rise again after a fall in the early 1950s, and in the separate chapter on drugs, alcohol and tobacco made specific mention of the danger of sexual misconduct arising from the 'loosening of control' following excessive drinking. The handbook therefore claimed that 'the demand for some more definite form of instruction does seem to reflect a real need' (54). There was also a first mention of the challenge to the traditional standards of behaviour from films and television, which brought boys and girls 'in closer contact with the outside world than we often realise'. There was the second objective of helping children come to terms with puberty, with the handbook suggesting that the problems that troubled boys and girls were 'seldom very novel' but they were 'anything but easy for the young people themselves to bear or tackle unaided' (ibid.: 57). There was particular concern for girls that the onset of menstruation caused 'emotional shock particularly if it comes without warning' and it pronounced that 'If parents are reluctant to explain, then it is for the teacher to make sure that the girl is emotionally prepared' (ibid.: 58).

The DFE handbooks of 1968 and 1977 showed that health concerns continued to underlie the recommended provision of sex education in the age of the permissive society, rather more than the desire to reassure pupils at what was being termed in society a time of storm and stress. They reiterated the physical and emotional pressures that did not exist in former generations, with now easily available oral contraception, the earlier age of physical maturity particularly for girls and the rejection of many of the scruples and taboos and of organized religion that had acted as constraints upon the behaviour of their parents (DFE, 1968: 100). The 1968 chapter dealing with the prevention of communicable diseases for the first time discussed venereal disease, explaining that this was caused by close sexual contact and providing graphic details of symptoms. The 1977 chapter on sex education began with a lengthy quote from the Crowther Commission, which showed the lack of restraints on the young. It also outlined statistics from 1974, when there had been 1,553 births to girls below the age of sixteen and 3,378 legal abortions (ibid.: 113). The incidence of gonorrhoea rose in England and Wales from 20,000 cases in 1955 to 59,000 by 1975, with most cases in the age range sixteen to twenty-five, and the report concluded, 'these facts show how far the religious ideal of chastity is from universal acceptance'. While again parents are recognized as having the chief responsibility here, the handbook suggested that this did not 'absolve the schools'. The handbook suggested that in these circumstances it was difficult to contest the argument for making knowledge of methods of birth control available to older boys and girls before they left school (ibid.: 114). Girls needed to understand that they might 'quite inadvertently impose great stresses on boys by arousing sexual reactions in them which they do not fully comprehend and may not be able to control' (ibid.: 117). Masturbation, contraception, venereal disease, sexual deviations and homosexuality were explicitly identified as potential, though not obligatory, topics within sex education.

The sex education of the early 1960s appears still not to have been particularly effective. Allen in her research in 1987 interviewed parents and found surprising stories of a continuing ignorance about the most basic facts of life, including menstruation. Over 10 per cent of the women said that they had known little or nothing about periods, and for some women the onset of menstruation had been a traumatic experience. A thirty-four-year-old mother illustrated the point: 'I remember when I started menstruating, mother said nothing. I was horrified and shocked. I thought I was bleeding to death. No one ever said anything' (Allen, 1987: 107). A mother of forty-two who went to school in the 1950s described the alarm: 'We were never told anything. The first girl to start screamed blue murder. She thought she was dying' (ibid.: 108). A father also commented: 'I would have liked more on things in general. It would have cut out all the standing on the corner asking other boys. It seemed rather smart then and it was difficult to imagine having a worthwhile relationship with a girl' (ibid.: 109).

The Plowden Report of 1967 referred to the paucity of primary sex education, which it said appeared rarely on the timetable and received little mention in schools (Plowden, 1967: 259). It again emphasized that the proper people to answer children's questions were parents and asserted that 'when the information is given in the context of a happy home by loving parents it may be more acceptable than if given by someone else, however well intentioned'. However, the report pointed out that not all homes were happy and that some parents still found it embarrassing to discuss the physical details of sex with their children. The question was then: 'Who, in such cases, ought to answer the questions and in what circumstances?' (ibid.: 260). The committee therefore recommended an informal method in schools, answering children's question when they arose, particularly for girls who were facing early menstruation. The coverage might also refer to relationships in such education, and the rationale for this again appeared to be to counteract the mass media, which 'are preoccupied with the physical aspects of sex and seem unable to put them into perspective'. Schools could not 'cure this sickness', but they could 'make a beginning' (Plowden, 1967: 261).

While sex education remained at the school's discretion, ministerial advice was still forthcoming, with increasing stress placed on the role of the family life. A 1986 Education Act had included a backbench amendment to ensure due regard to moral considerations and the value of family life, and Education Department Circular 11/87 thus advised schools that the physical aspects of sexual behaviour should be set within the 'clear moral framework' of 'the benefits of stable marriage and family life and the responsibilities of parenthood'. DfEE Circular 5/94 again stressed that sex education could not be value-free. Both highlighted that that pupils should be encouraged to consider 'the importance of self restraint, dignity and respect for themselves and others' and helped to recognize 'the physical, emotional and moral risks of casual and promiscuous sexual behaviour'. The advice gave a specific warning about advocating homosexual behaviour, which, it claimed, many saw as 'not morally acceptable' (DES, 1987: para. 22).

The first detailed (and surprisingly still current in 2015) guidance on the subject was issued in 2000, displaying yet again a clear public health motivation for the delivery of the subject, after a National Opinion Poll survey had indicated that young adults were becoming complacent about the importance of safer sex and over a quarter believing that the contraceptive pill would protect them from sexually transmitted infections (DfEE, 2000: 16–17). The nomenclature was changed to 'Sex and Relationships Education' (SRE) to acknowledge that children and young people were entitled to more than just the biological basics, although the guidance was non-statutory, and emphasized that 'schools *might* need to address' certain specific issues' in order to be effective in the subject (ibid.: 11). The document highlighted the aim of reducing the incidence of HIV/AIDS, and sexually transmitted infections, after genital chlamydial infection, genital warts and gonorrhoea had increased significantly since 1995, particularly in the sixteen- to nineteen-year-old range. Thirty-nine per cent of those with AIDS in the UK were reported to be in their twenties, most having contracted HIV in their teens (ibid.: 17). The issue of underage pregnancy was again in the forefront of government considerations, with the assertion of the unacceptability of 100,000 conceptions to teenagers in 1998, of which over 8,000 were to girls under sixteen (ibid.: 15). The advice therefore moved from a former restrictive approach to stating unequivocally that young people should be informed about condom use and that there should be instruction in the different types of contraception, 'including emergency contraception, and their effectiveness' (ibid.: 15). The document expressed concern at relying on parents for sex education, noting that fathers in particular 'rarely take responsibility for giving sex and relationship education to their sons' (ibid.: 25) and that children from black and other minority ethnic communities were less likely to talk to their parents about sex and relationships. Some young women and young men from minority ethnic communities were seen to rely on schools as their main – and sometimes only – source of sex education (ibid.: 11).

The 2000 guidance outlined the second objective of helping young people to 'move with confidence from childhood through adolescence into adulthood'. Ten per cent of girls were shown to receive no preparation at all before their first period and thus in primary schools all children needed to know about puberty 'before they experience the onset of physical changes' (ibid.: 15). In the early primary school years, education about relationships was described as focusing on 'friendship, bullying and the building of self-esteem' (ibid.: 9). There was throughout constant reference to the nature and importance of marriage for family life and bringing up children, while accepting that there were 'strong and mutually supportive relationships outside marriage' (ibid.: 4). In secondary school young people needed to be given 'a clear understanding of the arguments for delaying sexual activity and resisting pressure and the benefits to be gained from such delay'. It was advised that care needed to be taken to ensure that there was 'no stigmatisation of children based on their home circumstances' or homophobic bullying (ibid.: 13).

Ed Balls, the minister for children, schools and families in the Labour government, met formidable opposition in 2009 when he attempted to make sex education compulsory for the first time in English schools. An external review of the delivery of SRE had reported in 2008 and its chair, Jim Knight concluded:

> Modern life is increasingly complex and we have a duty to equip our young people with the knowledge and skills to deal with it. It's vital that this information doesn't come from playground rumour or the mixed messages from the media about sex. We need structured classroom teaching, set within a clear understanding of right and wrong that emphasises the importance of family relationships. Parents bring up children, not schools or Governments, but schools can help guide them through the maze of issues and prepare them for the difficult transition from childhood through to adulthood. (DCSF, 2008b)

Balls accepted that sex education started too late and that earlier lessons were needed 'to counter teenage pregnancy, increasingly explicit storylines in films and television soap operas, as well as exposure to pornography online and through mobile phones'. His Children, Schools and Families Bill of 2009 proposed to force all schools, including faith schools, to teach the 'full, broad, balanced curriculum on sex and relationship education'. Classes in the first three years of secondary school would cover sexually transmitted diseases, contraception, pregnancy, abortion, and the importance of stable relationships such as marriage and civil partnerships. The emphases again appeared to be to counteract the social and health problems caused by early sexual experiences. More crucially, the bill proposed to remove the statutory right granted to parents since 1993 to 'opt out' and withdraw their children from lessons once they had reached the age of fifteen. Sex education itself would start at the age of seven. Balls did concede, before the third reading, that the school's governing body would still be allowed to teach PSHE in a way that reflected the school's religious character. In the event, with the general election just a month away, all the sex education provisions were lost from the Children, Schools and Families Act in April 2010.

The Coalition government between 2010 and 2015 had to deal with even greater health and safeguarding concerns – about internet pornography, and about child safety after a series of revelations of historic paedophilia in Rotherham and Greater Manchester and the predatory actions of Jimmy Savile and others. Ofsted also reported in 2013 that a half of all secondary schools and a third of primary schools were not preparing young people adequately in SRE. In secondaries, there was too much emphasis on 'the mechanics' of reproduction with the avoidance of any discussion of sexual and emotional feelings and the controversial issues of sexual abuse, homosexuality and pornography. Only 39 per cent of children had learned about abortion. In primaries, 'too much emphasis was placed on matters such as maintaining friendships and this left pupils ill-prepared for puberty and lacking in knowledge about reproduction and how babies are born' (Ofsted, 2013c: 11–12). Pressures therefore grew to redraft the Guidance on Sex Education. However, when the DES launched a review of PSHE in 2011, it explicitly ruled out making the subject as a whole a statutory one within the national curriculum. The issue led to a dispute between the Coalition's deputy prime minister, Nick Clegg and the education secretary, Michael Gove in 2013, after the former had said publicly that the guidance on sex education should be updated to take account of the 'explosion' in internet pornography. Gove told *The World at One* on BBC Radio 4 that he had been advised that, 'rather than attempting to update guidance when technology changes so rapidly, the most important thing was to provide the resources teachers needed and to rely on them' (*Guardian*, 5 September 2013). However, with government backing, new (non-statutory) supplementary guidelines were issued by the PSHE Association which emphasized that younger pupils should learn to respect their own and other people's boundaries, 'that their body belongs to them' and 'that they can say who has access to it'. As recommended by Ofsted, the new guidance stressed that primary pupils needed to learn the correct biological names for the genitalia, as this, along with knowing how to seek help if they are being abused, was vital for safeguarding and could 'support girls at risk of female genital mutilation' (PSHE, 2013: 9). The issue of pornography was addressed, with the recommendation that secondary teaching should emphasize that this did not portray real life and could be 'worrying, confusing and frightening for young people' (ibid.: 10):

Pupils should understand that pornography shows a distorted image of sex and relationships, including 'perfect' bodies and exaggerated sexual prowess. SRE provides opportunities to discuss body image and understand how pornographic pictures and videos are routinely edited and 'photoshopped'. (PSHE, 2013: 11)

The practice of 'sexting' (sending sexual content and images by mobile phone) was said to raise 'particular issues of safety, privacy, peer influence and personal responsibility' (ibid.: 12). Throughout, there are references made to the Equality Act of 2010, advising schools to ensure that teaching is accessible to all, including those who are lesbian, gay, bisexual and transgender, that 'inclusive SRE will foster good relations between pupils, tackle all types of prejudice – including homophobia – and promote understanding and respect'.

Throughout the whole period covered above, there was a reluctance to make SRE teaching compulsory. Before 1986, headteachers had the responsibility to decide if sex education was to be taught in their schools and the 1986 Education Act made the decision a statutory right of the governing body. In the 1988 Education Reform Act, teaching about the biological aspects of human reproduction became compulsory within the new statutory curriculum for science, although all non-biological aspects of sex education remained at the discretion of the governing body. In 1993 the government made it compulsory for governors to make, and keep up to date, a separate written statement of their policy with regard to the provision of sex education and to make this available for inspection and for parents. The 2000 Framework pointed out that Ofsted had a statutory obligation, under the School Inspections Act of 1996, to evaluate and report on the spiritual, moral, social and cultural development of pupils at any school they inspected and that this included 'evaluating and commenting on a school's sex and relationship education policy' (DfEE, 2000: 7). Schools do have a statutory obligation under the 2004 Children Act to promote their pupils' well-being, which Ofsted can use to assess safeguarding policies. As a school 'subject', it remains in the bizarre state of being non-statutory, while simultaneously being an expectation as an integral part of a good school. The biological aspects of puberty, reproduction and the spread of viruses are compulsory for all maintained schools as part of the science curriculum, and there is a statutory requirement, since 1994, for secondary schools to teach about HIV/AIDS and sexually transmitted infections. Governors still have a statutory obligation to create a school policy on SRE which includes information about sexually transmitted diseases and Ofsted has a duty to inspect these policies.

New guidance on safeguarding published in April 2014 contained a single reference to SRE, reaffirming that governors and headteachers were responsible for how children were taught about safeguarding and adding that in maintained schools this 'may include covering relevant issues ... through SRE' (House of Commons, 2015: 31). Moreover, there is no obligation on academies and free schools to deliver any of this content whatsoever. These 'semi-independent' schools, directly funded by central government, have greater freedoms than maintained schools, including freedom from the national curriculum. There is similarly no requirement on them to have up-to-date policy on SRE. Over all is the right of parents to withdraw their children from sex education lessons, except (in maintained schools) for those parts included in the statutory national curriculum.

The objections to sex education being delivered in schools

The objections which were voiced in the Dronfield case of 1913 have been echoed throughout the century. They centre largely on the concept of the innocence of children, which was perceived as being jeopardized by discussions of sex in school, and the desire of parents to deal with the issue themselves. There was a feeling that any such education might act as a cause for promiscuity rather than a response to children's needs. In the contemporary debate, the topics of homosexuality, contraception and abortion have caused particular controversy. In 1988, a backbench amendment adopted by the government as 'Section 28' prohibited the promotion of homosexuality and the teaching of the acceptability of homosexuality as a 'pretended family relationship'. Some teachers were concerned that they might unwittingly fall foul of the law in their lessons, while others reacted with fury at the perceived prejudice implicit in this phrase. It was not until 2003 that Section 28 was finally abolished under New Labour. Further complaints emerged in 1991, when the secretary of state changed the boundary between biological and non-biological instruction by amending the national curriculum for science to include the study of HIV/AIDS. This led again to a political storm over fears that this would expose children to inappropriate information about homosexuality. It prompted Ashraf in 1991 to express the Muslim view that 'the religious perspective on sexual behaviour and relationships should be fully and properly presented'. He felt this was often disregarded or 'treated in a casual manner' and his particular concern was that homosexual acts were 'sometimes presented as something entirely natural without any mention that from the religion's point of view they are regarded as other than normal'. The ethos of sex education was central to his objections, as he believed that too often the sex education given in schools concealed 'value controversiality and under the guise of openness imposes determinant values on pupils at variance with their own or family and religious beliefs' (Reiss, 1993: 131).

The issue of abortion has been particularly contentious. The 2000 Framework showed that 38 per cent of teenage pregnancies ended in abortion in 1998, but that Roman Catholics in particular had 'strongly held views and religious beliefs' about abortion and that 'some schools will apply a particular religious ethos through their sex and relationship education policy to the issue which will enable pupils to consider the moral and personal dilemmas involved' (DfEE, 2000: 16). Sarwar in 1989 had shown the Muslim concerns at the subject, as abortion was not allowed in Islam 'except in circumstances of threat to the mother's life' (Sarwar, 1993: 14). Roman Catholics have similarly objected to the detailed analysis of contraceptive methods in maintained schools. In 1994, one Vatican spokesman complained that:

> sex education programs are in no way any solution, but rather a significant part of the problem of today's sexual permissiveness – for when new attitudes about sex are purveyed in the classroom and under the authority of the school, the kids can be affected even more decisively than they are affected by the sexual permissiveness they regularly encounter in the media. Modern contraception, along with the availability of abortion, makes the very idea of sex without consequences possible – which thus lies at the heart of the modern sexual revolution. (Whitehead, 2006)

Ed Balls met a firestorm of opposition when he proposed to make the subject compulsory in his Children, Schools and Families Bill of 2009. The chief opposition centred on the dual issues of the age at which compulsory sex education would begin, seven years old, and the removal of the parental right of withdrawal when children reached fifteen years of age. The latter was intended to ensure that all children received at least twelve months of sex education before finishing compulsory schooling. The parental rights of withdrawal had been jealously guarded. The 1943 ministry guidance suggested that when special talks were given on sex education, parents were usually given the opportunity to withdraw their children if they wished to do so (Board of Education, 1943). The 1977 handbook had again advised that cooperation between parents and schools was 'not only essential but often highly effective in encouraging mutual understanding and trust' (DES, 1977: 118). Parents were, however, warned against withdrawing their children from lessons, because their children would merely obtain information from their friends and would 'almost certainly receive a garbled report' (ibid.: 118). In Circular 11/87, although parents had no statutory right to remove their children from sex education lessons, governors were given the non-statutory discretion to consider requests from parents for their children to be withdrawn from any sex education to which they objected. There was much disgruntlement that the issue of HIV/AIDS was added to the science curriculum and was therefore not subject to parental withdrawal; the 1993 Act had reversed this decision and had also allowed parents an unconditional right to withdraw their child from sex education. The 2009 proposals would for the first time have withdrawn this right after the pupil reached fifteen years of age. Sex education would also have become statutory in all schools, including faith schools. In the official consultation on the proposals, carried out by the QCA, only 32 per cent agreed that sex education should be compulsory. In a letter to the *Sunday Telegraph*, 2,000 signatories, including Catholic bishops, parish priests, university professors, councillors and doctors, called for the legislation to be dropped (Wells, 2010). The letter claimed the plans sought to impose a 'particular ideology' and undermined parents' rights to bring up their children in accordance with their own values and culture. Norman Wells, Director of the Family Trust, added:

> There is widespread disquiet among head teachers, school governors and faith leaders about moves to reduce the influence of parents over what is taught in such a sensitive area ... increasingly parents find themselves sidelined and effectively told they must bring up their children by Government diktat. It is time to stand up to the encroachment of an overbearing state and say enough is enough. (*Telegraph*, 28 March 2010)

The Muslim view was shown in a further petition that stressed that sex education was the responsibility of the parent and therefore 'should be imparted within a domestic framework where it can be taught based on Islamic teachings that prohibit premarital sexual relations'. It questioned the moral basis of the government's plans, asserting that 'SRE should not be taught within the model of moral relativism, where right and wrong does not factor ... Our concern is that these teachings are prematurely sexualizing children at a psychological level.' Tahir Alam, a spokesperson for the Muslim Council in Britain's education committee, commented: 'Such teachings erode the innocence of children ...The whole subject is not taught from a values framework, but from a value-free framework. It says "you children you make your own minds up"' (*Independent*, 23 July 2009). Because of the strength of the opposition, faith schools won a concession that Roman Catholic, Anglican, Jewish and Muslim schools would still be able to teach sex lessons that reflected their religious character. This would allow them to make clear to pupils their opposition to contraception, abortion or homosexuality (*Telegraph*, 28 March 2010). Balls still maintained that there would be no opt-out for any faith school from teaching the full, broad, balanced curriculum on sex and relationship education. Catholic schools would be allowed to say to their pupils that, as a religion, they believed contraception to be wrong, but they would still have to address the subjects of contraception, homosexuality and civil partnership (*Telegraph*, 23 February 2010). As mentioned above, the opposition was so strong that Conservative MPs refused to follow usual practice before an election and allow a bill in its final stages to be quickly moved onto the statute book. The SRE clauses of the bill had to be surrendered.

A large number of witnesses to the parliamentary enquiry of 2015 expressed concern at age-inappropriateness in school sex education. The Christian Institute complained that 'many resources produced for primary schools contained graphic material that was highly unsuitable for classroom use'. The Association of Catholic Women claimed that some material was so explicit that 'if it were shown by an adult to a child in a non-school setting, it would be regarded by many as child abuse' (House of Commons Committee, 2015: 25). The age-appropriateness of sex education classes has been a disputed area for many years. The 1943 guidance suggested that most instruction came in the final year of schooling, when pupils were thirteen years old, although it suggested this should be determined by the understanding of the child and that as soon as questions were being asked they should be answered honestly. There was a hint at relationships education, with the guidance suggesting that instruction in the physiology of sex was only a beginning, and that the oldest pupils should be given advice about controlling their impulses and establishing 'mutual understanding and respect between the sexes', as an adequate preparation for marriage (Board of Education, 1943). Bibby suggested in 1944 that the age of instruction could not be prescribed, because of the different rates of development of children, but he did suggest:

> if left until the age of 14 or 15, most modern boys and girls will already have picked it up from other sources. But it will be garbled accounts that they have heard, and the facts will have been coated with some of the slime of the gutter-channels through which they have been passed … Street corner and playground companions must not be given a year or two's start over parents and teachers. (Bibby, 1948: 8)

The 1956 Handbook recognized what it called the serious issue that in any one class there would be children at 'very different stages of physical and sexual development, so that what may help one child may not be right for another … No two boys or girls are the same and their questions cannot be solved in the mass by rule-of-thumb answers' (57). Similarly in 1977, the handbook cautioned against creating 'even more damaging anxieties in boys and girls who still prefer their hobbies and interests while some of their contemporaries are blatantly attracted to the opposite sex, by implying that they are not developing normally and so making them feel themselves forced into patterns of precocious experimentation which are an affront to their innate sense of modesty and decency' (ibid.: 117). Nevertheless, a decade later, Sarwar was still complaining that no allowances were made for the fact that children develop physically and psychologically at different ages and that 'children should only be given potentially disturbing information when they and their parents feel they are ready to receive in the right frame of mind instead of the present situation whereby sex education is given to all children at a certain age, regardless of their mental readiness' (Sarwar, 1993: 18).

The same sentiments can be seen today. Giles Fraser, the former canon chancellor of St Paul's cathedral, typified the views of many in 2015 when he declared:

> There is something about childhood, something about play ... having imagination, that gets encroached upon by this doing things by numbers, official guide to relationships. We should allow children to be children, whatever that means ... We don't over-commercialize or over-sexualise at a ridiculously early age. (*Moral Maze*, 2015)

Fraser, too, questions the efficacy of current guidelines which stress that coverage should be age-appropriate but which fail to acknowledge that children develop physically and sexually at different rates. The development of more graphic sex education in primary schools has exacerbated the problems. Yusuf Patel, founder of SREIslamic, told MPs that that 'the idea of what is inappropriate or not largely hinges on what parents believe is developmentally and culturally sensitive to their children', and Philip Robinson noted that 'what is age-appropriate is actually child-specific, not just age-specific, because children develop at different rates'. Sarah Carter, a trustee of the Family Education Trust, explained to MPs that developmental differences applied even to older children, and that in a classroom of year eleven students, 'half of the classroom are mortified and the other half you are too late for. When it comes to self-esteem, exploitation or drug awareness, every child is going to be on a completely different level' (House of Commons Committee, 2015: 25–6). Such a problem appears insurmountable in the context of large classes.

For many, the issue strikes at the very heart of parental rights and responsibilities. Many deponents to the Education Standing Committee in 2015 emphasized that the moral and legal duty for children's education lies not with the state but with parents, and that, although the overwhelming majority of parents delegate most education provision to a state or independent school, 'parental primacy should be recognized' (House of Commons Committee, 2015: 18). Those who accept this contention argue that parents are in the best position to discuss these matters with children, as they have potential opportunities for spontaneous discussion, can transmit their personal and community values, and can better understand the child's developmental stage and level of understanding of sexual matters. Yusuf Patel reasoned that parents were the best providers of SRE 'because they are emotionally invested in their children'. Similarly, Sarah Carter posited that 'schools should not be compensating for bad parenting'. There is a fear that the state is overstepping the mark in assuming such a role, and that SRE might become even more prescriptive over time as subsequent governments added to the list of topics. The Catholic view was expressed by Antonia Tully of the Safe at School campaign, who complained: 'Parents constantly find themselves having to battle with schools in order to protect their children from inappropriate sex education ... Parents are the primary educators of their children, they are natural sex educators of their children and they are the experts on their own children' (Catholic Education Service, 2015).

The future of sex education in schools

In the current debate, sex education continues to be largely an issue of safeguarding and health. In February 2015, the House of Commons Committee on Education published its report on SRE, *Life Lessons*, which called again for the subject to be statutory, highlighting the problems of the rise of social media, increasing access to pornography and new trends such as 'sexting', which were changing the way pupils thought about sex. Children, it was argued, were being bombarded with sexually explicit images on the internet and even on mainstream television, with the implicit message that early sexual activity was the norm. One witness to their enquiry claimed that access to internet pornography had increased incrementally and was significantly shaping young people's behaviours and self-image:

> It affects young women and their body image – self-objectification. It affects young men and the expectation that they have of sexual partners. Therefore, it is incumbent on schools to address that issue and talk with young people about it as part of PSHE. (House of Commons Committee, 2015)

The report concluded that even primary school children should be taught which kinds of physical contact are acceptable and unacceptable, as well as the proper names for genitalia, the ignorance of which, Ofsted had argued, presented a risk to their safety. Those who favoured statutory status argued that it was important as a child protection measure, following child abuse cases in Rotherham and Greater Manchester. The NSPCC expressed specific concerns at the spread of the practice of sexting, 'the exchange of sexual messages or images' and the 'creating, sharing of forwarding of sexually suggestive nude or nearly nude images' through mobile phones or the internet, which they argued was often coercive, linked to harassment, bullying, and even violence (House of Commons Committee, 2015: 16). The PSHE Association Report of March 2015 similarly emphasized the influence of peer pressure, alcohol, drugs and technology in abuse and unhealthy relationships. There was particular concern that the concept of consent now had to be taught:

> Learning about consent should begin before young people are sexually active, otherwise it is too late ... Pupils must learn that the law is clear that sexual activity is illegal for young people under the age of 16 ... some young people are sexually active before the age of 16 and learning about healthy relationships is crucial to keeping them healthy and safe from abuse and exploitation. (PSHE Association, 2015)

In a speech to the Tory group Bright Blue in March 2015, the education secretary, Nicky Morgan, admitted the challenges:

> I can almost hear the screams from some quarters, the printing presses starting up with their negative stories, the howls of derision from elsewhere. You only have to look at some of the headlines this weekend when we suggested ... we ought to teach young people about the concept of consent ... that sparks strong and impassioned debates about what is and isn't age appropriate; what is and isn't right. But good PSHE teaching is also essential to keeping pupils safe, inside and outside the school gates ... Some say we should wrap them in cotton wool and not expose them to the realities of the world, but in the internet age that is increasingly hard to do. The question is how we provide them with the emotional resilience to cope. (Morgan, 2015)

Morgan ruled out further attempts to make the subject statutory, and instead insisted that she would rely on schools and teachers to design their own PSHE curriculum to meet the specific needs of their pupils and communities. Nevertheless, she stressed that educating children about healthy relationships and consent could help them to 'make sense of situations that can often be confusing and distressing for young minds to comprehend, and teach them how to keep themselves and others safe'. After the recent revelations of child abuse, she concluded that 'the stakes are too high to let our young people leave school without this knowledge'.

Points to consider:

- Should SRE be statutory and at what age would you expect this to be appropriate?
- SRE is crucial in schools because society is changing and children are increasingly vulnerable. How would you respond to both parts of this premise?
- 'SRE is now too important to be left to parents.' How far do you agree with this statement?
- There has been much pressure that the subject should now be called Relationships and Sex Education. What issues are behind such a name change?

10

Should schools be feeding their pupils?

... no medical testimony is required to establish the necessity of feeding children before exercising their muscles

SIR JOHN ELDON GORST, 1906

The issue of poor food in school and at home has been much publicized in recent years, particularly by TV chef Jamie Oliver, with the Coalition government introducing free meals for all infants in schools in 2014. This chapter discusses this issue and shows the origins and rationale behind the beginnings of school meals and the arguments of those who feel that measures taken to ensure that children eat healthily have crossed the line of basic parental responsibilities.

Food is a serious issue for children's health. For several years, health experts have been concerned that their diet is unbalanced, with too much salt, sugar and fat, and not enough fruit and vegetables. The Medical Research Council has reported that sugar consumption rose by 30 per cent between 1980 and 2000, and in 2012, 28 per cent of children aged between two and fifteen were declared to be either overweight or obese. In response, Michael Gove launched a new set of mandatory standards for food served in schools in 2014, to try to ensure that children were able to eat healthy meals. Previous standards were introduced between 2006 and 2009 to improve school food, but they had been expensive to enforce, with school cooks complaining of having to use computer programs to analyse the nutritional content of every menu. The new standards included a statutory portion of vegetables or salad every day, with at least three different fruits and three different vegetables each week; there was an emphasis on wholegrain foods in place of refined carbohydrates, an attempt to make water the drink of choice, limiting fruit juice portions and restricting the amount of added sugars in other drinks to 5 per cent; there were to be no more than two portions a week of deep-fried, batter-coated or breadcrumbed food, and no more than two portions of pastry. These standards had been devised by an expert panel of cooks, teachers, caterers and dieticians. In addition, in 2014 the Coalition government introduced free hot lunches for all four- to seven-year-olds, costing £600 million a year, with a further £3 million set aside to help schools set up breakfast clubs. The Liberal Democrat deputy prime minister, Nick Clegg claimed that the evidence of pilot studies in Durham and Newham had shown that free school meals not only helped to ease parents' household budgets but also encouraged positive eating, helped concentration and raised educational performance.

The principal opposition to these measures in 2014 centred on cost. In the previous year, the Labour-run Southwark Council had pioneered a free school meal scheme for all its primary children, and even the Liberal Democrat deputy leader, Simon Hughes, expressed concerns at the expense there (£15 million a year), with meals going to the borough's richest families irrespective of their ability to pay (*Telegraph*, 18 September 2013). Gove's special advisor leaked that the secretary of state himself had written to the treasury that the national initiative was an abuse of taxpayers' money and that 'we must not risk forcing schools to subsidize meals by reducing their spending on teaching and learning'. He feared they would be directing scarce resources away from the maintenance of buildings (*Daily Mail*, 9 May 2014). However, there was also a philosophical objection, expressed by Claire Fox, director of the Institute of Ideas, in the *TES* of 9 September 2014 that parents were not being trusted to feed their own children without the teacher's paternalistic supervision. She deplored the fact that some teachers had no qualms about sending notes in lunch boxes to reprimand parents for serving inappropriate snacks to their own children. She rejected the declaration by the president of the Royal College of Paediatrics and Child Health that, while people might argue the merits of giving schools freedom over the curriculum and pedagogy, when it came to school food there could be no debate. She felt that too many teachers had blindly followed this mantra and that this was a direct assault on the rights and responsibilities of parents.

The issue of healthy eating for children is not a modern phenomenon. John Locke in the seventeenth century expressed concern at children devouring sweets, over-eating and eating between meals, and even suggested that infants under four should not be given meat. Echoing the health experts of today, he condemned the 'over-much use of salt' which had 'ill effects upon the body', and suggested that bread should be the only snack between meals so that 'you will not teach him to eat more and oftener than nature requires' (Locke, 1693: 14). As today, he highly recommended apples, pears, strawberries, cherries, gooseberries, currants and dried fruit, as long as the latter was dried without sugar (ibid.: 20), although he was wary of the 'unwholesome' juice of melons, peaches, plums and grapes. But these were recommendations for the rich who could afford obesity. The majority of children had to suffer the deprivations of poor harvests and food shortages and the issue of such malnutrition became visible to the middle classes only with the advent of popular schooling in the nineteenth century. Responses to this child malnutrition were underscored by concerns for self-reliance and parental rights.

Charities were active by the mid-nineteenth century to try to alleviate the worst excesses of child poverty. The Destitute Children's Dinner Society began work in London in 1864 and had opened fifty-eight centres by 1870, providing meals once or twice a week in winter and as a matter of principle charging a penny per meal, though this was not always paid. The 1870 Education Act and subsequent compulsory schooling highlighted the distress of children on a scale hitherto unknown. However, in the debates on education in 1873, Sir Michael Hicks Beach reminded MPs that the law 'sanctioned the principle that a parent was bound to provide sufficient food for his child' and Forster stressed that in the new schools the children would be taught but not clothed and fed (*Hansard*, 1873: 502–90). From 1876, Sir Henry Peek did begin supplying the children at his own national school at Rousdon with a penny dinner on the five days of the week that they attended. The children, who had previously been ill-fed and unable to learn their lessons, were said to become much healthier. They succeeded so well in the annual examinations that they were mentioned by Vice-President of the Committee on Education, A. J. Mundella, who told the Commons in November 1884 that this was 'an excellent experiment'. He reiterated that school boards were not themselves allowed to expend money in feeding children, but he had 'the fullest confidence that voluntary effort will supply all that is needful' (*Hansard*, 1884: 1581–2). The idea did spread sporadically and by the 1880s twelve kitchens had been opened in London and there was a call for a network to be established. The Catholic journal, the *Tablet*, wrote in 1884 that starvation or semi-starvation was at the root of listlessness in half of the poorest children in London. They had no dinner in school, and took with them a crust of bread and a draught of weak tea:

> Those only who have worked among the small, tattered starvelings of outcast London, can realise the dullness of children worn out from want of food, with sensations benumbed by the over-mastering cravings of hunger. Often in an out-of-work season, children come famishing to school ... Well [teachers] know it is not stupidity so much as starvation that renders

unavailing their efforts to bring the school up to the required standard of excellence. (*Tablet*, 1 November 1884: 26)

The Council for Promoting Self-supporting Penny Dinners was established in 1884, at a time when there were still only two centres providing these lunches in London. Thirteen others were begun during the year and by 1889 they had been created in Birmingham, Gateshead and Carlisle. While private philanthropists were attempting to relieve the suffering, there was still a clear expectation that a contribution would be made by parents. It was seen to impinge too much on parental responsibilities to provide free food.

The meals of all the dinner societies were provided by voluntary agencies, not by schools, although some local authorities allowed the use of rooms. At Liverpool in 1885, the local council offered grants to school managers for the supply of 'appliances' for the penny dinners, although it stressed that 'the payment of a penny should absolutely cover the cost of each dinner, so as not only to avoid pauperising the recipient, but also to render the scheme entirely self-supporting' (London School Board, 1889: 383). The Birmingham school board allowed a voluntary committee to erect kitchens on school premises but again would not finance meals. At Gateshead, the school board arranged for a supply of dinners to schools in the poorest parts of the town. Catholic schools, too, undertook to minister 'on business principles to the wants of the little ones' and the *Tablet* article quoted above empha-sized that the fundamental principle at the root of the penny dinner scheme required that it 'should not be a form of almsgiving, but the organisation of an economical method of providing food for children'. The London Destitute Children's Society explained in *The Times* in 1889 that in the previous winter it had provided 367,000 dinners, costing £1,796, and had received £760 from the children's pennies. The Rev. William Harrison wrote that it was 'a touching sight to see the gratitude of the parents, who rejoice to know that their children are provided with a meal, even though they themselves have been obliged to go without one'. The headteacher of one board school commented: 'It is quite impossible for the children to accomplish the mental work required of them in preparing for the government examinations unless the bodies of the scholars are well nourished' (*The Times*, 15 November 1889: 4).

In 1884, Dr James Crichton-Browne advocated free milk and school meals for poor children, in order to end serious undernourishment and 'brighten up the sluggish intellects'. He concluded: 'The children want blood, and we offer them a little brain-polish; they ask for bread and receive a problem; for milk, and the tonic-sol-fa system is introduced to them.' There was, though, a clear boundary that it was felt the state should not cross, and supplying free meals or milk was seen by many as going too far. Sir Joshua Fitch, a senior school inspector, claimed that the school boards should ensure a good environment for learning, but 'could not control all the conditions which affect a child's life', and that proposals for free dinners were a 'radical misconception of the very limited function of a public elementary school', which was to provide instruction and should not be mixed up with the administration of food. There were fears that the provision of schooling (which still itself required school pence) already threatened to 'diminish the sense of parental responsibility', but that 'the responsibility of caring for the food and health of young children belongs properly to the parent' (Goldstrom, 1972: 156). Nevertheless, from 1886 one charitable organization, the Birmingham Schools Dinner Society, did indeed provide free meals for needy children, as did the London School Dinner Association from 1889, although with no assistance from their respective school boards. The Board School Children's Free Dinner Fund felt that the poorest children needed to be fed even when the parents were unable to pay a penny contribution:

> our work does not cross the hues of the penny dinner movement. It was started before that movement and has been in some cases carried on side by side with it, its object being to feed those children whose parents have neither pennies not half-pennies to pay for their dinners. Free dinners are restricted to the children of widows, and to those whose parents are ill or out of work. (Bulkley, 1914)

By the 1890s, only 10 per cent of these agencies were in fact still expecting the penny contributions and yet Charles Booth was claiming that 10 per cent of the capital's school children remained underfed. The board estimated that during the winter of 1899 there were 30,930 children in its schools 'in want of food'.

There remained much criticism of the voluntary efforts, especially if they failed to compel parents to make any contribution to the food costs. The Charity Organisation Society, for example, continuously opposed free meals, claiming it pauperized families and denied parental responsibilities. The point was made quite forcibly in *The Times* in 1890:

> They temporarily mitigate suffering, but increase it in the long run by leading the workers to depend on eleemosynary aid instead of upon work and thrift ... the labourer, with few exceptions, has no pride in or love of his work. He would not do a stroke if he could help it. And how are we to get him to work if his wants and those of his family are supplied by charity? The mission or soup kitchen will provide food. The School Board will educate his children free, or Dr Barnardo will take charge of them altogether ... It is hard on the children, but the sins of the fathers have fallen upon them in all time ... these increasing and competitive charitable

agencies are just sapping the energy and industry of the English people. (*The Times*, 26 December 1890: 11)

Margaret McMillan and Fred Jowett were of a different mind. They were members of the Bradford school board, which took the technically illegal action of introducing free school meals in its schools at the start of the twentieth century. They tried to persuade Parliament to introduce legislation to encourage all education authorities to provide meals for children, the former arguing that if the state insisted on compulsory education it had to take responsibility for the proper nourishment of its pupils. Debates were intensified after concerns over the poor health of recruits to the Boer War, with many young men considered too small and sickly to enter the army. Malnutrition was identified by some as a cause of ill health and poor physical and mental performance and studies were conducted to estimate the numbers of malnourished children in different areas. The Report of the Royal Commission on Physical Training of 1903 and the Report of the Interdepartmental Committee on Physical Deterioration of 1904 both again drew attention to the lack of nourishment of children. Some of the witnesses appearing before the latter repeated the familiar claims that lazy housewives relied on tinned food and fish and chips, but the Board's inspector Dr Eichholz concluded that in London children remained seriously malnourished. The final report recommended that the evils arising from underfeeding were so widespread and so pressing that 'some authoritative intervention' was needed to ensure that the education of the children would not be hampered by their physical condition. The time had come for the state to ensure 'adequate nourishment to children in attendance at school' (PP, 1904b: 66).

In society generally, there continued to be a heated debate on school meals between those who favoured state intervention and those who maintained that malnutrition was a problem of poor parental care and opposed any school meals funded out of the rates. Sir John Gorst was vociferous in his advocacy of school meals. His arguments have an echo of those in the current debates over free meals for infants, with the appeal that the child had rights and that if the parents failed in their responsibilities, then the state had to secure these rights. Moreover, as the state had compelled school attendance, he declared that it was imposing added pressure onto the children:

No child is fit to receive such instruction if it is starving for lack of food. Forcing a hungry child to effort, physical or mental, is an act of cruelty, which if practised on a horse would bring the perpetrator within the penalties of the Criminal Law. Thus by forcing starving children to attend and receive instruction in its schools the State is not only failing in its general obligation to secure the children's rights, but is inflicting on them an additional and cruel wrong. (*The Times*, 17 September 1904)

In the Commons, Gorst constantly badgered the government and summarized his argument that they should not waste schooling by giving it to ill-fed children (*Hansard*, 1905: 1184–5). However, the opposition to his ideas was equally vocal, with a 1905 editorial in *The Times* arguing that he was exaggerating the problem. More philosophically, while not denying the evil of undernourishment, it asked for him to consider 'the good of the community at large', that it was wrong that 'the state is to do everything for everybody and nobody is to do anything for himself that he is disposed to shirk doing'. The editorial accused Gorst of 'social quackery'. There is an echo here with the puritan belief of the previous century that poverty itself was an indication of the personal failing of the beggar and that charity encouraged and compounded this failing. Hence the paper complained that free meals placed 'a premium upon laziness, meanness, and self-indulgence; and, at the same time, discouraged all who still endeavour to resist these degenerate vices'. The concept of self-help was still strong in British society:

> We have already made a serious inroad upon personal responsibility and personal independence by relieving parents of the duty of educating their children. That is now used as an argument for relieving them of the duty of feeding their children. When we have done that, the argument will be stronger than ever for relieving them of the duty of clothing their children. From that it is an easy step to paying for their proper housing ... It is a race of fatherless and motherless foundlings to which Sir John Gorst's proposals point ... Everyone who does not do his share in providing is a dead loss to the State, and a dead weight upon those who do play their part as citizens. The encouragement of the non-effectives does more than throw a burden upon the industrious. It demoralizes them. It is an erosive force always operating upon the margin of industry, and seducing those nearest the boundary to cease their efforts. (*The Times*, 2 January 1905)

The Liberal government elected in 1906 was, however, committed to social reform and Jowett, who was elected to the Commons as Labour MP for Bradford, dedicated his maiden speech to the subject of school meals. He eventually convinced Parliament that hungry children had trouble learning and in 1906 the Provision of School Meals Act was passed, allowing – though not obliging – local authorities to offer school feeding on their school premises. In spite of this limitation, Gustafsson notes that it was a significant ideological break with the past laissez-faire free market approach (Gustafsson, 2002: 686).

Fig. 10: The first free school meals at White Abbey Feeding Centre, Bradford, in 1907 served by headteacher, Jonathan Priestley (father of J. B. Priestley). Courtesy of Bradford University Archive

The money for the meals had to be raised by local taxation and there was an expenditure limit imposed by central government. In reality, the provision of meals varied between LEAs and many children were overlooked. By 1912, only 131 out of the 322 LEAs had established a service. Issues with the quality and distribution of free meals also remained a concern, with paying children given better food than those who were given the free dinners. Meals were described as soup or stew, with breakfast of porridge or bread and jam served in some areas instead of lunch. The 1914 Provision of Meals Act finally gave the Chancellor of the Exchequer the power to make available grants to cover half the cost of meals and to compel local authorities to make some provision.

By 1918, nutritional science had progressed and fruit, vegetables and milk were classified as 'protective foods', and the value of vitamins was recognized (James, 2004). Many children had a deficiency of vitamin D that was found to be responsible for the spread of rickets, with as many as 83 per cent of children in Durham suffering from the disease. The evidence of milk as a protective food also led to the introduction of a school milk scheme, providing this for those children considered needy, subsidized by local authorities or local charities. Other children were able to purchase a third of a pint of milk at cost price. As well as a means to improve children's health, farmers were pleased to dispose of a glut of milk at this time. In 1930 it was decided to provide free school milk to all children in Scotland, but in 1933 the Board of Education repeated the danger of offering any free sustenance to all pupils, which might lead to demands for free school dinners. Under the 1934 Milk Act, the Board of Education gave the Milk Marketing Board a subsidy of £500,000 for two years, and the milk scheme which came into operation made milk available to schoolchildren at a halfpenny for a third of a pint. By 1939, over 55 per cent of elementary school children were offered milk, with 20 per cent given this free. Under the 1944 Education Act it became a statutory duty for local authorities to offer school milk, which finally became free to all children under the Labour government in 1946.

In 1937, the former arguments were again aired in the Commons after the Labour Party introduced a proposal for free school meals. The major objection was on the ground of the cost, which was seen as considerable. However, in introducing the measure, Manny Shinwell argued that thousands of children were going short of food because prolonged unemployment prevented their parents from affording the meals they needed. For him, 'no price is too high to pay for the assurance that our school children are being properly nourished' (*Hansard*, 3 February 1937: vol. 319: 1623). Shinwell taunted his fellow MPs that they all were well nourished and that 'the question of food rarely troubles them', but he wanted the same assurance for all children attending school. The promise was for the whole nation to gain 'in health, in vigour, in physique, and above all in food production ... It will serve as an important contribution to social wellbeing, to the safeguarding of child life, and to the future of the nation.' His fellow Scottish Labour MP, James Brown echoed the argument of the previous century that 'if the child is not properly fed, it is almost impossible for the child to absorb the education that is offered to it in schools'. Both men denied the accusation that it demoralized parents by showing they could not support their offspring. Shinwell caustically pointed out that it would certainly not demoralize the children and that when he was a child from a poverty-stricken home, 'the provision of a meal would not have caused me the slightest perturbation of mind, although it might have done my stomach a great deal of good':

> about demoralisation, the sapping of independence, the loss of our national characteristics, and the like – all very fine-sounding phrases, but in view of the existing situation they have nothing whatever to do with the case. If we have an assurance that all will eat when they require to eat, that will far outweigh any trifling consideration of that kind. (*Hansard*, 3 February 1937)

However, those who opposed the measure ruled the day. The Conservative MP Thelma Cazalet found the expense too great, and the proposal too extensive to feed all children 'irrespective of whether they require it or not, whether their parents wish them to have it or not, and whether they are being properly fed in their own homes'. She felt it was a gross interference with the functions of the home. Edward Keeling similarly claimed:

'The virtue of parents is a great dowry'. That was said 2,000 years ago, and I do not think that the nature of parents has changed since then ...would [it] increase the spiritual and moral welfare of the people to be relieved of the duty of feeding their own children ... I assert on the other hand, that it is a right and proper thing, a deep-rooted human instinct, even a law of nature, that parents should themselves feed their children. Are we to sweep away this fundamental principle because a small proportion of the children of this country are underfed? The right course is to lubricate and tighten up the existing machinery, which provides that any child whose health or education is suffering should be given a free meal if the low income of the parent justifies it. (*Hansard*, 3 February 1937: 1637)

With the outbreak of the Second World War, raising the standards of the nation's health was seen as an essential prerequisite to maintain morale. Food rationing was introduced in 1940 as part of the war effort to ensure fair distribution of the food that was available and also to ensure a healthy nation and a productive war machine. The school meals service was expanded under guidelines issued in 1940 and 1941 and by the end of the war more than 1.6 million meals were being served daily to a third of the school population, with 14 per cent of these free and the rest being charged at 4d. or 5d. (the cost of the ingredients). The 1944 Education Act finally made it a statutory duty rather than optional entitlement for local authorities to provide school meals. In 1945 school meals were described by the Ministry of Education as having 'a vital place in national policy for nutrition and well-being of children' and Lord Woolton told the Warwickshire Women's Institute: 'The young need protection and it is proper that the state should take deliberate steps to give them opportunity ... Feeding is not enough, it must be good feeding. The food must be chosen in the light of knowledge of what a growing child needs for building a sound body' (*Guardian*, 3 December 1999).

The Labour government of 1945–51 had wanted to provide all meals free of charge but eventually decided that this was unrealistic on grounds of cost. By 1951, 49 per cent of all pupils ate school meals and 84 per cent drank school milk. In 1955, the nutritional standards for school lunches were updated, with government Circular 290 recommending that they should provide 650–1,000 kilocalories (depending on the age and sex of the child), 20 g of 'first class' protein and 25–30 g of fat, with 'fruit of some kind' served at least once a week. In a reference to parental neglect, it added that the school dinner 'must also provide a sound diet for growing children and must take into account the possibility of deficiencies in a child's home diet' (Ministry of Education, 1955). There was, though, a reaction against this march of state involvement in the diet of the young, and subsequent governments, including the 1964 Labour government, expressed concerns at the growing costs of the school meal service and again attempted to make it self-financing. In 1968 the price rose from 1s. to 1s. 6d. and in the following year to 1s. 9d. and the supply of milk to children in secondary schools was ended.

In June 1970, Margaret Thatcher became secretary of state for education in the new Conservative government at a time of economic crisis, and she felt compelled to raise school meal charges and to end the surviving free milk allowance to all children over seven years old. She argued that free milk was costing £14 million a year, twice as much as the budget for school books, and that ending this for all but nursery and primary children would save £9 million. She also told MPs that the chief medical officer had been consulted on the plans and had advised that it was impossible to predict whether the withdrawal of free milk would harm children's diets and overall health. Regardless of his reticence, the plans went ahead. As prime minister from 1979, Thatcher's overwhelming desire was to cut public spending further and school meals proved to be an easy target, with a 1979 White Paper estimating the cost of the service to be £380 million. The 1980 Education Act therefore finally eliminated the free school milk entitlement altogether and initiated a deregulated approach to school meals policy. It removed the duty on LEAs to provide school lunches at all, except to those children entitled to a free school meal, and also dispensed with the fixed pricing system of school meals, as well as the designated nutritional standards which had been introduced from 1906. To make further cuts, the government introduced commercial competitive tendering (CCT), which obliged local authorities to choose the most 'competitive' catering on offer. Passmore and Harris note that CCT shifted attitudes about school meals and instead of being a service provided for the child's benefit, it was now intended to be a commercial service (Passmore, 2004: 223). Many schools which had provided set meals switched to free choice cafeteria systems, with services outsourced to private companies. The requirements of competition, profit and cost-cutting measures proved to have an impact on the nutritional quality of school meals. Children could now spend as much or as little as they wanted and there was no method of controlling what they ate. Half a million children lost the right to free meals and general uptake fell rapidly from an average of 64 per cent in 1979 to 47 per cent in 1988. The effects of these reforms were various, with many school kitchens closing completely and more processed food items entering school menus. Gustafsson has since concluded that children's diets worsened during this period, with increased consumption of fat and sugar and decreased consumption of fruit and vegetables (Gustafsson, 2002).

Food standards also changed within the children's homes, with the development of microwave meals and a reduction in home cooking. After its establishment in 1998, the Food Standards Agency conducted a detailed survey of the diet and nutrition of 1,700 children aged between four and eighteen. Its report showed that in general they were eating far less fresh fruit and vegetables than ever before, consuming on average less than half the recommended daily amount of five portions, with a fifth of the children not eating a single piece of fruit in the week in which the survey was carried out. There appeared to be a prevalence of processed or convenience foods, white bread, savoury snacks, crisps, biscuits, potatoes and chocolate, all of which led to excessive amounts of salt and sugar. Nine out of ten drank fizzy drinks and the children were found to be getting a third of their energy from sugar (as compared with a recommended level of 11 per cent). Boys consumed up to 12.5 g of salt a day, twice the recommended daily intake. Of particular concern, it was noted that children from poorer backgrounds had much worse diets, were fatter and did less exercise than children from better-off families.

This report precipitated government action and education secretary David Blunkett issued new draft nutritional guidelines for school meals which specified, for example, that baked beans should not be served more than once a week and chips not more than three times a week in primary schools, and that fish should be on the menu at least once a week (*Guardian*, 15 December 1999). There was, though, widespread criticism of the government's approach, reminiscent of that seen in the Victorian era, with Conservative politicians describing it as 'Nanny Stateism'. New Labour also intervened in the health issue by pioneering the National School Fruit Scheme, breakfast clubs, healthy tuck shops, improved access to drinking water, free milk for under-fives and a 'National Healthy School Standard'. The age-old argument went on – that feeding children was entirely a matter for parents and not something the state should be involved in.

Public interest in the nutritional quality of meals served to children was sparked off again in 2005 by the television programmes of celebrity chef Jamie Oliver, who condemned schools still serving processed foods of low nutritional value and spending as little as 37 p per meal on ingredients. The topic attracted a great deal of media interest, focusing attention on the turkey twizzler, an item that became synonymous with cheap processed food served for school lunches. The campaign led to a 300,000-signature petition and brought the issue into the May 2005 general election campaign, with the Labour government promising again to review school meals policy and to increase spending on ingredients. Tony Blair made it a central part of a speech in Nottingham in July of that year:

> But in respect of obesity, the issues are really quite stark. For Type 2 diabetics, around half of whose condition is attributable to obesity, life expectancy is reduced by as much as ten years. Amongst children obesity is growing at a rapid, indeed alarming, rate. This is the reason

why campaigns like those run by Jamie Oliver on School Dinners are not a passing fad, they are central to the nation's future health. (Blair, 2006)

After this poll success, education about healthy eating became part of the Ofsted school inspection process, although inspectors were not expected to assess the quality of food on offer in school canteens. Attention was linked to growing concerns with obesity among children and an array of physical and mental health problems associated with poor diet. Nutrient-based standards were finally made mandatory in all state schools in England in September 2009, specifying that for the children who opted for school meals there should be two portions of fruit and vegetables per pupil per day, food cooked in fat or oil should not be provided more than three times a week, and no sugary soft drinks should be served. There were fourteen nutrient-based standards, including maximum intake levels for fat, saturated fat, salt and added sugars, minimum intake levels for calcium, carbohydrate, fibre, folate, iron, protein, vitamins A and C and zinc, and the energy intake from a school lunch (for example, 530 calories for primary pupils) (POST, 2009).

In 2004, Hull City Council had acted ahead of impending school meal legislation and begun to provide free school breakfasts, morning fruit and free lunches to all 20,000 children in its primary and special schools in the *Eat Well Do Well* initiative. The move was so radical that they had to obtain 'Powers to Innovate' from the DfES to implement it. A healthy menu was introduced two months before the free meals scheme started, with children eating less fat and salt and receiving more vitamins, and by 2007 an average of 64 per cent of pupils were eating the dinners. Children reported that they felt more alert and ready to learn and teachers felt that classrooms were a calmer environment for learning (Colquhoun et al., 2008). The scheme overall was regarded as a success by the Labour-controlled local council, although the scheme was abolished in 2007, ironically by a new Liberal Democrat council, to save the considerable costs. It was impossible to attribute improvements in educational performance solely to diet and there have been other support projects in the schools, but it was noted that Key Stage 2 results in primary schools in Hull were the best recorded and Derek Colquhoun judged that hunger remained an important problem nationally, that 'we were so obsessed with obesity, we have taken our eye off the hunger problem'.

The arguments on both sides of the current debate are those recurring throughout the last 150 years. Tony Blair summarized in 2006 that the defining division in politics in Britain was about the limitations on the role of the state, and this was – and still is – central to the provision of school meals:

Essentially progressives believed in its ability to improve society; Conservatives feared its interference stifled personal liberty. The division became caricatured as between those who favoured a 'Big' state and those who favoured a 'minimalist' one ... about the precise level at which public spending started to crowd out private investment. (Blair, 2006)

Over a century and a half before Blair's words were spoken, a *Times* leader had asserted that the British people remained wary of the power of the state, to the extent that 'we prefer to take our chances with cholera and the rest than be bullied into good health' (*The Times*, 1 August 1854: 8). The question on school food remains that of 1854 and of 2006 – about whose responsibility it is to feed *all* children, and whether it should be a proper area for government intervention at all.

Points to consider:

- In June 2015, there was an outcry from parents when teachers at Cherry Tree primary school in Colchester confiscated Scotch eggs from pupils' packed lunches. Did the teachers go too far in this attempt to make children eat healthily?
- Should free school meals be provided to all children, irrespective of their parents' incomes?
- What are the advantages and disadvantages of state intervention in the healthy food debate?

11

Has elementary teaching ever been a profession?

Teachers desiring to criticise the Code were as impertinent as chickens wishing to decide which sauce in which they would be served.

(THOMPSON, 1927: 76)

There has been much debate over the last two decades over whether teaching can be construed a profession. A number of criteria have been proposed that purport to define the meaning of the term. This chapter addresses the discussions that began over 150 years ago on the issue and continue to this day. It shows how the status of the occupation of teaching gradually rose in the nineteenth and twentieth centuries and then fell back from the 1970s, until the current situation, with recent research showing how poor teachers' morale now is, and many feeling they can no longer claim that title.

The above quote was made by Robert Lowe, the architect of payment by results, in 1861. It shows the lowly position in ministerial regard of the schoolteachers of the day, who had just begun their battle to be recognized as professionals. There has been much debate in recent decades about the concept of the current 'professionalism' of teachers. This debate has intensified as governments have sought to impose new measures of accountability and new concepts of professionalism. There have indeed been disagreements about which occupations should define themselves as professions, but by the middle of the twentieth century, there was some consensus that they should be self-regulating in the entry, exit and behaviour of their members, have autonomy in practice and be protected from lay interference (Wilkins,

2011). They usually have a code of practice, a professional body and a shared commitment to continuing development and there is also a presumption of a specialized knowledge and language. Thus, Forsyth and Danisiewicz, for example, argued in 1985 that the tasks of professionals are so exclusive and complex that they should have autonomous decision-making powers free from external pressures (Demirkasimoglu, 2010: 2048). Each of the above features has been found wanting in relation to teaching, particularly with regard to the responsibility for, ownership, and regulation of its own members (Swann et al., 2010: 550). Mausethagen and Granlund argue that the recent introduction of new accountability regimes is an expression of public and political scepticism towards teachers' competence and that this contradicts the requirement for trust in professionals (Mausethagen, 2012: 818). Given the anomalous position of teaching in respect of some of the agreed criteria, Etzioni characterized it as a 'quasi-profession' and the New Labour government from 1997 promoted the concept of a 'new professionalism' which involved greater accountability to outside agencies. For Townsend, one of the key current questions is whether teaching should now be designated not as a profession but a craft (Townsend, 2011). However, Hanlon has argued that professionalism is now 'a shifting, rather than a concrete phenomenon', while Whitty posits that a profession is whatever people think it is at any particular time. So, for him, the commonly held perception of teaching as a profession means that it is so, even when the core characteristics cannot be perceived (Whitty, 2000: 282).

The status of the elementary schoolteacher in history has depended on a number of factors. It has been enhanced by training, increases in salary, the creation of professional organizations and even the granting of pension rights. However, at the start of the nineteenth century, provision of elementary schooling was patchy and anyone could set themselves up as a teacher since no qualifications were obligatory. It could not be said that teachers possessed any specialist knowledge of any kind. Many ran little schools as a part-time supplement to other occupations such as baking, weaving, shopkeeping or even stonemasonry. It was a common practice for men and women to resort to teaching after failing in other professions and, as late as 1847, one MP pronounced in the Commons that men were 'generally made schoolmasters' because they were unfit for anything else and that 'if a man lost an arm or a leg, the first thing he did was to look for a turnpike; or failing an empty turnpike, he next applied for a situation of village schoolmaster' (Hurt, 1972: 144). David Stowe, who began his own training institution in 1837, wrote disparagingly of the condition of his contemporary elementary teachers:

> We have been sowing hay seed and expecting to reap corn ... teachers have not been trained to their art, but left to make out one of their own

more or less efficient, and to cut and curve upon their pupils just as they pleased ... until our future teachers undergo a previous course of training ... under experienced masters, popular education must continue, as has hitherto been, too much a mere name, and the working classes sink below the level of sober, honest, upright, intelligent and sound-hearted Christians. (Stowe, 1847: 59–60)

There were numerous dame-schools but the education provided by the widows, discharged soldiers and bankrupts was at its best the three Rs and the Bible and often was no more than baby-minding. There was no system of training, no educational techniques for a teacher to acquire, and no system of inspection which would enhance the status of the occupation. The first elementary teachers who might be loosely termed 'professional' came with the charity schools of the eighteenth century. They had the common aim of teaching the children the basic beliefs of the Christian religion, and along with this went the teaching of reading, but the charity schools themselves complained of a lack of competent masters and mistresses. The SPCK recognized the need for some form of training and planned a college for teachers, although this had to be abandoned through lack of finance. It did though in 1708 encourage all its newly elected school-masters to 'consult with some of the present schoolmasters ... for the more ready performance of [their] duty' (Downing, 1708: 5). Clearly some form of acquisition of specialist knowledge, though limited, was being seen as useful.

The introduction of the monitorial system in the early nineteenth century might arguably be said to diminish the status of teachers further, as the teaching was undertaken by child monitors. This naturally raised questions about the amount of skill involved in the activity, if it could be done largely by a pupil, and the *Educational Expositor* described that it required little else of the teacher than 'an aptitude for enforcing discipline, an acquaintance with mechanical details for the preservation of order, and that sort of ascendancy in his school which a sergeant-major is required to exercise over a batch of raw recruits before they can pass muster on parade' (*Educational Expositor*, March 1853). Where any training existed at all, it still consisted of no more than a week or two attached to the school of an experienced teacher, or simply a visit by an experienced practitioner to initiate the intending teacher into the 'system' of monitors. The teacher had little standing in society, as a select committee reported in 1834 that the elementary schoolmaster was 'thought very little of' and was so despised that men of respectable attain-ments would not undertake the office. Kay-Shuttleworth, the first secretary to the committee of the Privy Council on Education, wrote in 1839 of the poor quality of teaching in the schools:

The quality of instruction is almost worthless, if not, in many instances, pernicious ... arising from their imperfect attainments, their ignorance of correct methods of instruction, and still more from their want of skill in training the habits and developing the characters of the children ... in many cases, the profession of the educator has fallen into the hands of persons who are destitute of means, not merely from want of ability, but from defects of character. And who resort to this calling after they have been proved to be unfit for any other. (Kay-Shuttleworth, 1839: 61–2)

Kay-Shuttleworth's book *Recent Measures for the Promotion of Education in England* is full of references to the envisaged professional nature of the role, 'the great responsibilities of their vocation', 'their honourable station', 'a mission of truth and civilization' and to be 'furnished with such skill in the practice of their art', to become 'the foster parents of their children whose temporal and eternal welfare is committed to their care'. He called for teachers to be trained in methods of teaching to make them become aware of the previous limits of a child's knowledge and to build on this, to make learning 'no longer a task, but a pleasure' appealing to the child's 'natural desire to know and combine' and making the pursuit of knowledge 'attractive by the simplicity and kindness with which it is imparted' (ibid.: 65). Teachers' salaries failed to recognize any professional status in society. Elementary schools were quite poor – one large British school had a total income of £131 a year, from which two teachers had to be paid, along with all other expenses. A select committee on education in 1845 even urged the voluntary schools not to let 'the wages of one who is fit to teach the children of the poor fall below those paid to a humble mechanic' and claimed that pay was too low to secure 'the zealous services of properly trained and qualified teachers':

While such pittance, in many cases less than the wages of an intelligent workman, continues to be paid, it will be in vain to expect efficient teachers. With no encouragement for exertion – no promotion for good conduct, it is not surprising that masters ... should be looking for more profitable employment. The consequence is that educated persons will not undertake the office, which but too generally is filled by men who have failed in other occupations. (Wardle, 1970: 102)

Kay-Shuttleworth himself complained in 1847 of 'the mean drudgery of instructing the rude children of the poor':

For what is the condition of the master of such a school? He has often an income very little greater than that of an agricultural labourer, and very rarely equal to that of a moderately skilful mechanic. Even the income is to a great degree contingent on the weekly pittances paid from the earnings of his poor neighbours, and liable to be reduced by bad harvests, want of employment, strikes, sickness among the children, or, worst of all, by the calamity of his own ill-health ... To build spacious and well-ventilated schools, without attempting to provide a position of honour and emolument for the masters, is to cheat the poor with a cruel illusion. (Kay-Shuttleworth, 1847: 17–18)

Clearly the role was not yet being recognized as a worthwhile occupation, let alone a profession.

The Revised Code of 1862 was a further blow to any improving morale and status in the occupation, as it introduced 'payment by results', with teachers compelled to cram their pupils for the yearly HMI examinations. There was clearly significant limitation in the 'autonomy of practice' expected of a profession, as the code laid down what s/he should teach and fostered unadventurous methods. The code also demanded much petty administration, adding to the burden of the work. Salaries were affected, with the average for a certificated teacher falling from £95 a year in 1862 back to £87 a year in 1865 owing to reduced grants. There were lowered standards of training, with school managers wanting to employ cheaper, under-trained teachers. Even the new colleges were affected by the Revised Code with a fall in applications and a resulting lowering of admission standards in 1865/6. However, the period of the school boards, from 1870 to 1903, did see improvements once more as appointments by a board gave a teacher a semi-official status. Rates of pay rose rapidly, as the headteachers of large urban schools required much administrative ability, which was recognized in their salaries. Each board (or Local Education Authority after 1903) decided its own salary scales and the first national salary scales were finally introduced in 1921.

Training

A first training college of the Church of England's National Society began work at Baldwin's Gardens in 1812, but training in these early days consisted almost entirely of learning the monitorial system. Any attempt to do more was hampered by the ignorance and general low quality of the students. David Stowe's Academy opened in Glasgow in 1828 and his Training Seminary followed in 1837 and there proved to be a great demand for Stowe's trainers. The English Wesleyans sent students to be trained there, while the National Society and the British and Foreign School Society sent deputations to study Stowe's methods. His organizing masters also visited schools, spending two or more months in each place, instructing the teachers, who were encouraged to visit each other's schools and to study in the evenings either alone or in local mutual improvement group. Kay-Shuttleworth tried to create a National Training College in 1839, but the plan failed through religious differences between church and dissenters. He did create his own, private training college at Battersea with a two-year course for eighteen-year-old future teachers. This was a forerunner of later colleges, although in practice the students concentrated on their own Bible knowledge and three Rs rather than teaching skills. Kay-Shuttleworth's pupil-teacher system, introduced in 1846, bolstered the standing of the role, by recognizing the need for some training to enhance competence. The pupil-teacher, a trainee usually of about thirteen years old, would be given supervised training by the headteacher of his or her school, with the latter receiving a salary enhancement of ten to thirty pounds a year, provided directly from a government grant. There were set hours of instruction out of school and these covered the pupil's own academic work and the study of teaching *per se*. The school day was then spent in actively teaching the younger children. An examination was set by the visiting HMI every year and the successful candidates could sit for the Queen's Scholarship for entry to a Training College. Their Certificate was recognized as a mark of technical competence and the teaching profession might be said to date from this period. The pupil-teacher system was then the first rung on the ladder of training and it spread widely.

Kay-Shuttleworth's own college was handed over to the National Society in 1843 and became St Mark's College for men. Whitelands College for women was established at the same time and other colleges began to emerge, including a Methodist training college at Westminster. A formalized network of denominational residential teacher training colleges emerged to meet the growing demand for qualified teachers and these greatly helped in the emergence of a sense of professional unity and the prestige of the career. At St Marks, the principal, Derwent Coleridge, felt it was necessary to give a high-class education to raise teaching standards, although the Newcastle Commission of 1861 felt students were actually being over-educated and this was targeted by the press with editorial complaints that 'we were overteaching our masters and under-teaching our children' (*Economist*, 21 September 1861), that the Privy Council 'have been long manufacturing razors for the purpose of cutting blocks, and in future the instrument must be better adapted for its purpose' (*Quarterly Review*, 1861, 220) and that 'the teacher must not be too far removed from his scholars' (*Edinburgh Review*, July 1861).

Training developed rapidly after the Cross Commission of 1888, which demanded better-trained teachers. It initiated Day Training Colleges connected to the universities and criticized the pupil-teacher system as now insufficient.

Pupil-teachers were encouraged to attend special centres and in 1884 their teaching commitment was reduced to only half-time. Nevertheless, in 1898, still 50 per cent of female and 30 per cent of male teachers were untrained. An enquiry in 1898 recommended raising the minimum age for pupil-teachers to fifteen and in 1902 this became sixteen. Pupil-teacher centres were also established at secondary schools, so they might receive a solid general education. The development of these centres led to a more sophisticated model of professional training with a much more rigorous commitment to the raising standards. The Board of Education began bursaries to any secondary school pupil who wished to become a teacher, tenable for a year, to be followed by a further year as a student teacher or entry to a training college. This became the normal pattern after the First World War. From 1904 LEAs were given grants to develop their own training colleges and the old pupil-teacher apprenticeship faded away.

At the NUT conference of 1920, the training of teachers was discussed at length and it declared its ambition to make teaching a graduate profession, with an added year of professional training. This did not become government policy and indeed there were continued complaints of the employment of untrained men and women. In 1922, for example, the London County Council employed 600 unqualified teachers in infant schools, which the president of the NUT condemned as 'a deliberate dilution of the teaching profession' and 'a definite degradation of the status of the qualified teacher' (Gosden, 1972: 277). The NUT conference of 1930 appealed once again that no more uncertificated teachers should be appointed, but to no avail. The NUT general secretary, as late as 1950, explained that before the Second World War the 'door was wide open to the untrained' but that it was at least by then 'only slightly ajar':

> Our task is now to slam the door and bar it and bolt it against the entrance of any more unqualified teachers. This would be a real service to children and to the teaching profession. (*Schoolmaster*, 13 April 1950: 157)

However, teacher shortage after the Second World War led the government to introduce an Emergency Training Scheme and a one-year training certificate; while this was accepted as necessary by the NUT, some teachers felt it again damaged their status. One wrote to the *Schoolmaster* that 'as long as teachers can be raised like mushrooms, wholly at the expense of the state, their value in public estimation must be two a penny' (Gosden, 1972: 287). The National Union of Women Teachers complained that it dangerously undermined their professional status and the president of the National Federation of Class Teachers feared that the new entrants would lack 'the standard of culture and knowledge which is regarded as an essential part of a teacher's equipment'. The feeling grew among teachers that doctors and dentists, who were also in short supply, had not relaxed their standards of entry and had thereby improved their status. By the time that the scheme was ended in 1951, some 15 per cent of all teachers had been trained by this one-year route.

In the same year, the NUT again called for a lengthening of the minimum period of training, underlining that the profession would not 'achieve its rightful status until the college courses on education and training are of four years' duration and until the normal qualification for recognition as a teacher includes a university degree' (Gosden, 1972: 284). At conference after conference in the 1950s teachers called for the extension of the minimum training period. A leading article in the *Schoolmaster* (14 June 1957: 1141) declared that there was no other reform which could do more to raise the status of the profession. The course was finally lengthened to three years in 1960 after the recommendations of the McNair Report. The Robbins Report of 1963 further proposed that by the mid-1970s a quarter of entrants to training colleges should study a four-year Bachelor of Education degree. Lord Eccles, a former minister of education, told the Lords that he fully approved of the recommendation to upgrade training colleges to end the situation of a quarter of a million teachers who suffered from being 'something more than a white-collar worker and something less than a professional man or woman' (307). Of the 326,000 teachers in England and Wales in 1970, 73 per cent were still non-graduates, 6 per cent were untrained graduates, and only 16 per cent were trained graduates. The DES finally announced an end to the employment of unqualified people even as temporary teachers and all graduates wanting to teach after 1973 were required to take a one-year PGCE course. Moreover, the James Report of 1972 envisaged an all-graduate profession, with the opportunity for teachers to 'top up' their teaching certificate to a BEd degree. These changes facilitated a rise in the proportion of graduates in primary schools to over 26 per cent by 1986, and to 47 per cent by 1995. In 2008, the Labour government went further in the Children's Plan by encouraging teachers to study for a Masters in Teaching and Learning, although this specific qualification was ended by the Coalition government.

The academy and free school programme of education secretary Michael Gove affected the qualification expectations of the profession. These schools are funded by the state but are semi-independent, outside of local authority control, and have substantial freedom over curriculum. Gove announced in 2012 that both types of school would be free once more to hire staff without standard qualifications. He claimed that this would free them up to employ professionals, such as scientists, engineers, musicians, university professors, and experienced teachers from overseas and the independent sector who might be well qualified, but did not have QTS (Qualified Teacher Status). By

2014 it was reported that as many as 6 per cent of the 141,000 teachers at such schools were untrained.

While achieving something of a professional goal in the expectations of educational standards, a related pillar of professionalism was denied to them. In 1983, the government had assumed greater control of teacher training itself, denying the profession self-regulation in entry standards. The Teacher Training Agency (TTA) was set up to inspect training quality nationally. DES Circular 9/92 demanded that teacher training institutions create partnership schemes with schools, with two-thirds of the students' time spent in school rather than in college, and stipulated that a new teacher had to complete a further year of supervised teaching in a state school to achieve QTS. Under the Labour government, Circular 4/98 created a model which atomized teaching into a measurable checklist that specified the skills needed to be accepted as a competent practitioner. This was condemned as 'de-profes-sionalizing', disregarding the professional expertise and autonomy of the field. In recent years, the standards required of new teachers have been revised several times, with Wendy Robinson positing that 'never before has there been so much detailed prescription of what student teachers should be taught, should know, and should be able to demonstrate in terms of technical skills and competence' (Robinson, 2008: 54).

Associations and registrations

Local teachers' associations became common in the 1850s, as social gatherings at first, with occasional lectures and discussions on educational topics. One association produced its own manuscript magazine. In 1855 the *Educational Expositor* gave a list of fifty-one local associations. There were 2,770 certificated teachers in England and Wales by this time, and 450 belonged to the Associated Body of Church Schoolmasters (ABCS), 250 to the United Association of Schoolmasters and 150 to the Metropolitan Church Schoolmasters' Association, which owned its own reading room and library. The opposition to the Revised Code was a fillip for some of these associations, with the ABCS membership rising to 1,200. The National Union of Elementary Teachers came into being in the 1870s and its fundamental aim was to create a true profession. One of its calls was for freedom from 'obnoxious interference', which was reflected in the words of its president, Graves, at its first conference, that there was 'no class of men whose daily duties and personal interests were more frequently interfered with by legislation and hence the teachers must by necessity unite to influence such legislation' (Tropp, 1957: 110). The union did work hard to achieve a voice and from 1880 Mundella consulted the union before announcing his proposals for a new code. Kekewich, who took over as secretary in 1890, sought teachers' opinions and it was he who finally abolished the remnants of the payment by results system. By 1904 the Code for Public Elementary Schools and in 1905 the *Suggestions for Teachers* showed a less authoritarian attitude from the centre. The preface of the latter asked that 'each teacher shall think for himself and work out for himself such methods of teaching as may use his powers to their best advantage and be best suited to the particular needs of the school' (PP, 1905: 6). Teachers were being trusted with a substantial measure of autonomy in their work in the classroom.

Teachers were long aware that their status depended upon self-government and there were early calls for a 'Scholastic Council' analogous to the General Medical Council to register qualified schoolteachers. There was, though, an enormous barrier in the mistrust between certificated teachers, uncertificated and 'higher grade' (grammar school) teachers. From 1880, the National Union of Elementary Teachers exerted steady pressure on the department to reduce the number of unqualified, who were being given posts as 'acting teachers'. In 1899 Parliament had explicitly enacted that a 'teacher's register' should be set up with the names of all grades of teachers arranged in alphabetical order and in 1902, without any discussion with teachers themselves, an Order in Council prescribed an alphabetical list of teachers. This antagonized the profession, as it was seen to be a caste register, after it appeared that it clearly designated in two lists those qualified to teach in elementary schools and those qualified to teach in secondary schools. When a Registration Council was established in 1912, it was given no power to compel registration or to impose any penalty on those who chose to remain unregistered. Registration was finally abandoned in 1948 only to re-emerge with the establishment in 2000 of the General Teaching Council for England (GTC). This again held a register of all qualified teachers and had powers to strike off teachers for serious misconduct or incompetence. It also produced a professional code of values and practice, the first incarnation of which, under much political pressure, asserted that:

1   (Teachers) have high expectations of all pupils; respect their social, cultural, linguistic, religious and ethnic backgrounds; and are committed to raising their educational achievement.

2   They treat pupils consistently, with respect and consideration, and are concerned for their development as learners.

3   They demonstrate and promote the positive values, attitudes and behaviour that they expect from their pupils.

4   They can communicate sensitively and effectively with parents and carers, recognising their roles in pupils' learning, and their rights, responsibilities and interests in this.

5   They contribute and share responsibly in the corporate life of school.

6   They understand the contribution that support staff and other professionals make to teaching and learning.

7   They are able to improve their own teaching, by evaluating it, learning from the effective practice of others and from evidence.

8   They are motivated and able to take increasing responsibility for their own professional development.

The New Labour government portrayed this at the time as an attempt to raise teachers' professional status, with explicit comparisons drawn with the self-regulation of 'high status' professions, although it failed to acknowledge that this had been imposed from above and the GTC had thirteen appointees of the secretary of state and seventeen appointed representatives from bodies such as the local authorities and the church, alongside the twenty-five elected teachers and nine union representatives. Unlike the General Medical Council or the Bar Council, it was not a self-regulating body of the teaching profession and the secretary of state retained responsibility for controlling teacher quality. The GTC was abolished in 2012 by the government, with some of its functions being assumed by a new body, the Teaching Agency, which was an executive agency of the Department for Education. Most teachers themselves did not lament its demise, having always regarded it as a tool of government and an indication that the profession had become little more than an extension to the civil service. The Teachers' Standards, imposed again by the department in 2011, reinforced this belief.

The Inspectorate

There had long been calls for promotion to the Inspectorate, which it was argued would be a clear move towards the 'craft' becoming a self-governing body. The Newcastle Commission of 1861 rejected outright the call on the grounds that the teachers were uncultured and that it was 'absolutely necessary that the inspectors should be fitted by previous training and social position to communicate and associate upon terms of equality with the managers of schools and the clergy of different denominations' (PP, 1861a: 160). The commissioners did accept that former teachers might relieve HMIs of most of the drudgery of payment by results and sixty inspectors' assistants' were appointed, although they were paid relatively low salaries and offered no chance at all of promotion to the full Inspectorate. It was not until 1882 that Mundella formed a sub-inspectorate from the ranks of the assistants and it took a further eleven years before the first sub-inspector was promoted to the full Inspectorate. Only six ex-elementary teachers had been promoted to the full Inspectorate by 1901, when the new grade of 'Junior Inspector' was introduced, recruited again not from teachers but from Oxford and Cambridge graduates. Local inspectors, who reported for local authorities after 1905, were appointed from the teaching body, but were not promoted to the Junior Inspectorate. Moreover, they were apparently resented by Robert Morant, the permanent secretary of the Privy Council on Education, who, together with the chief inspector, composed a strictly confidential memorandum to HMI in 1910, that 'the wrong sort of people' were being appointed. The memorandum reported that of 123 local inspectors, 104 were ex-elementary school teachers and that only a couple of the whole cohort had the qualifications normally expected of junior inspectors – education at a public school and then Oxbridge. The document asserted: 'Apart from the fact that elementary teachers are as a rule uncultured and imperfectly educated, and though many, if not most, of them are creatures of tradition and routine, there are special reasons why the bulk of the inspectors in this country should be unequal to the discharge of their responsible duties.' When this came to light, the NUT was furious and demanded Morant's removal. His successor attempted to calm the issue, announcing that they needed first-rate men, 'and a first-rate man, if he has experience of teaching in elementary schools, is more suited for the post of inspector in elementary schools than if he has not had that experience' (Gosden, 1972: 335).

The Inspectorate between the wars was clearly delineated between secondary and elementary inspectors. Most of the inspecting of elementary schools was undertaken by assistant inspectors (AIs) who were mainly former elementary heads and were under the authority of the HMI. The AIs were paid on a lower scale, travelled third class and were not allowed to put their signature to reports, and had little chance of advancement to HMI status. In 1944 the Inspectorate was finally reorganized and the rank of AI was abolished, although those who were now promoted did not automatically move onto the HMI pay scale and they were at times disparaged by their existing HMI colleagues. The period also saw an expansion in the Inspectorate with large numbers of new recruits, who in some areas soon outnumbered the incumbents. They were mainly drawn from the pool of headteachers, with many invited into the post by existing HMIs. Moreover, the HMI role was defined clearly by the senior chief inspector of the time, showing that he did not expect undue interference in schools. They were instructed to keep themselves to the 'proper limits of considerate inspection', clearly showing the trust in the teachers themselves at this particular time (Maclure, 2000: xxxi).

The basic organization of the Inspectorate continued without fundamental change until 1992, when this collegial monitoring was replaced by the more draconian inspections of the new inspection body, Ofsted. Once again teachers' autonomy began to be undermined. In 1999, a union survey, *Looking up the Microscope* again renewed the pre-war complaints of inexperienced inspectors, who, for example, were asking to hear three-year-olds read and enquiring about their homework and teaching syllabuses. At primary level there was unease at being examined by inspectors who had spent their entire teaching career in secondary schools. A particular bugbear was the lay inspectors who were introduced in the 1990s to allow non-professionals to work with Ofsted to look at non-core areas of provision. After much opposition, the role was ended in 2005, when it was made statutory that all new inspectors had to have a teaching qualification. However – and once again – the issue of those unqualified to teach reporting on schools is still a controversial one. Inspectors already in post remained on inspection teams and in 2012 it was highlighted that Tribal, one of three private companies that had conducted 7,000 school inspections since 2005 on behalf of Ofsted, employed at least five lead inspectors who did not have QTS and that it had never asked inspectors to provide them with information about their teaching background. Ofsted also admitted in April 2012 that it did not have details of whether their senior inspectors held QTS, whether they had worked in primary or secondary phase, or how many of them had experience of leading schools. All the teachers' unions expressed exasperation at the situation, with Russell Hobby, general secretary of the National Association of Head Teachers, questioning how anyone without qualification could provide a meaningful assessment of the quality of teaching and the ATL union, adding:

> anyone who makes judgements about teaching must have the ability to do that themselves and understand what it's like to do the job. If inspectors are coming to schools, they need to be experts. No wonder they cannot command teachers' respect. (*TES*, 20 July 2012)

Sir Michael Wilshaw, the Ofsted chief inspector, did act quickly on the matter and introduced a ban in October 2012, telling MPs that this was because school inspections were now to be more focused on lessons (*TES*, 5 April 2013).

Post-Callaghan autonomy

Hargreaves has claimed that in the post-war period teachers enjoyed a kind of 'licensed autonomy', when the words 'professional' and 'autonomy' became increasingly inseparable and teachers were granted 'a measure of trust, material reward, occupational security and professional dignity and discretion in exchange for broadly fulfilling the mandates the state expected of them' (Hargreaves, 2000: 159). Bottery and Wright concur that the period from the 1940s to the 1970s was generally seen as the golden age of teachers' autonomy – that teachers accepted the broad legislative framework from the government, but enjoyed interpreting this framework (Bottery and Wright, 2000: 12). Le Grand (1997) similarly suggests that parents were expected to trust that teachers knew what was best for their children and the state did not seem to want to intervene, even though effectively it paid teachers' salaries (Le Grand, 1997). The extent of this autonomy was ultimately questioned in the 1970s by the Black Papers, the William Tyndale Inquiry and then by Prime Minister James Callaghan, who, in his Ruskin College speech, called for a more thorough monitoring of the use of resources and emphasized the role of an inspectorate 'in relation to national standards':

> Public interest is strong and legitimate and will be satisfied. We spend £6 billion a year on education, so there will be discussion. But let it be rational. If everything is reduced to such phrases as 'educational freedom' versus State control, we shall get nowhere. I repeat that parents, teachers, learned and professional bodies, representatives of higher education and both sides of industry, together with the government, all have an important part to play in formulating and expressing the purpose of education and the standards that we need ... To the teachers I would say that you must satisfy the parents and industry that what you are doing meets their requirements and the needs of our children. (Callaghan, 1976)

The idea that professionals could be trusted to act competently was increasingly questioned, and those favouring a market economy approach – not least the Conservative party elected into government in 1979 – pressed for 'customers' to have the power to hold professionals to account. The aspiration of teachers to have a similar professionalism to that of doctors and lawyers was therefore dashed by government interference in the 1980s. Kenneth Baker announced in 1988 that the country could not continue with a system under which 'teachers decide what pupils should learn without reference to clear, nationally agreed objectives', with the result that a national curriculum was imposed in all state schools, removing the flexibility previously enjoyed by teachers. The core characteristic of classical professionalism, the control of the body of knowledge, was undermined by the presumption that this curriculum provided a 'complete canon of knowledge' (Leaton Gray, 2006: 307). As in 1862, teachers' professional reputations and even financial security became dependent on favourable Ofsted reports, which affected the popularity of the school among prospective parents. Teachers themselves were expected to implement the government agenda, with professional judgement undermined by a culture of 'coercive compliance' (Graham, 1999: 392). Even professional development became a 'top-down' imposition rather than a genuine personal and collegial enterprise. The *Professional Standards* of 2007 demanded that teachers at every stage of their career demonstrate that they had 'a creative and constructively critical approach towards innovation' and are prepared to 'adapt their practice where benefits and improvements are identified', but these standards were imposed upon teachers by the TDA (TDA, 2007: 8).

Subsequent government reforms significantly changed the working lives of teachers along with conceptions of their professional identity. There was the emphasis on performance indicators (performativity), with a business ethos demanded in schools which emphasized competition and efficiency. Teachers were no longer in control of the curriculum and the publication of the results of tests (SATs) at seven, eleven, fourteen and at GCSE emphasized their growing accountability. Many commentators saw these measures as signalling the deprofessionalization of teachers, with a loss of autonomy and status. Other observers argued that a new professionalism had emerged, concentrating on the improvement of standards, responsiveness to the market forces and target-setting. The Labour secretary of state in 2001, Estelle Morris addressed teacher concerns in her pamphlet *Professionalism and Trust: The Future of Teachers and Teaching*. After asserting 'Gone are the days when doctors and teachers could say, with a straight face, "trust me, I'm a professional"', she articulated six characteristics of this new professionalism. These focused on high standards, regular training, efficient management of assistants, effective use of technology, rewards for excellence and (with something of a sting) 'relentless focus on what is in the best interests of those who use the service – in education, pupils and parents – backed by clear and effective arrangements for accountability and for measuring performance and outcomes' (DfES, 2001). Morris praised the standards for QTS which had been introduced, again by government imposition, in 1998 and which many teachers had seen as no more than craft skills. They had been revised in 2002 at least to include reference to broader 'professional values and practice' (TDA, 2002).

Bottery and Wright identified in particular the 1999 imposition not only of content, but of teaching methods in the primary literacy and numeracy hours, as a challenge to the very bases of teacher autonomy. They claimed that a decade of constant change, combined with a reluctance by the profession to engage in critical debate, had 'neutered most dissident voices', even as regards the proposals for performance-related pay (Bottery and Wright, 2000: 482). Even the drive by the TTA to encourage a 'research-and evidence-based' culture was seen paradoxically as part of this same process. The essence of a profession is the grounding of expertise on a solid evidence base, but Bottery and Wright challenged the TTA's limitation solely to research into teaching method, school organization and assessment. This, they argued, was research for the 'restricted professional, the imple-menter of others' policies and not for a profession which is envisaged as making any significant contribution to the formation of education policy and direction'. What was expected was 'non-critical research' and the disregard for critiques of policy echoed the previous dismissal by Chris Woodhead, chief inspector of schools, of educational research as a vast waste of public money if not directed at classroom issues. Bottery and Wright concluded therefore that 'being truly professional involves a belief that teaching transcends the classroom ... becoming more informed on the forces at work in society that are steering education ... [and] independent critical inquiry' (ibid.: 484). Ironically, the sentiment was echoed ten years later by Woodhead himself, who showed exasperation at the lack of challenge from teachers of government initiatives. He described the silence from the profession at the imposition of standards for all teachers, whether at initial training or core, post-threshold, advanced skills and excellent teacher level. All these, for Woodhead, were 'spelt out with bureaucratic exactitude' by the TDA, 'an organisation that exists to ensure nobody can become a teacher, or be promoted as a teacher, if they do not dance to the government's tune'. He finally challenged the proposed new primary curriculum of Jim Rose and asked: 'Where is the debate about these issues? We have all been programmed to believe the official line, or have learnt to keep quiet. Teaching is no longer a profession' (*TES*, 15 May 2009).

In its survey of the profession, the *Teacher Status Project* of 2007 found that all teacher respondents perceived a steady and significant decline in status between 1979 and 1988. The teachers saw a large discrepancy between the positive working conditions of a high-status profession and those of the teaching profession, and ratings placed them in the lowest rankings of a list of fifteen occupations, with secondary teaching at 12th and primary at 14th (Hargreaves, 2006: x, xiii). Teachers consistently felt less rewarded and more controlled and regulated than a high-status profession (Hargreaves, 2007: 9). Participants in the corresponding case study research felt that teachers, whom they perceived as once venerated and similar in stature to doctors, had been reduced to the much lower status of service sector professionals.

Since 1988 there has been a clear shift in accountability from teacher self-regulation to being answerable to agencies such as the QCA, Ofsted and the TTA. The demands of Ofsted currently involve standards, quality, efficiency, value for money and performance. Jane Perryman uses the idea of 'panoptic performativity' to describe the regime in which the frequency of inspection and the sense of being perpetually under surveillance leads to teachers performing in ways dictated by the discourse of inspection; lessons are taught to a rigidly prescribed routine and school documentation and policies closely mirror the diktats of the Inspectorate (Perryman, 2006). She argues that, in a special measures regime in particular, schools need to accept that this discourse is the only way forward and that there is no room for schools to 'do their own thing' in terms of improvement.

Recent Coalition government reforms draw heavily on the discourse of teaching as a 'craft' to be learnt as an apprenticeship. Michael Gove pronounced that 'watching others, and being rigorously observed yourself as you develop, is the best route to acquiring mastery in the classroom' (Gove, 2010). His vision for teacher training was that this should be 'practical' and in 2013 over half of all training places were switched to schools and away from universities, with all college postgraduate trainees obliged to spend at least 60 per cent of their time in schools. A national network of Teaching Schools was designated to take lead responsibility for providing and quality assuring initial teacher training in their area, and the Coalition government's revised Teachers' Standards have been said to perpetuate the defining of teacher professionalism in performative terms (Edmond, 2013: 212). The interference is likely to continue. In 2014, Tristram Hunt, shadow secretary of state for education promised that if his party became the government, he would establish by statute a Royal College of Teachers, a teacher oath, and expect teachers to revalidate their qualifications at regular intervals by undertaking professional development (Hunt, 2014b). The irony that this was again an imposed professionalism – and thus no professionalism – was not lost on many teachers. Hunt rejected any curtailment of Ofsted in favour of a form of peer quality review.

It appears that neither of the major political parties can accept a profession which is self-regulating and autonomous in practice. For almost 200 years teachers themselves have struggled for a true recognition, which involves their autonomous and trusted status in society and the confidence to challenge impositions from government. Teachers retain a niggling conviction that they, rather than transient politicians, should be determining educational initiatives. The current plight of teachers suggests that their struggle, which began over 150 years ago, will continue for many more years.

Points to consider:

- Why do some teachers now doubt that they belong to a true profession?
- How important is it that teachers and inspectors have been trained in pedagogy, rather than simply trained in their own subject area?
- What should be included in any Professional Standards for teachers and what should be outside their purview?

12

What might schools be like in the future?

This chapter speculates on the future of education in the UK, looking at the possible changes to school buildings, school curricula, the impacts of new media on children's learning, and the possible challenge to the authority of teachers as gatekeepers of knowledge. It reflects the issues outlined in other chapters but also considers predictions made by Prensky, Greenfield and many others about what schools might be like if current trends continue apace.

At the beginning of the twentieth century, the French artist Maximilian Villemard (1865–1931) designed a series of cartoons to be published as cigarette cards under the title of 'L'an 2000' ('the year 2000'). One of these portrayed a group of children in a classroom, long before the invention of computers, with their teacher, suitably garbed in spectacles and gown, feeding books into a machine. The contents were then fed directly into the pupils' brains. The first premise has now been achieved, with the feeding of almost all books, including those several hundred years old, into a 'machine': the internet. The second has not yet been attained but it has indeed been frighteningly contemplated with the implanting of memory chips into brains. Children still need to utilize the age-old skills of reading and memorization to access information, admittedly using a screen rather than paper.

Not all predictions are successful, but there has been much recent speculation about what schools will be like in the not-distant future. The constant revolutions in information technology have telescoped such prophesies, but it is of value to speculate on potential change over the next quarter-century. Many writers see four areas where significant evolution is likely: the curriculum, the role of teachers, the school buildings and the funding of schools. There are other more contentious questions which cannot be ignored, as to whether children's brains and the way they learn will have

Fig. 11: A vision of the future in a cigarette card drawn by Villemard in 1900

transformed, whether will there be any need for teachers at all, and how the social, legal and political structures might be affected by such fundamental upheavals.

Curriculum and pedagogy

Literacy and numeracy have been central to schools for 200 years, but what skills will be needed by future children? New technologies will with ease be able to print out our spoken words and the need for reading could be comparatively rare, as our machines increasingly speak to us. Handwriting has already become rather archaic (and neatness in handwriting an increasingly quaint skill), as word-processors begin to assume a monopoly in the composition of essays, letters and other scripts. As for numeracy, it was claimed that the hand calculators of the 1980s would make arithmetic unnecessary, but this has not proved to be the case. The shelved Rose Review of the primary curriculum of 2009 continued to emphasize the importance of literacy, numeracy and ICT skills at the expense of other areas of study.

There has been much discussion, precipitated by the former secretary of state for education Michael Gove, of what constitutes the bedrock of cultural knowledge expected in schools. In a future national curriculum there will need to be renewed discussion of what history, geography, languages or science should and need to be taught. Moreover, in the light of the very current discussions of citizenship, will schools need to be seen, as they are now, as a natural vehicle to 'socialize' and 'citizenize' children, and indeed to act as the most effective bulwark against social fragmentation and a crisis of values? The compulsory nature of the institution itself has given the school a clear role in creating a collective ideal which tempers the individualism prevalent in the wider society. The school has been seen as administering the 'social glue' in society, although this role might be assumed by increasingly ubiquitous social media communities such as Facebook, uniting individuals in smaller interest groups.

The young live in a world where access to information is entertainment, unlike the school of yesteryear where academic achievement was often based on memorization. Marc Prensky has argued that children are now incrementally different from those of the past, in that they have become 'digital natives', who have spent their entire lives surrounded by and using computers, video games, digital music, cell phones and the toys of the digital age (Prensky, 2001). They need images as much as text. Printed books have been used in schools for the last 200 years, but there has already been a clear change from written text to image-based knowledge. Comparisons of current school textbooks with those of only fifty years ago show increasing illustration and much less text-based data. However, in many schools, textbooks are themselves a thing of the past and they have been replaced with screen data, with websites needing to be image-rich to attract their customers. Children have already come to expect such illustrative material, and their browsing has been nicknamed *edutainment*. Prensky also described the circumstances in which students who were starting university in 2001 had grown up:

> Unfortunately for our Digital Immigrant teachers, the people sitting in their classes grew up on the 'twitch speed' of video games and MTV. They are used to the instantaneity of hypertext, downloaded music, phones in their pockets, a library on their laptops, beamed messages and instant messaging. They've been networked most or all of their lives. They have little patience for lectures, step-by-step logic, and 'tell-test' instruction. (Prensky, 2001: 4)

The 2007 report of the Committee of Inquiry into the Changing Learner Experience similarly concluded (admittedly on higher education students rather than school pupils) that it has led them to 'impatience – a preference for quick answers – and to a casual approach to evaluating information and attributing it and also to copyright and legal constraints' (CLEX, 2007: 9).

Susan Greenfield's vision of future children is much darker. In *Tomorrow's People* she expresses fears that overexposure to new technologies is having lasting effects on children, generating short attention spans, sensationalism and an inability to empathize. She observes a marked preference for the here-and-now in children 'where the immediacy of an experience trumps any regard for the consequences', the emphasis is on 'the thrill of the moment, the buzz of rescuing the princess in the game' and a failure to develop 'real face-to-face human relations'. She warns that a move to more virtual schooling with 'a solitary student working alone on a computer for their entire education' will be that pupils 'will fail to develop an understanding of their own emotions and those of others' (Greenfield, 2004: 175). Greenfield has been criticized for not having a reliable evidence base for her assertions, but she continues to warn of the dangers to children. In the House of Lords in February 2009 she expressed concerns at the reduction in the attention span of pupils:

> If the young brain is exposed from the outset to a world of fast action and reaction, of instant new screen images flashing up with the press of a key, such rapid interchange might accustom the brain to operate over such timescales. Perhaps when in the real world such responses are not immediately forthcoming, we will see such behaviours and call them attention deficit disorder. It might be helpful to investigate whether the near total submersion of our culture in screen technologies over the last decade might in some way be linked to the threefold increase over this period in prescriptions for methylphenidate, the drug prescribed for ADHD. (*Hansard*, 2009: 1291)

Greenfield's conclusion was that 'the child's brain, devoid of cohesive narrative', will be 'almost infantilised, characterised by short attention spans, sensationalism, inability to empathise and a shaky sense of identity ... It is hard to see how living this way on a daily basis will not result in brains, or rather minds, different from those of previous generations' (*Hansard*, 2009: 1290–1).

There are also implications on the way we learn, and indeed the very essence of understanding. The age-old form of information gathering was by narrative, and much understanding was by narrative sequence, with the ordering of text itself often creating meaning. However, when children visit websites, they can choose the order and sequence of their visit, as the muse takes them; they pick information at random and follow interesting knowledge 'horizontally' rather than 'vertically'. The terminologies of books and websites show a very different culture, in that a book has a contents list, whereas a website has a menu, the latter implying choice and the randomness of reading. A book has a reader, whereas a website has a visitor. We do not read a website, we scroll it. So does this media scatter a learner's attention and diffuse concentration, or, as has been argued, does it improve selectivity in an individual, the ability to scan in order to extract the required information? There are drawbacks as magazines and newspapers shorten their articles, 'introduce capsule summaries, and crowd their pages with easy-to-browse info-snippets' (Carr, 2008). In March 2008, the *New York Times* decided to devote the second and third pages of every edition to article abstracts, its design director Tom Bodkin explaining that the shortcuts would give harried readers a quick taste of the day's news, sparing them the 'less efficient' method of actually turning the pages and reading the articles: 'Old media have little choice but to play by the new-media rules.' Carr concludes that the internet is beginning to change the way people think, making it harder even 'when we're offline to read books as skimming takes over and displaces our modes of reading'.

Selwyn et al. argue that the use of ICT results in an 'intellectual dumbing down' in accessing information and knowledge and that excessive use 'is now hampering many children's ability to gather information in a *discerning* manner' (Selwyn et al., 2010: 26). Seel and Dijkstra *claim* that it induces a 'non-sequential way of thinking and this may be an obstacle to learning' (Seel, 2004: 234). Greenfield herself describes information organized in the non-linear, more hypertext style of free association, expressed in rich visual media to convey experiences 'in stark contrast to words which convey ideas', and that this will have a profound effect:

> So the next generation may well have more visual sensibilities, and be as proficient at manipulating images as their parents or grandparents ... were once agile with words. Once literacy is truly as outdated as the slide rule and log tables are today, education will be transformed entirely into an experience rather than a thought process ... As the children of the future no longer need a long attention span to follow a linear narrative of words but rather are trapped by the immediacy of the 'now' – ever stronger flashing lights and bleeps may be needed to sustain motivation or concentration over time frames of seconds. (Greenfield, 2004: 172)

Greenfield argues that information is not the same as knowledge, and that there will need to be solid guidance for children about how to read this information and to understand core concepts. Many commentators argue that the emphasis of schooling will have to be *how* to learn – with children discerning the reliability of information given in websites, learning how to read images, thinking critically, mastering concepts, and expressing themselves effectively. Moreover, Greenfield speculates that future generations might not be generalists as they are now and that the Information Age could lead to more specialization, not less, as the specific needs of diverse aspects of society are met by appropriate technologies, needing ever-changing skills. 'We could be on the brink of returning to the mood of the mid-nineteenth century, when most of the workforce were apprenticed at a young age and learnt one vocational skill that fitted the needs of society.'

There have been more optimistic predictions for over a decade that simulations and game-based learning would become a boon within the classroom. In recent years, simulations have been introduced to healthcare education, where they can provide students with experiential learning opportunities and repeated practice without risk; these include simulated operations with virtual patients. Such learning is also used in the military and flight simulators are a common vehicle for training. Virtual reality scenarios within the classroom are claimed to foster communication and collaboration, if these 'soft' skills are seen to be vital in the future. While simulations are still regarded by many as peripheral to traditional practice, the increasingly pervasive nature of gaming in the home and the demographic advance of 'digital natives' themselves becoming classroom teachers, are likely to encourage more use in schools. Research commissioned by the Scottish government in 2010 reported that learning-oriented games can harness the motivational power of leisure games to 'make learning fun'. Simulations were also seen potentially to foster personal skills such as initiative and persistence, motor skills such as coordination and speed of reflexes, social skills such as teamwork and communication, and intellectual skills such as problem-solving (Groff et al., 2010: 15). Pupils enter environments that would be impossible to access in any other way, with even virtual visits to the past. Many barriers would need to be overcome, not least the initial acceptance by teachers and school leaders. The Scottish research, however, found that existing educational simulations were still too simplistic, and that they were unlikely to be able to compete with the sophistication of leisure gaming, which had enormous budgets for development. Nevertheless, education has often benefited in the past from the spin-offs from such industries. The amount of rigour needed to create an accurate simulation of a historical period, for example, is immense. Leisure gaming does not require this rigour and hence anachronisms and historical errors can be overlooked, as historical accuracy is not the intended objective of the game. Proliferation will therefore depend on the advances in hardware and on increasingly realistic educational software. Nonetheless, simulations could be used to allow children to undertake virtual science experiments, to learn languages in an immersive environment, to experience business practices in increasingly realistic ways and to be virtually present almost anywhere on the planet or even beyond it. The result would be learning by doing, but also learning by 'being there'.

School buildings

The traditional classroom has endured throughout the last 200 years, with the teacher at the front and pupils in rows. There are still many classrooms of thirty children in desks sometimes facing forward to a now white board, although schools have experimented with the geography of the classroom, moving desks, removing desks, having circle times and creating working groups. The Royal Society of Arts has claimed that the strong grip of the conventional teaching model has preserved a system no longer fit for purpose:

> The model is a Platonic one; the teacher as the fount of knowledge passing on information to his pupils. The concept is hard to reconcile with the availability, electronically, of floods of information; children may access more than their teachers. School management is hierarchical, still based on the command-and-control model fast disappearing from the business world. The school day channels learning for all pupils into the same hours. And the school year still matches the rhythms of an agricultural society. (Bayliss, 1998)

Changes in building design have been recommended to make schools more appropriate for modern learning. As students no longer need to face a board, learning stations could be distributed along walls, in island clusters, or in zigzag patterns, and for small study groups there might be triangular rather than square work spaces. It has been envisaged that the classroom might resemble a television studio with monitors and cameras, to display presentations broadcast both from within and from outside the classroom. Movable partitions would permit teachers to shift from small to large group activities. A research study carried out by NOP on behalf of City and Guilds predicted that technology's effect on education during the next hundred years will be a transition from the current highly structured and standardized system to a more fluid and informal system. The blackboard and the playground could become things of the past as new technology revolutionizes the face of teaching. Telepresent teachers and lifelong learning could become the norm. Holographic lecturers could enable remote learning, putting the student in control of their own timetable and in touch with world experts in their chosen subjects.

School buildings are often closed for much of the year, in the evenings and during school holidays, and their expensive facilities are often lost to children and the community. Already many schools now have sports centres which are open to the public 'out of hours' and it has been proposed that there might be more integration on site of other services, such as health clinics, family advice centres, cinemas and museums, making the building itself the centre of the community. The survival of the school building itself has been questioned. Parents in the UK are already allowed to educate their children at home and the existing increase in 'home learning' (because of parents' worries over poor schools and poor discipline) shows a trend which might boom in future years. For all children, integrated networks mean that there is less and less necessity for learners to be physically present in a particular location. Forms of video-conferencing can easily facilitate discussions with other pupils, teachers or learning advisors at a distance and, as noted above, virtual science and technology experiments dispense with the need for labs. Seymour Papert in *Mindstorms* forecasted such changes over thirty years ago:

> I believe that the computer presence will enable us to so modify the learning environment outside the classroom that much, if not all, the knowledge schools presently try to teach with such pain and expense and such limited success will be learned, as the child learns to walk, painlessly, successfully, and without organised instruction. (Papert, 1993: 8)

This implies that school buildings as we know them today will have no place in the future. But education has been essentially conservative in the past. In essence, it has been the preservation from one generation to the next of what was thought to be the most useful knowledge, both instrumentally and culturally, and the most acceptable conventions of behaviour to ensure social order. Some would argue that it preserved the power of a ruling class or intelligentsia. In all these aims, there is a need for the meeting of individuals to form a true community, and many feel this necessitates a school building. The choice of knowledge and skills have been taken out of the hands of individual teachers and defined by the state for over a century, and with increasing specificity since 1988. This demonstrates that governments themselves have recognized the enormous value of an institutionalized system as a facilitator of social engineering. They have a vested interest in preserving the old models to ensure that social cohesion and national culture can be retained.

Funding

In view of the 2008 global economic crash, the question of financing of schools, if they remain as institutions, is becoming even more critical. As well as unemployment and government debt crises, the UK is facing a demographic time-bomb of a reducing pool of working age people. Currently, 16 per cent of the population is over sixty-five, but by 2050, this is predicted to rise to 25 per cent, when there will be eight million octogenarians. The working base will be reduced and there will be fewer taxpayers, who are likely to question the rising government expenditure needed to finance pensions and the health care of the increasing numbers of the old. Education will have to fight to safeguard its finances in a shrinking available pot. It is feasible that in this situation other alternatives to existing funding models will be contemplated. There might be a renewal of the private sponsorships of schools, as in the past by churches or charitable organizations, or by large industrial conglomerates or billionaires. There have been fanciful predictions that there might be Adidas classrooms, McDonalds gyms, and, more unconvincingly, Microsoft exercise books. There are already public–private partnerships with privately owned and managed schools, receiving part-payment from the state and adhering to a nationally defined and inspected standard (much as it was after 1861). The school buildings themselves might be used as 'for profit' institutions, with proceeds subsidizing the children's education. There also might be a return to a partly privatized education with schools expecting fees from their pupils, as universities now expect fees from their students. Fees were charged in board schools until 1891, even though the state had made attendance compulsory some years before, so there is precedent for parents who could afford to pay to make contributions, with the government acting as a 'safety net' for the poorest families. The fully private sector is still a viable alternative to state schools in the UK and their numbers might increase incrementally as a state system starved of finance disintegrates. Many middle-class parents are dissatisfied with the existing school system and home schooling is increasing. So this trend might snowball, as the OECD have envisaged in one of its scenarios of the future:

> Dissatisfaction with institutionalised provision and expression given to diversified demand leads to the abandonment of schools in favour of a multitude of learning networks, quickened by the extensive possibilities of powerful, inexpensive ICT. The de-institutionalisation, even dismantling, of school systems as part of the emerging 'network society'. (OECD, 2001)

The problem would remain with those parents who would not voluntarily educate their children. It is unfeasible to contemplate the return of uneducated, feral children of the early nineteenth century. Perhaps it is equally unfeasible to accept that governments would willingly give up so many of the powers they have acquired over the young over the last hundred years.

The role of teachers

A crisis in teacher recruitment that has been predicted for over fifteen years has so far failed to materialize to any significant extent, although still almost half of all newly trained teachers leave the profession within five years. In

2014 there was repeated concern that teacher training had failed to meet its targets for three consecutive years and that there would be a shortage of 27,000 teachers by 2017. Figures released in 2015 showed that only 62 per cent of newly qualified teachers were still in teaching a year later, which Ofsted chief inspector Sir Michael Wilshaw describes as a 'national scandal'. Many solutions have been offered to reduce the education system's expensive dependence on teachers. The Major government of the 1990s thought of a 'mum's army' of teacher helpers; the Blair government created teaching assistants to take full responsibility for classes under the guidance of the 'experts', and the very existence of closely defined curricula and schemes of work from the 1990s facilitated their delivery by non-professionals. Moreover, the pool of young people who might teach has diminished, as the population is aging and teachers' retirement age has had to be extended, perhaps in the future to 70. There is a presumption here that the current systems will remain, and that schools will still be employing the old to teach the young, in classes of thirty pupils. A survey by Demos (Green and Hannon, 2007) suggested that children are actually more competent at finding information and sharing it with others than previously. This has implications for the boundaries between teacher and learner, which will become increasingly blurred as pupils discover and help peers on the internet. The 'googlization' of information has deprived the teacher of the role of the 'gatekeeper' of knowledge, with the Google Books digitization project reaching over thirty million texts in 2013 and Google's stated aim to scan every one of the estimated 130 million unique books in the world by the end of the present decade. Other libraries and organizations are also adding to the stock of accessible web-books. Almost all surviving books published before 1900 have already been digitized and recent publications, both journals, books and newspapers, are invariably issued digitally. New PhD theses in the UK are deposited in digital format in the British Library, whose EThOS project has embarked on the scanning of all previous theses as demand is made. Increasing numbers of archival manuscripts are being digitized by record offices and museums. It has been predicted that in the not-distant future, the sum total of human knowledge will be available at the tap of a key.

No longer then can teachers, or indeed any professionals, claim that they are the gatekeepers of knowledge. Indeed, Augusto and Michaela Odone, who had no previous medical training, became famous in the 1980s for discovering a treatment using Lorenzo's oil for their son's incurable illness. Such individual research is ever more easily accessible through the internet and medical experts are increasingly being challenged in their judgements. It is not surprising that the disposition of 'authority' on the part of educators is no longer seen as appropriate and, as Stephen Heppell points out, this is 'a transparent age' where there are no longer secrets (Heppell, 2006). Prensky posited that there must be a new pedagogy of children teaching themselves with a teacher's guidance (Prensky, 2008). Michelle Selinger similarly claims that teachers will need to adapt to a new role, as they will no longer be in control of the content of education (Sellinger et al., 2001). Their main aim will be to teach how to learn, how to question, to foster curiosity and to model the learning process. The pupil will be the 'novice learner' who is guided by the 'expert learner' (the teacher). The teacher as 'access-agent to scarce information' is redundant and this might lead to the death knell of the deference to the schoolteacher that had sustained the schooling structure for centuries. John Adcock, in *In Place of Schools*, predicted over twenty years ago that teachers would not work in schools at all, but remotely, devising and servicing the personal learning plans of a group of pupils (Adcock, 1994).

However, many believe that teachers will still be needed. Lee Shulman passionately holds that the teachers must remain the key to schooling, feeling that 'No microcomputer will replace them, no television system will clone and distribute them, no scripted lessons will direct and control them, no voucher system will bypass them' (Shulman, 2004: 162). Chris Woodhead, the former chief inspector of schools also has a conservative view of the resilience of the role:

> The purpose of education in the twenty first century is exactly what it was in the nineteenth and twentieth: to initiate the young into those aspects of our culture upon which their (and our) humanity depends. Good teachers ... know that their effectiveness as teachers depends upon their ability to secure order, explain things clearly, ask the right question of the right pupil, joke, urge, coax, encourage, and so on. There is nothing intellectually mysterious about these essential teaching skills. The teachers I know and admire simply laugh at self-indulgent nonsense of this kind! The challenge, as they see it, is to become better at the traditional craft of the classroom: better at explaining new ideas, better at asking questions and responding to their pupils' answers, better at dealing with the hundred and one unexpected possibilities that arise in every lesson they teach. (*TES*, 7 January 2000)

Perhaps a final word needs to be given to Jonathan Sachs, who, in a book on the future of schooling, has concluded more philosophically:

> Long ago the Jewish people came to the conclusion that to defend a country you need an army. But to defend a civilisation you need schools. The single most important social institution is the place where we hand on our values to the next generation – where we tell our children where we have come from, what ideals we fought for, and what we learned on

the way. Schools are where we make children our partners in the long and open-ended task of making a more gracious world ... Teachers open our eyes to the world. They give us curiosity and confidence. They teach us to ask questions. They connect us to our past and future. They're the guardians of our social heritage. We have lots of heroes today – sportsmen, supermodels, media personalities. They come, they have their fifteen minutes of fame, and they go. But the influence of good teachers stays with us. They are the people who really shape our life. (Alexander, 2004: 155)

These extracts show that many see the teacher's role as something much more than a conduit of information. They are motivators, encouragers, critical experts on how to read text and discern the reliability of data. This should ensure that there will be a teacher–pupil relationship in the future.

References

Acland, A. H. D. (1883), *The Education of Citizens*, Manchester: Central Cooperative Boards.

Adamson, J. W. (1907), *The Practice of Instruction*, London: National Society.

Adcock, J. (1994), *In Place of Schools: A Novel Plan for the 21st Century*, London: New Education.

Alexander, R. (2004), 'Still no Pedagogy? Principle, Pragmatism and Compliance in Primary Education', *Cambridge Journal of Education* 34 (1): 7–33.

Allen, I. (1987), *Education in Sex and Personal Relationships*, London: Policy Studies Institute.

Annual Register (1871), *A Review of Public Events at Home and Abroad for the Year 1870*, London: Rivington.

Archer, R. L. (1916), *The Teaching of History in Elementary Schools*, London: Black.

Aries, P. (1962), *Centuries of Childhood*, London: Cape.

Arnold, M. (1868), *Schools and Universities*, London: Macmillan.

Arnold, M. (1873), *Literature and Dogma*, London: Macmillan.

Arnold, M. (1908), *Reports on Elementary Schools, 1852–1882*, London: HMSO.

Arnold-Forster, H. O. (1896), *Things New and Old, III*, Montreal: Grafton.

Arnot, M., Gray, J., James, M., Rudduck, J. and Duveen, G. (1998), *Recent Research on Gender and Educational Performance: Ofsted Reviews of Research*, London: HMSO.

Barnardos (2008), 'The shame of Britain's intolerance of children'. Available online: https://www.barnardos.org.uk/news_and_events/media_centre/press_releases.htm?ref=42088 (accessed 3 June 2015).

Barnes P. (2014), *Education, Religion and Diversity. Developing New Models of Religious Education*, Abingdon: Routledge.

Barrow, R. (1981), *The Philosophy of Schooling*, Brighton: Wheatsheaf.

Bayliss V. (1998), *Redefining Schooling. A Challenge to a Closed Society. Discussion Paper 6*, London: Royal Society of Arts.

Becon, T. (1823), *Writings of the Rev. Thomas Becon*, London: Religious Tract Society.

Becon, T. (1844), *The Catechism of Thomas Becon, and Other Pieces*, Cambridge: Cambridge University Press.

Bell D. (2004), 'Change and continuity: Reflections on the Butler Act', 21 April 2004. Available online: http://www.theguardian.com/education/2004/apr/21/ofsted.schools (accessed 29 April 2015).

Bell, D. (2005), 'What does it mean to be a Citizen?' *Hansard Lecture*, 17 January 2005. Available online: http://dera.ioe.ac.uk/5245/1/Citizenship.pdf (accessed 23 May 2015).

Bell, D. (2015), *Today* [Radio Programme], BBC Radio 4, 5 January 2015. Available online: http://www.bbc.co.uk/programmes/p02gkf5j (accessed 24 May 2015).

Best, S. (1849), *Manual of Parochial Institutions*, London: Darling.

BHA (British Humanist Association) (2014), 'Faith Schools'. Available online: https://humanism.org.uk/campaigns/schools-and-education/faith-schools (accessed 8 December 2014).

Bibby, C. (1948), *Sex Education: A Guide for Parents, Teachers and Youth Leaders*, London: Macmillan.

Blair, T. (2001), 'Speech on Education', 23 May 2001. Available online: http://www.theguardian.com/politics/2001/may/23/labour.tonyblair (accessed 5 January 2015).

Blair, T. (2006), 'Speech on Healthy Living', 26 July 2006. Available online: www.theguardian.com/society/2006/jul/26/health.politics (accessed 21 October 2014).

Blunkett, D. (2001), *Today* [Radio Programme], BBC Radio 4, 12 July 2001.

Blunt, J. H. (1880), *Directorium Pastorale*, London: Rivington.

Blunt, J. J. (1856), *The Acquirements and Principal Obligations and Duties of the Parish Priest*, London: Murray.

Board of Education (1923), *Differentiation of Curricula between the sexes in the Secondary school*, London: HMSO.

Board of Education (1927), *Handbook of Suggestions for the Consideration of Teachers and others concerned in the work of Public Elementary Schools*, London: HMSO

Board of Education (1931), *Report of the Consultative Committee on the Primary School*. London: HMSO.

Board of Education (1937), *Handbook of Suggestions for the Consideration of Teachers and Others Concerned in the Work of Public Elementary Schools*, London: HMSO.

Board of Education (1943), *Sex Education in Schools and Youth Organisations*, London: HMSO.

Bottery, M. and Wright, N. (2000), 'The Directed Profession: Teachers and the State in the Third Millennium', *Journal of In-Service Education* 26 (3): 475–87.

Bottery, M. and Wright, N. (2012), *Teachers and the State: Towards a Directed Profession*, London: Routledge.

Boyd, C. W. (1914), *Mr Chamberlain's Speeches*, London: Houghton.

Braby, M. C. (1908), *Modern Marriage and How to Bear it*, London: Werner Laurie.

Brighouse, H. (1998), 'Why Should the State Fund Schools?' *British Journal of Educational Studies* 46 (2): 138–52.

Brinsley, J. (1917), *Ludus Literarius*, London: Constable.

Brougham, H. (1838), 'Practical Observations Upon the Education of the People' in *Speeches of Lord Brougham Upon Questions Relating to Public Rights, Duties and Interests*, Edinburgh: Black.

Brown, G. (2006), 'Speech to the Fabian New Year Conference'. Available online: www.britishpoliticalspeech.org/speech-archive.htm?speech=316 (accessed 3 December 2014).

Bruner, J. (1983), 'Play, Thought and Language', *Peabody Journal of Education* 60 (3): 60–69.

Bruner, J. S. and Haste, H. E. (1987), *Making Sense: The Child's Construction of the World*, London: Methuen.

Bulkley, M. E. (1914), *The Feeding of School Children*, London: Bell.

Butler, R. A. (1943), *Address delivered on 30 March to the Third Annual Congress of the Free Church Council*, Cambridge.

Callaghan, J. (1976), 'Towards a national debate', Speech given at Ruskin College. Available online: http://www.ukpolitics.org.uk/node/3508 (accessed on 9 September 2014).

Carlile O. and Jordan, A. (2009), 'The centre cannot hold: Challenging student-centred learning', Proceedings, AISHE Conference, NUI Maynooth, 2009. Available online: http://ocs.aishe.org/index.php/international/2009/paper/view/90 (accessed 18 June 2015).

Carr Lane (n.d.), 'School Punishment Book'. Available online: http://www.sblha.com/carr_lane_punish.html (accessed 29 December 2014).

Carr, D. (2003), *Making Sense of Education*, London: Routledge.

Carr, N. (2008), 'Is Google Making Us Stupid?', *Atlantic Monthly*, July/August 2008. Available online: http://www.theatlantic.com/magazine/archive/2008/07/is-google-making-us-stupid/306868/ (accessed 21 May 2015).

Carrington, B. (2008), 'Role Models, School Improvement and the Gender Gap', *British Educational Research Journal* 34 (3): 315–27.

Catholic Education Service (2015), 'Catholic groups reject call for sex education lessons from age of five', *Catholic Herald*, 18 February 2015. Available online: http://www.catholicherald.co.uk/news/2015/02/18/catholic-groups-reject-call-for-compulsory-sex-education-from-age-of-five (accessed 28 May 2015).

Chadwick, P. (1997) *Shifting Alliances, Church and State in English Education*, London: Cassell.

Children's Society (2006), 'Good Childhood. A National Enquiry'. Available online: https://www.childrenssociety.org.uk/sites/default/files/tcs/research_docs/Summary%20Good%20childhood%20launch%20report.pdf (accessed 16 December 2014).

Christodoulou, D. (2013), *Seven Myths about Education*, London: Routledge.

Church of England (2000), 'Churches state expectations on sex education guidance'. Available online: (https://www.churchofengland.org/media-centre/news/2000/02/churches_state_expectations_on_sex_education_guidance.aspx (accessed 27 May 2015).

Church of England (2001), *The Way Ahead: Church of England Schools in the New Millennium*, London: Church House.

Church, A. J. (1894), *Stories from English History*, London: Seeley.

CLEX (2007), 'Higher Education in a Web 2.0 World'. Available online: http://www.webarchive.org.uk/wayback/archive/20140614222117/http://www.jisc.ac.uk/media/documents/publications/heweb20rptv1.pdf (accessed 24 May 2015).

Colquhoun, D., Wright, N., Pike, J. and Gatenby, L. (2008), 'Evaluation of Eat Well Do Well, Kingston upon Hull's School Meal Initiative'. Available online: http://www2.hull.ac.uk/IFL/pdf/IFL-R_finalreport.pdf (accessed 2 December 2014).

Committee of Council (1841), *Minutes of the Committee of Council on Education, 1840–1*, London: Clowes.

Cook, H. (2012), 'Emotion, Bodies, Sexuality and Sex Education in Edwardian England', *Historical Journal* 55 (2): 475–95.

Copley, T. (2005), *Indoctrination, Education and God*, London: SPCK.

Crowther, G. (1959), *15–18. A report of the Central Advisory Council for Education (England)*, London: HMSO.

Cunningham, H. (2005), *Children and Childhood in Western Society since 1500*, London: Pearson.

Cunningham, H. (2006), *The Invention of Childhood*, London: BBC Books.

Curtis, W. and Pettigrew, A. (2009), *Learning in Contemporary Culture*, Exeter: Learning Matters.

Dawkins, R. (2007), *The God Delusion*, London: Black Swan.

DCSF (2007), *School Discipline and Pupil-behaviour Policies – Guidance for schools*, London: DCSF

DCSF (2008), *Personalised Learning – A Practical Guide,* London: DCSF.

DCSF (2008b), *Press* Release, 23 October 2008. Available online: http://www.nepes.eu/?q=node/389 (accessed 8 July 2015).

DCSF (2010), *Religious Education in English Schools: Non-Statutory Guidance*, Nottingham: DCSF.

De Montmorency, J. E. G. (1902), *State Intervention in English Education*, Cambridge: Cambridge University Press.

Demirkasimoglu, N. (2010), 'Defining "Teacher Professionalism" from Different Perspectives', *Procedia*, 9: 2047–51.

DES (1968), *A Handbook of Health Education*, London: HMSO.

DES (1975), *Curricular Differences between the Sexes*, London: DES.

DES (1977), *Education in Schools*, London: HMSO.

DES (1977), *Health Education in Schools*, London: HMSO.

DES (1987), *Sex Education at School, Circular 11/87*, London: DES.

DES (1992), *Curriculum Organization and Classroom Practice in Primary Schools*, London: DES.

DES (2003), *Excellence and Enjoyment: A Strategy for Primary Schools*, London: DfES.

DES (2006), *A Vision for Teaching and Learning in 2020*, London: DES.

Dewey, J. (1915), *The School and Society*, Chicago: University of Chicago.

Dewey, J. (1938), *Experience and Education*, New York: Macmillan.

DfE (2012), *Pupil Behaviour in Schools in England*, London: DfE.

DfE, 2013, *Citizenship Programme of Study, Key Stage 3 and 4*, London, DfE.

DfEE (2000), *Sex and Relationship Education Guidance 0116/2000*, London: DfEE.

DfES (2001), *Professionalism and Trust. The Future of Teachers and Teaching. A Speech by the Rt Hon Estelle Morris Secretary of State for Education and Skills to the Social Market Foundation*, London: DfES.

DfES (2003), *Excellence and Enjoyment,* London: DfES.

DfES (2007), *Diversity and Citizenship.* London: DfES.

Downing, J. (1708), *An Account of the Charity Schools Lately Erected in England and Wales.* London: Downing.

Durkheim, E. (1956), *Education and Sociology*, London: Simon and Schuster.

Edmond, N. and Hayler, M. (2013), 'On Either Side of the Teacher: Perspectives on Professionalism in Education', *Journal of Education for Teaching: International Research and Pedagogy* 39 (2): 209–21.

Elton (1989), *Discipline in Schools, Report of the Committee of Enquiry Chaired by Lord Elton*, London: HMSO.

Epstein, D. (1998), *Failing Boys? Issues in Gender and Achievement*, Buckingham: Open University.

Feeney, P. (2009), *A 1950s Childhood*, Stroud: History Press.

Finlay-Johnson, H. (1912), *The Dramatic Method of Teaching*, London: Ginn.

Fitch, J. (1880), *Lectures on Teaching*, Cambridge: University Press.

Froissart, J. (1870), *Oeuvres de Froissart, Poésies, (L'Espinette amourouse)*, Brussels: Devaux.

Gingell, J. and Winch, C. (1999), *Key Concepts in the Philosophy of Education*, London: Routledge.

Goldstrom, J. M. (1972), *Education: Elementary Education, 1780–1900*, Newton Abbot: David and Charles.

Gosden, P. R. J. H. (1969), *How They Were Taught*, Oxford: Blackwell.

Gosden, P. R. J. H. (1972), *Evolution of a Profession*, Oxford: Blackwell.

Gove, M. (2009), 'What is Education for?', Speech to the RSA, 30 June 2009. Available online: http://www.thersa.org/__data/assets/pdf_file/0009/213021/Gove-speech-to-RSA.pdf (accessed 4 December 2014).

Gove, M. (2010), 'Speech to the National College Annual Conference', Birmingham, 16 June 2010. Available online: http://www.gov.uk/government/speeches/michael-gove-to-the-national-college-annual-conference-birmingham (accessed 4 December 2014).

Gove, M. (2013), 'The importance of teaching', Speech delivered to Policy Exchange. Available online: https://www.gov.uk/government/speeches/michael-gove-speaks-about-the-importance-of-teaching (accessed 28 December 2014).

Gove, M. (2014), 'Interview by BBC News'. Available online: http://www.bbc.co.uk/news/education-26003722 (accessed 4 December 2014).

Grantham, T. (1644), *The Brainbreaker's Breaker*.

Green, H. and Hannon, C. (2007), *Their Space. Education for a Digital Generation,* London: Demos.

Greenfield, S. (2004), *Tomorrow's People: How 21st-Century Technology is Changing the Way We Think and Feel,* London: Penguin.

Groff J., Howells C. and Cranmer S. (2010), *The Impact of Console Games in the Classroom: Evidence from Schools in Scotland*, Available online: http://archive.futurelab.org.uk/resources/documents/project_reports/Console_Games_report.pdf (accessed 28 June 2015).

Gustafsson, U. (2002), 'School Meals Policy: The Problem with Governing Children', *Social Policy and Administration* 36 (6): 685–97.

Hadley, G. (1788), A New and Complete History of the Town and County of the Town of Kingston-Upon-*Hull*, Hull: Briggs.

Hadow (1923), *Report of the Consultative Committee on Differentiation of the Curriculum for Boys and Girls Respectively in Secondary Schools*, London: HMSO.

Hall L.A. (2012), 'In Ignorance and in Knowledge. Reflections on the History of Sex Education in Britain', in D. H. Lutz and R. Davidson (eds), *Shaping Sexual Knowledge: A Cultural History of Sex Education in Twentieth Century Europe*, 19–29, London: Routledge.

Hallinan M. T. (ed.) (2013), *Restructuring Schools: Promising Practices and Policies*, New York: Springer.

Hargreaves, D. (1994), *The Mosaic of Learning: Schools and Teachers for the Next Century*, London: Demos.

Hargreaves, A. (2000), 'Four Ages of Professionalism and Professional Learning', *Teachers and Teaching: Theory and Practice* 6 (2): 151–82.

Hargreaves, L. (2006), *The Status of Teachers and the Teaching Profession: Views from Inside and Outside the Profession Interim Findings from the Teacher Status Project*. London: DfES.

Hargreaves, L., Cunningham M., Hansen A., McIntyre D. and Oliver C. (2007), *The Status of Teachers and the Teaching Profession: Views from Inside and Outside the Profession. Final Report of the Teacher Status Project*. London: DfES

Hastings, A. (1986), *A History of English Christianity, 1920–1985*, London: Collins.

Heater, D. (2001), 'The History of Citizenship Education in England,' *Curriculum Journal* 12 (1): 103–23.

Heppell, S. (2006), 'Learning 2016', RSA Boyle Lecture. Available online: https://www.tes.co.uk/teaching-resource/teachers-tv-stephen-heppell–learning-2016-6083931 (accessed 3 June 2015).

Heywood, C. (2001), *A History of Childhood*, London: Polity.

HMI (1977), *Curriculum 11–16*, London: DES.

Holland, V. (1998), 'Underachieving Boys: Problems and Solutions', *Support for Learning* 13 (4): 174–8.

Holmes, E. ([1912] 2008), *What Is and What Might Be*, London: Bibliobazaar.

Hoole, C. (1913), *A New Discovery in the Old Art of Teaching Schoole*, Liverpool: Liverpool University Press.

Hopkins, K. (1939), 'Punishment in Schools', *British Journal of Educational Psychology* 9 (1): 8–28.

Horn, P. (1989), *The Victorian and Edwardian Schoolchild*, Gloucester: Sutton.

House of Commons Committee on Education, (2015), *Life Lessons: PSHE and SRE in Schools*, London: HMSO.

Hull, J. M. (1991), *Mishmash. Religious Education in Multi-Cultural Britain. A Study in Metaphor*. Available online: http://www.bibelwelt.de/html/mishmash.html (accessed 28 May 2015).

Hunt, A. (1975), *Fifth Form Girls: Their Hopes for the Future*, London: HMSO.

Hunt, T. (2014a), *A Tale of Two Classrooms, a Demos Collection on Educational Inequality*. Demos.

Hunt, T. (2014b), *Speech to Demos*, 8 December 2014. Available online: https://socedassoc.files.wordpress.com/2014/06/tristramhuntdemosdec2014.pdf (accessed 3 June 2015).

Hutchings, M. (2015), 'Exam Factories?'. Available online: http://www.teachers.org.uk/files/exam-factories.pdf (accessed 7 July 2015).

Institute of Christian Education (1954), *Religious Education in Schools*, London: SPCK.

Ipsos MORI and Nairn, A. (2011), *Children's Well-being in UK, Sweden and Spain: The Role of Inequality and Materialism, a Qualitative Study*, UNICEF.

James, A., Jenks, C. and Prout, A. (1998), *Theorizing Childhood*, Cambridge: Polity.

Johnson, A. (2007), 'Schools must teach Britishness', Available online: http://news.bbc.co.uk/1/hi/education/6294643.stm (accessed 24 June 2014).

Johnson, D. W. and Johnson, R. T. (1999), *Learning Together and Alone: Cooperation, Competitive and Individualistic Learning*, Boston, MA: Allyn and Bacon.

Johnson, R. (1979), 'Really Useful Knowledge: Radical Education and Working Class Culture, 1790–1848', in J. Clarke, C. Critcher and R. Johnson, *Working Class Culture: Studies in History and Theory*, London: Hutchinson.

Jones, H. (1866), *Priest and Parish.*

Jones, S. (2005), 'The Invisibility of the Underachieving Girl', *International Journal of Inclusive Education* 9 (3): 269–86.

Kamm, J. (1958), *How Different From Us: A Biography of Miss Buss and Miss Beale*, London: Bodley Head.

Kay-Shuttleworth, J. (1839), *Recent Measures for the Promotion of Education in England*, London: Ridgway.

Kay-Shuttleworth, J. (1847), *The School and its Reactions to the State, the Church*, London: Murray.

Kelvedon Hatch (nd), 'School Log Book'. Available online: http://www.historyhouse.co.uk/kelvedonhatch/school_log_book.html (accessed 28 December 2014).

Kerr, D. (2000), 'The Making of Citizenship in the National Curriculum'. Available online: http://www.leeds.ac.uk/educol/documents/00001643.htm (accessed, 7 January 2015).

King, A. (1993), 'From Sage on the Stage to Guide on the Side', *College Teaching* 41 (1): 30–5.

Ladurie, E. L. (2002), *Montaillou*, London: Penguin.

Landon, J. (1908), *The Principles and Practice of Teaching and Class Management*, Holden.

Lawson, D. and Dufour, B. (1976), *The New Social Studies,* London: Heinemann.

Lawson, J. (1973), *A Social History of Education in England*, London: Methuen.

Lawton, D. (1988), *The Education Reform Act: Choice and Control*, London: Hodder and Stoughton.

Le Grand, J. (1997), 'Knights, Knaves or Pawns: Human Behaviour and Social Policy', *Journal of Social Policy* 26 (2): 149–64.

Leach, A. F. (1971), *Educational Charters and Documents*, Cambridge: Cambridge University Press.

Leaton Gray, S. (2006), 'What Does it Mean to be a Teacher? Three Tensions within Contemporary Teacher Professionalism Examined in Terms of Government Policy and the Knowledge Economy' *Forum* 48 (3): 305–16.

Locke, J. (1693), *Some Thoughts Concerning Education*, London: Churchill.

London School Board (1889), *Report of Special Sub-Committee on Meals for School Children, Minutes of London School Board, 25 July 1889*, SBL/1467, London Metropolitan Archives.

Mandeville, B. (1724), *The Fable of the Bees: Or Private Vices Public Benefits. With an Essay on Charity and Charity-schools*. 3rd Edition, London: Tonson.

Manson, J. (1762), *A New Pocket Dictionary; Or, English Expositor*, Belfast: Blow.

March, N. (1915), *Towards Racial Health: A Handbook for Parents, Teachers and Social Workers on the Training of Boys and Girls*, London: Routledge.

Mausethagen, S. and Granlund, L. (2012), 'Contested Discourses of Teacher Professionalism: Current Tensions between Education Policy and Teachers' Union', *Journal of Education Policy* 27 (6): 815–33.

Mayhew, H. (1842) *What to Teach and How to Teach it,* London, Smith.

Methodist Conference (1997), *Agenda: 'School Education: the State and the Churches'.*

Meyer, B. (2008), *Independent Learning: a Literature Review*, London: DCSF.

Ministry of Education (1947), *The New Secondary Education, Pamphlet* 9, London: HMSO.

Ministry of Education (1955), *School Meals Service. The Nutritional Standard of School Dinners*, London: HMSO.

Ministry of Education (1956), *Health Education*, London: HMSO.

Ministry of Education (1963), *Half our Future. A Report of the Central Advisory Council for Education, England*, London: HMSO.

The Moral Maze (2015) [Radio programme] BBC Radio 4, 4 March 2015.

Morgan N. (2015), 'Preparing young people for life in modern Britain', speech delivered to Bright Blue: 10 March 2015. Available online: http://www. brightblue.org.uk/index.php/blog/ourvoice/item/460-speech-by-the-rt-hon-nicky-morgan-mp (accessed 20 May 2015).

Morris, M. C. F. (1922), *Yorkshire Reminiscences*, London: Milford.

Mulcaster, R. (1888), *Positions*. London: Green.

NASUWT (2006), 'Report of National Association of Schoolmasters and women teachers' Conference'. Available online: http://news.bbc.co.uk/1/hi/education/5074794.stm (accessed 28 September 2014).

NS (National Society For Promoting The Education Of The Poor In The Principles Of The Established Church) (1812), *Annual Report of the National Society*, London: National Society.

O'Day, R. (1982), *Education and Society, 1500–1800*, Longman.

OECD (Organisation for Economic Co-operation and Development) (2001), '*Schooling for Tomorrow Scenarios*'. Available online: www.oecd.org/site/schoolingfortomorrowknowledgebase/futuresthinking/scenarios/theschoolingfortomorrowscenarios.htm (accessed 12 December 2014).

Ofsted (2003), *Boys' Achievement in Secondary Schools*, London: Ofsted.

Ofsted (2005), *Managing Challenging Behaviour*, London: DfES.

Ofsted (2007), *Making Sense of Religion*, London, HMSO.

Ofsted (2010), *The Quality of Teaching and the Use of Assessment to Support Learning*, London: Ofsted.

Ofsted (2013a), *Religious Education: Realizing the Potential*, London: HMSO.

Ofsted (2013b), *Subsidiary Guidance: Supporting the Inspection of Maintained Schools and Academies*, London: Ofsted.

Ofsted (2013c), *Not Yet Good Enough: Personal, Social, Health and Economic Education in English Schools in 2012*, London: Ofsted.

Ofsted (2014), *Below the Radar: Low-level Disruption in the Country's Classrooms*, London: Ofsted.

Orme, N. (2003), *Medieval Children*, Yale University Press.

Painter, F. V. N. (1889), *Luther on Education*, St.Louis: Concordia.

Palmer, S. (2007), *Toxic Childhood*, London: Orion.

Papert, S. (1993), *Mindstorms: Children, Computers and Powerful Ideas*, New York: BasicBooks.

Passmore, S. and Harris, G. (2004), 'Education, Health and School Meals: A Review of Policy Changes in England and Wales Over the Last Century', *Nutrition Bulletin* 29 (3): 221–7.

Peal, R. (2014), *Playing the Game: The Enduring Influence of the Preferred Ofsted Teaching Style*, London: Civitas. Available online: http://www.civitas.org.uk/pdf/PlayingtheGame.pdf (accessed 22 May 2015).

Perryman, J. (2006), 'Panoptic Performativity and School Inspection Regimes: Disciplinary Mechanisms and Life under Special Measures', *Journal of Education Policy* 21 (2): 147–61.

Pilcher, J. (2004), 'Sex in Health Education: Official Guidance for Schools in England, 1928–1977', *Journal of Historical Sociology* 17 (2/3): 185–208.

Pinchbech, I. and Hewit, M. (1973), *Children in English Society,* London: Routledge.

Plato (1892), *Dialogues of Plato*, vol. 2, trans. B. Jowett, London: Oxford University Press.

Plato (1914), *Dialogues of Plato*, vol. 3, trans. B, Jowett, London: Oxford University Press.

Plowden, B. (1967), *Children and their Primary Schools,* London: HMSO.

Pollock, L. (1983), *Forgotten Children*, Cambridge: Cambridge University Press.

Pollock, L. (1987), *A Lasting Relationship. Parents and Children over Three Centuries*, London: Fourth Estate.

POST (Parliamentary Office of Science and Technology) (2009), 'Nutritional Standards in UK schools'. Available online: http://www.parliament.uk/documents/post/postpn339.pdf (accessed 24 May 2015).

Postman, N. (1982), *The Disappearance of Childhood*, New York: Vintage.

PP (Parliamentary Papers), (1861a), *Report of the Committee of Council on Education, 1860–1*, C2794–I.

PP (1861b), *Reports of the Assistant Commissioners, Vol. II, 1861*, C2794–II

PP (1868), *Report of Schools Inquiry Commission, (Taunton Commission), IX*, C3966–VIII.

PP (1870), *Report of the Committee of Council on Education, 1870–1*, C1019.

PP (1874), *Report of the Committee of Council on Education, 1873–4*, C1019.

PP (1877), *Report of the Committee of Council on Education, 1876–7*, C1780.II.

PP (1879), *Report of the Committee of Council on Education, 1878–9*, C2342.

PP (1892), *Report of the Committee of Council on Education, 1891–92*, C6746.1.

PP (1894), *Report of the Committee of Council on Education, 1893–4*, C7437.1.

PP (1895), *Report of the Bryce Commission*, C7862.

PP (1899), *Report of the Committee of Council on Education, 1897–8*, C9400.

PP (1900), *Report of the Board of Education for 1899–1900*, Vol iii, C328.

PP (1904a), *Board of Education, Regulations for Secondary Schools*, C2128.

PP (1904b), *Report of the Inter-Departmental Committee on Physical Deterioration*, C2175.

PP (1904c), *Board of Education, Code of Regulations for Public Elementary Schools*, C2074 .

PP (1905), *Suggestions for the Consideration of Teachers*, C2638.

PP (1906), *Code of Regulations for Public Elementary Schools*. C3043.

Prensky, M. (2001), 'Digital Natives, Digital Immigrants', MCB University Press. Available online: http://www.marcprensky.com/writing/Prensky%20-%20 Digital%20Natives,%20Digital%20Immigrants%20-%20Part1.pdf (accessed 22 May 2015).

Prensky, M. (2008), 'The Role of Technology in Teaching and the Classroom', *Educational Technology* 48 (6). Available online: http://www.marcprensky. com/writing/Prensky-The_Role_of_Technology-ET-11-12-08.pdf (accessed 24 May 2015).

PSHE Association (2013), *Sex and Relationship Education for the 21st Century. Supplementary Advice to the Sex and Relationship Education Guidance,* London: PSHE Association.

PSHE Association (2015), *Teaching about Consent in PSHE Education at Key Stage 3 and 4,* London: PSHE Association.

QCA (2000), *Religious Education. Non-statutory Guidance,* London, DfE.

QCA (2007), *Citizenship. Programme of Study for Key Stage 3,* London: DfES.

Quintilian (1920), *Institutio Oratoria,* trans. H. E. Butler, London: Harvard University Press.

Reiss, M. (1993), What are the Aims of School Sex Education?' *Cambridge Journal of Education* 23 (2): 125–36.

Ricks, G. (1895), *Object Lessons and How to Give Them: First Series for Primary Schools,* Boston: Heath.

Roberts, R. (1971), *The Classic Slum,* Manchester: Manchester University Press.

Roberts, R. (1997), *A Ragged Schooling,* Manchester: Mandolin.

Robinson, J. (1851), *The Works of John Robinson,* London: Snow.

Robinson, W. (2008), 'England and Wales' in T. O'Donoghue and C. Whitehead (eds), *Teacher Education in the English-speaking World: Past, Present and Future,* 45–60, London: Information Age.

Roud, S. (2010), *The Lore of the Playground: One Hundred Years of Children's Games, Rhymes and Traditions,* London: Cornerstone.

Rouseau, J. J. (1918), *Emile.* London: Appleton.

Royden, A. M. (1922), *Sex and Common Sense,* New York: Putnam.

Sandford, J. (1845), *Parochialia, or Church, School, and Parish,* London: Longman.

Sarwar, G. (1992), *Sex Education: The Muslim Perspective,* London: Muslim Educational Trust.

Schools Council (1965), *Working Paper 2. Raising the School Leaving Age,* London: HMSO.

Schools Council (1971), *Working Paper 36, Religious Education in Secondary Schools,* London: Methuen.

Seel, N. and Dijkstra, S. (2004), *Curriculum, Plans, and Processes in Instructional Design: International Perspectives,* London: Routledge.

Selinger, M. and Yapp, C. (2001), *ICT Teachers,* London: IPPR.

Selwyn, N., Cranmer, S. and Potter, J. (2010), *The Primary Schools and ICT,* London: Continuum.

Shorter, E. (1976), *Making of the Modern Family,* London: Collins.

Shulman, L. (2004), *The Wisdom of Practice: Collected Essays on Teaching, Learning and Learning to Teach,* San Francisco: Jossy-Bass.

SIC (Social Integration Commission) (2015), *Kingdom United, Thirteen Steps to Tackle Social Segregation, Final Report of the Social Integration Commission.* Available online: http://socialintegrationcommission.org.uk/images/sic_kingdomunited.pdf (accessed 24 May 2015).

Simon, B. (1974), *The Two Nations and The Educational Structure, 1780–1870,* London: Lawrence and Wishart.

Simpson, R. (1842), *The Clergyman's Manual,* London: Groombridge.

Smith, J. T. (2009), *Victorian Class Conflict,* Brighton: Sussex Academic Press.

Smith, J. T. (2014), 'Picturesque and Dramatic or Dull Recitals of Threadbare Fare: Good Practice in History Teaching in Elementary Schools in England, 1872–1905', *Journal of Educational Administration and History* 46 (1): 93–107.

Snell, G. (1649), *The Right Teaching of Useful Knowledge, to Fit Scholars for some Honest Profession,* London: Du Gard.

Steer, A., 2009. *Learning Behaviour, Lessons Learned,* London: DCSF.

Stowe, D. (1847), *National Education.The Duty of England in Regard to the Moral and Intellectual Elevation of the poor and Working Class,* London: Hatchard.

Swann, M. (1985), *Education for All: Report of the Committee of Enquiry into the Education of Children from Ethnic Minority Groups,* London: HMSO.

Swann, M., McIntyre, D., Pell, T., Hargreaves, L. and Cunningham, M. (2010), 'Teachers' Conceptions of Teacher Professionalism in England in 2003 and 2006', *British Educational Research Journal* 36 (4): 549–71.

Sylvester, D. W. (1970), *Educational Documents 800–1816,* London: Methuen.

Talbott, J. (1707), *The Christian Schoolmaster,* London: Downing.

TDA (Training and Development Agency) (2007), *Professional Standards for Teachers.* London: TDA.

Thatcher, M. (1987), 'Speech to the Institute of Directors, 24 May 1987', Available online: http://www.margaretthatcher.org/document/106753, (accessed 21 May 2015).

Thompson, D. (1927), *The Professional Solidarity among the Teachers of England,* New York: Columbia University Press.

Thornton, A. (2014) Available online: http://www.democraticlife.org.uk/2013/09/18/citizenship-is-here-to-stay-reactions-to-the-dfe-final-national-curriculum-for-2014 (accessed 10 June 2015).

Tomlinson, S. (2001), *Education in a Post-welfare Society,* Buckingham: Open University Press.

Tooley, J. (2000), *Reclaiming Education,* London: Cassell.

Topping, K. J. (2005), 'Trends in Peer Learning', *Educational Psychology* 25 (6): 631–45.

Tosh, J. (2008), *Why History Matters,* London: Macmillan.

Townsend, T. (2011), 'Searching High and Searching Low, Searching East and Searching West: Looking for Trust in Teacher Education', *Journal of Education for Teaching* 37 (4): 483–99.

Tropp, A. (1957), *The School Teachers,* London: Heinemann.

Vaughan, R. (2014), 'Irritated Wilshaw Writes to Inspectors to tell them not to Prescribe Teaching Styles', *Times Educational Supplement,* 27 January 2014.

Walford, G. (ed.) (2010), *Blair's Educational Legacy,* Abingdon: Routledge.

Wardle, D. (1970). *English Popular Education, 1780–1975.*Cambridge: Cambridge University Press.

Weisz, J. (2004), *Psychotherapy for Children and Adolescents,* Cambridge: Cambridge University Press.

Wells, N. (2010), 'Hundreds of heads and church leaders oppose sex education for seven year olds', *Sunday Telegraph,* 28 March 2010. Available online: http://www.christian.org.uk/news/compulsory-sex-education-undermines-free-society (accessed 28 May 2015).

Wesley, S. (1732), 'Some Thoughts on Raising Children'. Available online: http://www.path2prayer.com/article/1042 (accessed 7 January 2015).

Whale, G. (1882), *A Fragment on Political Education,* London: Ridgeway.

Whitehead, K. (2006), 'Sex Education: The Vatican's Guidelines'. Available online: http://www.catholiceducation.org/en/marriage-and-family/sexuality/sex-education-the-vatican-s-guidelines.html (accessed 28 May 2015).

Whitty, G. (2000), 'Teacher Professionalism in New Times', *Journal of In-Service Education* 26 (2): 281–95.

Wilkins, C. (2011), 'Professionalism and the Post-performative Teacher: New Teachers Reflect on Autonomy and Accountability in the English School System', *Professional Development in Education* 37 (3): 389–409.

Wilkinson, E. (1946), 'Speech on Education'. Available online: http://labourlist.org/2014/04/england-expects-a-strategy-for-improving-all-its-schools (accessed 24 December 2014).

Wilshaw, M. (2012a), 'The Good Teacher, Speech to the RSA'. Available online: www.thersa.org/fellowship/journal/archive/summer-2012/features/the-good-teacher (accessed 20 May 2015).

Wilshaw, M. (2012b), 'The importance of teaching – Ofsted's view', speech given at the London Festival of Education', 17 November 2012. Available online: http://www.dysky.org/wp-content/uploads/2012/11/121117-London-Festival-of-Education-speech-HMCI.pdf (accessed 20 May 2015).

Woodward, E. (1649). *Of the Child's Portion, viz: Good Education*, London: Underhill.

Wragg, E.C. (2006), *Classroom Teaching Skills*, London: Routledge.

Wyse, D. and Torrance, H. (2009), 'The Development and Consequences of National Curriculum Assessment for Primary Education in England', *Educational Research* 51 (2): 213–28.

Younger, M. and Warrington, M. (2005), *Raising Boys' Achievement*, London: HMSO.

Younger, M. and Warrington, M. (2007), 'Closing the Gender Gap? Issues of Gender Equity in English Secondary Schools', *Discourse: Studies in the Cultural Politics of Education* 28 (2): 219–42.

Index

Lightning Source UK Ltd.
Milton Keynes UK
UKHW020029230922
409278UK00004B/838